INTERPRETING WTO AGREEMENTS

The case law of the World Trade Organization is now extensive, running into more than one hundred cases and thousands of pages. The interpretative process involved in this jurisprudence constitutes a form of legislative activity, and is therefore of great significance not only to the parties to disputes but also to the membership of the WTO as a whole. Asif H. Qureshi sets out here to identify some of the principal underlying problems of interpreting the WTO Agreements, within the context of various issues, problems, objectives and disciplines, and comprehensively to examine the underlying conditions for the interpretation of the WTO Agreements. He focuses on the apparatus of interpretation in the WTO; the manner of interpreting institutional norms, national measures and exceptions in the WTO; the manner of facilitating the development objective in the WTO; the manner of reconciling conflicting norms through interpretation; and the manner of interpreting the trade remedy agreements. Various perspectives on interpretation are proffered, particularly those of justice and development. This book is an essential tool for WTO trade specialists, as well as government and judicial officers concerned with interpreting these agreements.

ASIF H. QURESHI is Professor of International Economic Law in the Law School at the University of Manchester, and a barrister at Quadrant Chambers, London.

INTERPRETING WTO AGREEMENTS

PROBLEMS AND PERSPECTIVES

ASIF H. QURESHI

CAMBRIDGE UNIVERSITY PRESS
Cambridge, New York, Melbourne, Madrid, Cape Town,
Singapore, São Paulo, Delhi, Mexico City

Cambridge University Press
The Edinburgh Building, Cambridge CB2 8RU, UK

Published in the United States of America by Cambridge University Press, New York

www.cambridge.org
Information on this title: www.cambridge.org/9781107406261

First published 2006
First paperback edition 2012

A catalogue record for this publication is available from the British Library

ISBN 978-0-521-84475-8 Hardback
ISBN 978-1-107-40626-1 Paperback

CONTENTS

PREFACE

My interest in the problems of interpreting the WTO Agreements is a long-standing one. My first monograph on the WTO focused on the implementation of the WTO Agreements,[1] and interpretation is very much a part of implementation. When that book was published, however, interpretation was not that big an issue. Some of the inspiration for this work also comes from my earlier research on IMF conditionality.[2] Anyone working on the legal aspects of IMF conditionality at that time had to engage with the works of Joseph Gold – in particular his work on interpretation.[3] Judge Rosalyn Higgins's work on problems and processes no doubt provided the idea for a problems-based approach to the subject,[4] although it is a matter of judgement whether my work is in any way process oriented. Another inspiration for the writing of the current book is irritation (which can also be a motivating factor for research) stemming from the preoccupation in the existing literature on the interpretation of the WTO Agreements with the interaction of international environmental and human rights norms with the WTO Agreements. Diverse perspectives even on a seemingly technical subject can have significance in the development of international law.[5]

This monograph was researched and written while I was visiting Fudan Law School, Shanghai, China; the Law School, University of Malaya, Kuala Lumpur, Malaysia; and the Graduate School of Law and

[1] See A. H. Qureshi *The World Trade Organization: Implementing International Trade Norms* (Manchester UP, Manchester 1996).

[2] See A. H. Qureshi *International Economic Law* (Sweet and Maxwell, London 1999) part two.

[3] See J. Gold *Interpretation: The IMF and International Law* (Kluwer Law International, The Hague 1996).

[4] See R. Higgins *Problems and Processes: International Law and How It Works* (Clarendon Press, Oxford 1995).

[5] See A. H. Qureshi (ed) *Perspectives in International Economic Law* (Kluwer Law International, The Hague 2002).

Politics, University of Osaka, Japan. Of course, a substantial part was also completed at my base in the Law School, University of Manchester. I am particularly grateful to Professor Lu Zhian, Professor Khaw Lake Tee and Professor Mari Nagata for their very kind hospitality during my sojourns in China, Malaysia and Japan, respectively. I am also very grateful to my colleagues in Manchester for facilitating these trips.

There are a host of others to whom gratitude needs to be expressed. I thank these people and apologise for not naming all of them here individually. I would, however, like to mention Finola O'Sullivan of Cambridge University Press for facilitating this publication and for her firm advice on deadlines! I am also grateful to Valerie Hughes, former Director of the Appellate Body of the WTO, for her comments on chapter 2, and to Willie Chatsika, Counsellor in the Technical Co-operation Division of the WTO, for his observations on an earlier draft of chapter 5.

Last but not least, this book would not have been possible without the love and care that sustained me while I worked on it. Mianghi 'Kamsa Hamnida', as they say in Korean.

ABBREVIATIONS

AB	Appellate Body
ADA	Agreement on Implementation of Article VI of the General Agreement on Tariffs and Trade 1994
ASCM	Agreement on Subsidies and Countervailing Measures
BIT	bilateral investment treaty
BOP Committee	Balance of Payments Committee
DSB	Dispute Settlement Body
DSU	Understanding on Rules and Procedures Governing the Settlement of Disputes
ECJ	European Court of Justice
FCN	friendship, commerce and navigation
GATS	General Agreement on Trade in Services
GATT	General Agreement on Tariffs and Trade
IBRD	International Bank for Reconstruction and Development
ICJ	International Court of Justice
ICSID	International Centre for Settlement of Investment Disputes
IIA	international investment agreement
ILC	International Law Commission
IMF	International Monetary Fund
ITO	International Trade Organization
LDC	least-developed country
MEA	multilateral environmental agreement
MFN	most favoured nation
MTN	Multilateral Trade Negotiations
NAFTA	North American Free Trade Agreement
PCIJ	Permanent Court of International Justice
RTA	regional trade agreement
SA	Agreement on Safeguards

S&D	special and differential treatment
SPS Agreement	Agreement on Sanitary and Phytosanitary Measures
TPR	trade policy review
TPRM	Trade Policy Review Mechanism
TRIMs	Trade-Related Investment Measures
TRIPS	Trade-Related Aspects of Intellectual Property Rights
UNCTAD	United Nations Conference on Trade and Development
VAT	value added tax
VC(LT)	Vienna Convention (on the Law of Treaties)
WIPO	World Intellectual Property Organization
WTO	World Trade Organization
WTO Agreements	The Results of the Uruguay Round of Multilateral Trade Negotiations: The Legal Texts

Introduction

Beware, beware the interpreter! Whether interpretation is viewed as an objective or a subjective process,[1] this caution is equally relevant. But it is as much counsel about the interpreter as it is counsel for the interpreter, because the process of interpretation can be fraught with dangers. It is well understood that many normative frameworks have met with disrepute, indeed disasters, in the process of their interpretation. Others, however, have endured and better stood the test of time, precisely as a consequence of the manner of their interpretation. Thus, with caution come opportunities. If evolution is the manner of mankind's development, interpretation is its equivalent normative vehicle for development – whether viewed as an objective or subjective process. This analogy is best understood if the objective and subjective standpoints on interpretation are placed in their respective temporal boxes. Thus, the objective view of interpretation is concerned more with the present. Consequently, it is less focused on the long-term legislative, impact of interpretation, despite that impact, given its incremental nature – sometimes in the blink of an eye, or in a decade of a time frame. In contrast, the subjective, constitutive perspective on interpretation best derives its clarity from the historical, retrospective context in which it observes evolution.

This book identifies some of the underlying problems of interpreting the WTO Agreements within the context of different spheres of issues, problems, objectives and disciplines. In this process, some perspectives on interpretation are proffered, and the scene is set for the development of appropriate approaches to various issues. This book is not about the substantive interpretations of the WTO Agreements as such.

[1] See for example R. Dworkin 'Law, Philosophy and Interpretation' in F. Atria and D. N. MacCormick (eds) *Law and Legal Interpretation* (Ashgate Publishing 2003), chapter 1, 3. See also R. Dworkin *Law's Empire* (Fontana, London 1987).

Interpreting the WTO Agreements involves focusing on the text of the WTO Agreements through customary norms of treaty interpretation as set out in Articles 31–3 of the Vienna Convention on the Law of Treaties. The process of understanding the WTO Agreements is augmented by considering them against the backdrop of the jurisprudence of the WTO. In practice, this has been greatly facilitated by the *WTO Analytical Index* and further work in the WTO that highlights different provisions of the WTO Agreements in the light of the WTO jurisprudence, namely, the *WTO Appellate Body Repertory of Reports and Awards.*

Chapter 1 focuses on the actual tools of treaty interpretation relied upon in the WTO. In particular, it considers how those very tools of interpretation have themselves been adopted and shaped within the WTO to facilitate the process of interpretation. Chapter 2 focuses on the institutional set-up within which interpretation takes place and considers the problems of treaty interpretation as they relate to institutional aspects of the WTO. Chapter 3 is a consideration of the interpretative issues within the national dimension. This national dimension is considered mainly as it has been analysed in the WTO.

Chapter 4 considers the interpretative issues that arise from the interplay and engagement of exceptions in the WTO Agreements. Here special and differential treatment provisions are drawn upon as an example. Closely allied to the question of interpreting exceptions is the challenge of facilitating development through the very process of interpretation. Thus, Chapter 5 focuses on interpretation from the perspective of the development dimension. Chapter 6 looks at a discourse much considered among WTO scholars, namely, the extent to which external concerns can be taken into account in the interpretative processes. Finally, Chapter 7 examines interpretative issues in the dimension of a particular discipline – trade remedies agreements.

1

Interpreting principles of treaty interpretation in the World Trade Organization

1.1 Introduction

The jurisprudence of the World Trade Organization (WTO) is replete with references to Articles 31–2 of the Vienna Convention (VC) on the Law of Treaties. This gospel for interpretation is often the starting-point of judgments in the WTO. Its use in the WTO became established with the Appellate Body (AB) decision in the US–Gasoline case. wherein it was pointed out that the general rule of interpretation set out in Article 31 of the VC had

> attained the status of a rule of customary or general international law. As such, it forms part of the 'customary rules of interpretation of public international law' which the Appellate Body has been directed, by Article 3(2) of the *DSU* [Understanding on Rules and Procedures Governing the Settlement of Disputes], to apply in seeking to clarify the provisions of the *General Agreement* and the other 'covered agreements' of the *Marrakesh Agreement Establishing the World Trade Organization*.... That direction reflects a measure of recognition that the *General Agreement* is not to be read in clinical isolation from public international law. (Footnotes omitted)

This statement is often religiously cited in other WTO cases. Indeed, in the same vein, Article 32 of the VC has also been acknowledged as having attained the status of a customary rule of interpretation of public international law.[1] This equation of customary rules of interpretation of public international law in Article 3 (2) of the DSU with Articles 31–2 of the VC is founded ultimately on the need to ensure certainty and clarity in the process of interpretation of the WTO

[1] See for example Mexico–Telecommunications (Panel) para 7.15; US–Cotton Yarn (Panel) para 7.17; US–Sardines (Panel) para 7.12; Japan–Taxes on Alcoholic Beverages (AB) 10; US–Anti-Dumping Measures on Oil Country Tubular Goods (OCTG) from Mexico (Panel).

Agreements. In effect it has rendered Articles 31–2 of the VC a Hart's 'rule of recognition' in the WTO which is binding on WTO members who are not party to the VC.[2] Similarly, the practice of other judicial organs operating in the sphere of international economic relations – for example, the European Court of Justice (ECJ),[3] North American Free Trade Agreement (NAFTA) Panels[4] and International Centre for Settlement of Investment Disputes (ICSID) arbitration[5] – involves frequent references to Articles 31–2 of the VC, accompanied by the observation that those provisions represent customary rules of treaty interpretation.[6]

In these circumstances, to question the adequacy of Articles 31–3 of the VC as aids to interpreting the WTO Agreements may well be considered heresy. The VC is certainly generally uncritically invoked. Yet there are sound reasons for a re-evaluation of the principles of treaty interpretation applicable to the WTO Agreements.[7]

First, it is the case that the drafting of the VC principles predates the spate of international agreements that have spawned international law, particularly international economic law, since 1969. Those principles were established against the background of a preoccupation with fundamental principles, in particular the principle of *pacta sunt servanda.* International relations, along with international economic relations, have since moved on to a higher level of consciousness to encompass fairness.[8] Fairness not only pervades all aspects of international economic discourse *de lege ferenda* but is also establishing itself as part of the very architecture of the international economic order.

Second, the dynamic but Byzantine manner in which international trade negotiations take place must in some measure inform the kind of aids to interpretation necessary for subsequent engagement with the agreement reached. Thus, the circumstances of the negotiations can

[2] See H. L. A. Hart *The Concept of Law* (2nd edn Oxford UP, Oxford 1994).

[3] Opinion of Advocate General Misho, Case C-257/99 (26 September 2000) para 63.

[4] NAFTA Arbitral Panel Established Pursuant to Chapter Twenty: In the Matter of Cross-Border Trucking Services (Secretariat File no. US-MEX-98–2008–01) para 220.

[5] See for example Salim Costruttori S.p.A and Jordan, ICSID Case no. ARB/02/13 para 75.

[6] See also *Case Concerning Kasikili/Sedudu Island* (Botswana/Namibia) ICJ 1999 para 18.

[7] A view shared by J. Jackson, although for somewhat different reasons – namely, that the VC 'is more suited to application to bilateral treaties' given that it was negotiated mainly against the backdrop of bilateral agreements. See J. Jackson *Sovereignty, the WTO, and Changing Fundamentals of International Law* (Cambridge UP, Cambridge 2006) 184.

[8] See for example T. M. Franck *Fairness in International Law and Institutions* (Oxford UP, Oxford 1995).

lead to incomplete arrangements or confusion over the nature of the provisions of the agreement.

Third, the very nature of trade and trade agreements must have a bearing on the canons of interpretation drawn upon. Thus, trade negotiations are often said to be founded on reciprocity. Equally, many trade norms are not contractual in nature but partake of a legislative character. Although it is received wisdom that insofar as interpretation is concerned it does not distinguish between such variations, nevertheless there have been calls for re-visiting this wisdom.[9]

Fourth, the diversity of the participants in multilateral trade negotiations is a factor that shapes trade agreements. The arrangements for the subsequent interpretation of these agreements must be sensitive to the fact that the agreements engineered have involved both powerful and weak members. This is not to detract from the *pacta sunt servanda* principle or the text of the agreement. Rather, it is to assert that when one group of participants in the negotiations lacks information, negotiating expertise, acumen and foresight regarding the consequences of some of its actions during the negotiations and at the time of the conclusion of the agreement, it has a certain interest in these circumstances being taken into account in some measure in the apparatus of interpretation. Thus, this group may well be clear as to the overall objectives and purposes of the agreement, which usually are apparent, but somewhat at a loss at the micro/technical detail level of the subject of negotiations. In such circumstances, the group may well have a legitimate expectation that the canons of interpretation subsequently drawn upon will re-balance in some measure their negotiating deficits. One manner of taking cognisance of this negotiating deficit in the interpretative process is to give more weight to the overall objects and purposes of the agreement – in other words, the canons of interpretation should iron out some of the consequences of the deficit in the negotiations at the micro level by reinforcing the consensus of the group with regard to the overall objectives and purposes of the agreement.[10] Equally, where a vulnerable group is invited to engage in

[9] See for example Sir Humphrey Waldock [1964] 1 *YILC* para 18 (ILC 765th Meeting A/CN.4/167/Add.3): 'It was difficult to distinguish between treaties laying down rules of conduct for States and those of a contractual type involving an exchange of benefits. The rules being drafted should not become a strait-jacket capable of frustrating, for example, the institutional development of international organizations.'

[10] Note that in domestic systems unfair contracts are protected by law through, for example, duties of disclosure. It is not being suggested here that agreements should be

negotiations whose objects and purposes motivate their engagement, there is legitimacy in their expectations that the interpretative apparatus will not detract from those objects and purposes. In summary, the objects and purposes, as opposed to the 'intentions' of the parties, provide a better basis for transparency, fairness and re-distributive justice in the interpretative process.

Finally, the built-in international power ratio in the administrative and adjudicative processes involved in the interpretation of WTO Agreements can have a bearing on the manner in which international principles of treaty interpretation are applied. In particular, the neutrality and resilience of the principles of treaty interpretation in terms of that power ratio are germane. The de-coupling of the interpreters from the principles of treaty interpretation is logically not coherent. Principles of treaty interpretation cannot be conceived of in isolation. A measure of their objectivity is the degree to which they lend themselves to the preferences of the interpreters. Thus, the more ambiguous the principles of treaty interpretation, the more susceptible they are to partisan use.

In conclusion, there is a case for principles of treaty interpretation to be founded on a number of factors – not necessarily confined to the traditional set of standards. Certainty, predictability and the intentions of the parties as manifested in the text of the agreement are indeed relevant factors by which to measure the adequacy of principles of treaty interpretation. However, the adequacy of the international customary principles of treaty interpretation needs to be evaluated from the perspective of a wider range of legitimate expectations and concerns. Thus, how the principles of treaty interpretation deliver in terms of the fulfilment of the objects and purposes of the negotiations, how they take into account the circumstances leading to the conclusion of the agreement (including disparity in the knowledge and expertise of the negotiators), the extent to which they lend themselves to manipulation by the power structure enshrined within the institution after the agreement is reached, and how indeed they further internationally agreed community goals are all relevant.

In particular, the principles for treaty interpretation set out in the VC ascribe a custodian role to an interpreter. The application of the principles involves judgements, in particular 'allocative' judgements, about the placement of material sources into the interpretative pool,

re-written, rather that to the extent there is scope in the interpretative process, such scope should be drawn upon for some measure of redress.

which ultimately informs the interpretation. Parties in litigation, as well as divergent policy claims, compete for the inclusion of particular sources as material within the parameters of the principles of treaty interpretation set out in the VC. Interpreters thus perform an allocative/gate-keeper function in this process. The interpretative process as set out in the VC partakes of a form of distributive justice. In the circumstances, expectations of fairness – albeit within the constraints of the interpretative process and the interpretative mandate – are indeed legitimate. Interpretation, contrary to popular belief, is not completely non-judgemental in terms of the substance of the agreement or in relation to the process of the conclusion of the agreement. Thus, good faith is an aspect of the process.[11] By the same token, the consensus arrived at is set against the background of the international legal order – wherein are to be found principles of justice and fairness.[12]

In international trade discourse there is much ado about trends in the interpretation of WTO Agreements. This may be a legitimate concern, but it certainly is a passing one. What is more, evaluating trends involves judgements and assumes objective criteria. In a sense, the more critical query is not so much about trends as such as about the underlying interpretative apparatus which facilitates trends. Focusing on how the principles of treaty interpretation have been applied and have themselves been interpreted within the WTO thus serves to shed light on the trends that might emerge. This is achieved here through a focus on the adequacy and propriety, both generally and specifically, of some of the aspects of the application and interpretation of the principles of treaty interpretation drawn upon in the WTO.[13]

1.2 Interpretation of the VC in the WTO generally

The practice within the WTO, and indeed other international organisations, of equating 'customary rules of interpretation of public

[11] See Article 31 of the VC. See also [1966] 1(Part II) *YILC* 205 para 30 (ILC 870th Meeting A/CN.4/186 7 Addenda; A/CN.4/L.107, L.115), wherein Mr Rosenne explained that it was impossible to arrive at a decision that was manifestly absurd or unreasonable if good faith was applied in the process of interpretation.

[12] See for example Article 31 (3) (c) of the VC. See also [1964] 1 *YILC* 312 para 41 (AC/CN.4/167Add.3): 'Mr Amado said that anyone interpreting a treaty in good faith could hardly help assuming that it had been drafted in the light of the rules of international law.'

[13] This focus here excludes an evaluation of Article 32 of the VC, on the basis that it is not at the core of the issues being considered.

international law' with Articles 31–2 of the VC invites the question whether it is appropriate, indeed permissible, to freeze in time such customary rules, at least within the WTO. The pace of international treaty-making, the length of time since the VC and the nature of customary international law all call into question such a rigid equation. It is this equation which has contributed in the WTO, and indeed in other organisations, to the paucity of references to practices of interpretation in other international organisations as well as to State practice which contributes to the formation of customary or general international law in this sphere. Indeed, the interpretation has been based mainly on the work of publicists and the International Law Commission (ILC) deliberations on the VC. This observation is valid despite the fact that the practice in certain comparable international organisations (e.g. NAFTA, the ECJ and the ICSID) is not necessarily exemplary. Thus, there is little evidence of 'subsequent practice' (subsequent to the VC) being taken into account in the development of the principles of treaty interpretation.

In the same vein, by limiting the scope of 'customary rules of interpretation of public international law' to Articles 31–2 of the VC, WTO practice has restricted the spectrum of rules of treaty interpretation to these provisions. It can be argued that the corpus of customary rules of interpretation of public international law may be at variance with these provisions.[14] Conversely, have customary rules of treaty interpretation not otherwise directly associated with Articles 31–2 of the VC been squeezed into this VC straitjacket?

From a starting-point of taking their cue in matters of interpretation from the VC, the judicial organs of the WTO have now acquired the confidence to clarify and formulate their own 'interpretative gloss' on Articles 31–2 of the VC. Indeed, in this respect, the WTO judicial organs can be said to be the most distinguished of all international judicial organs with respect to their imprint on international agreements. However, this contribution needs to be evaluated in terms of the adequacy of the set of standards drawn upon in the clarification process.

The process of interpretation of the VC in the WTO has been essentially in response to the exigencies of particular disputes. This practice is indicative of a judicial acknowledgement of the need for a clear set of rules

[14] A view shared by A. Lindroos and M. Mehling 'Dispelling the Chimera of "Self-Contained Regimes": International Law and the WTO' (2005) 16(5) *JIEL* 857–77, 869: 'Article 3.2 of the DSU refers to "customary rules of interpretation of public international law". By itself , this wording would seem to allow the application of other rules of treaty interpretation than those stipulated in Articles 31 and 32 VCLT.'

for interpretation with respect to the WTO Agreements. It is the case that some aspects of the principles set out in the VC are not clear, even when properly interpreted. Be that as it may, it is legitimate to enquire whether, in this process of interpretation, the organs of the WTO are engaged in interpreting the VC, in developing customary rules of interpretation of public international law, in formulating special rules of interpretation under Article 31 (4) of the VC or in establishing subsequent practice in the interpretation of the VC. Are such interpretations of the VC *qua* convention binding on non-signatories to the VC?

1.3 Interpretations of the VC

1.3.1 Purpose of interpretation

According to the WTO jurisprudence, the purpose of interpretation is to identify the common intention of the parties.[15] However, this common intention of the parties can be ascertained only by applying the process set out in Article 31 to the text of the agreement. Thus, the AB has stated:

> The legitimate expectations of the parties to a treaty are reflected in the language of the treaty itself. The duty of a treaty interpreter is to examine the words of the treaty to determine the intentions of the parties. This should be done in accordance with the principles of treaty interpretation set out in Article 31 of the *Vienna Convention*. But these principles of interpretation neither require nor condone the imputation into a treaty of words that are not there or the importation into a treaty of concepts that were not intended.[16]

This also means that the common intentions cannot be determined with reference to the 'subjective and unilateral' expectations of one of the parties alone.[17]

[15] See EC–Chicken Classification (Panel) para 7.94, wherein the Panel observed: 'The Panel also understands that the primary purpose of treaty interpretation is to identify the common intention of the parties and that the rules contained in Articles 31 and 32 of the *Vienna Convention* have been developed to help assessing, in objective terms, what was or what could have been the common intention of the parties to a treaty.' Confirmed by the AB (para 7.254). See also EC–Computer Equipment (AB) para 93.

[16] India–Patent Protection for Pharmaceutical and Agricultural Chemicals Products (AB) para 45.

[17] EC–Computer Equipment (AB) para 84.

A number of observations need to be made here on this apparent identification of the purpose of interpretation with ascertaining the common intentions of the parties, albeit with some caveats. First, the common intentions are by no means the only or sole purpose of interpretation. As the ILC pointed out in its deliberations on the VC:

> Writers . . . differ to some extent in their basic approach to the interpretation of treaties according to the relative weight which they give to –
>
> (a) the text of the treaty as the authentic expression of the intentions of the parties;
> (b) the intentions of the parties as a subjective element distinct from the text; and
> (c) the declared or apparent objects and purposes of the treaty.[18]

Second, this reference to common intentions in the WTO can be said to mark a departure from the textual/restrictive approach to interpretation to which the institution might have been more wedded in its early days. Third, the reference to common intentions must be considered against the background of other, related assertions which touch upon the purpose of interpretation in the WTO. Thus, references to the expressed objects and purposes are to be found in AB jurisprudence.[19] The relative importance of objects and purposes was widely recognised by the ILC in its preparatory work on the VC.[20] This importance has been somewhat dwarfed (but not diminished) by the concern over the potential for relying too much on, or giving undue weight to, the objects and purposes. The relative significance of the objects and purposes is implicit in the following observation with respect to the intentions of the parties made by Mr Lachs in the deliberations of the ILC: 'The burden of the operation of a treaty, in the light of the realities of international relations, fell upon all its signatories; there was therefore no reason for giving a higher standing to the intentions of the original parties in the matter of interpretation.'[21] Similarly, the affirmation of the principle of effectiveness, founded on the principle of good faith,[22] as an aspect of the interpretative apparatus of the WTO incorporates the function of the objects and purposes as expressed in the WTO Agreements. Finally, that objects and purposes and the

[18] Sir Humphrey Waldock [1964] 2 *YILC* para 4. [19] See for example US–Shrimp (AB).
[20] See for example Mr Bartos [1964] 1 *YILC* para 77 (ILC 766th Meeting).
[21] [1964] 1 *YILC* para 46. [22] See section 1.3.2.

common intentions of the parties are equally relevant is confirmed by the deliberations of the ILC, when it observed:

> The majority of modern writers, however, insist upon the primacy of the text as the basis for the interpretation of a treaty, while at the same time giving a certain place to extrinsic evidence of the intentions of the parties and to the objects and purposes of the treaty as a means for correcting or, in limited measure, supplementing the text. It is this view which is reflected in the 1956 resolution of the Institute of International Law . . .[23]

This need for the common intentions to be subordinated to the objects and purposes, or at most juxtaposed with them, subject to the text being the basis for their determination, also has a basis in transparency, fairness and good faith. Thus, common intentions are more opaque than objects and purposes. Weaker developing countries in negotiations have the safeguard that their bargain will be protected by the very nature of the enterprise of the bargain, as mirrored in its objects and purposes, as opposed to the common intentions, which are more susceptible to dispute afterwards. The priority of the objects and purposes as a function of the interpretative process is also reinforced by the absence of any mention of 'intentions' in Article 31 of the VC.

The relevant time of the common intentions, which has to be ascertained, depends, according to WTO jurisprudence, upon the sources that are being considered. This was explained as follows by the Panel in the EC–Chicken Classification case:

> The *Vienna Convention* does not expressly stipulate the time at which or period during which the common intentions of the parties are to be assessed when interpreting a treaty term. However, the Panel notes that the various sources to which a treaty interpreter may have regard under Articles 31 and 32 of the *Vienna Convention* are, in general terms, identified by reference to when they were created, finalized and/or existed as compared to when the treaty being interpreted was concluded. The Panel infers from this that the relevant time for assessment under Articles 31 and 32 of the *Vienna Convention* depends upon the source for treaty interpretation being referred to. In our view, the 'ordinary meaning' is to be assessed at the time of *conclusion* of the treaty in question, being the time which is at the focus of both Articles 31 and 32 of the *Vienna Convention*. Regarding 'context' under Article 31(2), Article 31(2) (a) refers to 'any agreement relating to the treaty which was

[23] [1964] 2 *YILC* 54.

> made between all the parties in connection with the *conclusion of the treaty*' and Article 31(2) (b) refers to 'any instrument which was made by one or more parties in connection with the *conclusion of the treaty*...'. The terms of Article 31(2) suggest that sources considered under that Article must have been created, finalized and/or existed *contemporaneously* with the conclusion of the treaty. Article 31(3) (a) refers to 'any *subsequent* agreement' and Article 31(3) (b) refers to 'any *subsequent* practice'. The terms of Article 31(3) suggest that sources considered under that Article must have been created, finalised and/or existed *following* conclusion of the treaty. Article 32 refers to 'the *preparatory work of the treaty* and the *circumstances of its conclusion*', suggesting that such sources considered under Article 32 must have been created, finalized and/or existed in *preparation of or in the lead up to* the conclusion of the treaty.' (Footnotes omitted)[24]

This analysis is somewhat problematic. It assumes that the common intentions can neatly be split into different time frames. It assumes that the different sources set in Articles 31 and 32 are sources in themselves, rather than aids to discerning the common intentions. In particular, it does not explain common intentions with reference to the underlying intentions of the parties with respect to the agreement. Above all, such an analysis is conducive to spurious strategic planning in litigation in the options it potentially opens for attributing a common intention at different times.

1.3.2 'Good faith' under Article 31 of the VC

Generally, there has been much focus on the concept of 'good faith' in WTO litigation.[25] Good faith in the context of interpretation has also received its due share of attention, although, as one observer has commented, in practice the principle has not changed 'the result found after applying the other interpretative criteria of Article 31, i.e., wording, context and object and purpose of the treaty'.[26] This is, of course, a matter of judgement and is dependent upon how good faith is conceived and invoked.

24 Para 7.99.

25 See for example US–Offset Act (AB) and US–Shrimp (AB). See also Helge Elisabeth Zeitler '"Good Faith" in the WTO Jurisprudence: Necessary Balancing Element or an Open Door to Judicial Activism?' (2005) 8(3) *JIEL* 721–58.

26 Zeitler '"Good Faith" in the WTO Jurisprudence' 727.

The various opportunities in the use of the concept in WTO litigation are not necessarily reflected in the degree to which it has received appropriate judicial elucidation. Nevertheless, the following elaboration is to be found. Good faith has been characterised as a 'core principle of interpretation of the WTO Agreement',[27] and it informs 'a treaty interpreter's task'.[28] It is a principle which should compel a treaty interpreter to opt for the interpretation which better gives effect to the treaty.[29]

More particularly, the requirement of good faith in Article 31 of the VC has been interpreted variously to include two propositions. First, it has been 'correlated with the principle of "effective treaty interpretation", according to which all terms of a treaty must be given a meaning'.[30] In other words, 'an interpreter is not free to adopt a reading that would result in reducing whole clauses or paragraphs of a treaty to redundancy or inutile'.[31] Furthermore, the principle of effective treaty interpretation involves 'the *duty*... to read all applicable provisions of a treaty in a way that gives meaning to *all* of them, harmoniously'.[32] The treaty should be interpreted 'as a whole, and, in particular, its sections and parts should be read as a whole'.[33] To this principle of effective interpretation has been attributed the 'potential for broad, teleological understandings of treaties, and even for judicial activism'.[34] However, it is a principle of customary international law and was accepted by the ILC as being implicit in the reference to good faith and the objects and purposes of the agreement in the draft VC. Second, good faith is also the basis for the proposition that 'interpretation should not lead to a result which is manifestly absurd or unreasonable'.[35]

Good faith is a concept that is potentially fairly open ended. Despite the gloss resulting from the WTO jurisprudence, it is still not clear what exact standard it encapsulates.[36] The practice of appending to it

[27] US–Gambling (Panel) para 6.50. [28] US–Offset Act (AB) para 296.

[29] See Japan–Taxes on Alcoholic Beverages (AB) footnote 21, referring to [1966] 2 *YILC* 219, wherein it is stated: 'When a treaty is open to two interpretations one of which does and the other does not enable the treaty to have appropriate effects, good faith and the objects and purposes of the treaty demand that the former interpretation should be adopted.'

[30] See for example US–Gambling (Panel) para 6.49; EC–Sugar Subsidies (Panel) para 7.151.

[31] EC–Sugar Subsidies (Panel) para 7.151.

[32] Ibid para 7.152, quoting Korea–Dairy Safeguard (AB).

[33] EC–Sugar Subsidies (Panel). [34] Zeitler 'Good Faith' 727. [35] US–Gambling.

[36] Zeitler 'Good Faith' 727.

principles which are underpinned by it facilitates elucidation whilst expanding its scope. The need for a certain caution with respect to the open-ended character of good faith has to some extent been taken on board. This is echoed in the following AB statement:

> Nothing, however, in the covered agreements supports the conclusion that simply because a WTO Member is found to have violated a substantive treaty provision, it has therefore not acted in good faith.[37]

In the same vein, with respect to the manner of discerning good faith, it has been stated:

> While Members are expected to negotiate, apply and interpret their treaty obligations in good faith, there are no provisions in the WTO Agreement that would allow a member's intentions to be probed and determined, except as reflected in the treaty language.[38]

Indeed, such is the reluctance to probe into 'bad faith' that it prompted one Panel to state:

> It is notoriously difficult, or at least delicate, to construe the requirement of the Vienna Convention that a treaty shall be interpreted in good faith in third party dispute resolution, not least because of the possible imputation of bad faith to one of the parties. We prefer, thus, to consider which interpretation suggests 'better faith' and to deal only briefly with this element of interpretation.[39]

This characterisation as 'delicate', occurring as it does in the WTO, may well echo the historical 'diplomatic character' of the WTO dispute settlement system. However, this hesitation or sensitivity marks a reluctance to engage with rigour in the judicial function. It detracts from the 'dirigiste' function of good faith for the interpreter. Bad faith preys on the vulnerable. This reluctance to police good faith reduces the standard of compliance by introducing minimal standards for the interpreter and for the protection of the weaker participants in the agreements. Opting for 'better faith' is not necessarily the same as ensuring 'good faith'.

Moreover, there is here a missed opportunity to clarify the role of good faith introspectively in terms of the partiality of the judges and of the 'guardian' or 'custodian' function of the interpreter in the process

[37] US–Offset Act (AB) para 298. [38] US–Gambling (Panel) para 6.50.
[39] US–Section 301 of the Trade Act (Panel) para 7.64.

of interpretation involving the interplay of diverse considerations. Thus, if interpretation is a process of determining the relevance of different sources, good faith involves not taking cognisance of those 'sources' which are underpinned by, or tainted with, bad faith or would result in taking into account considerations that would give rise to an unfair advantage or injustice. The injunction of good faith in the process of interpretation is very closely aligned to, if not coterminous with, the injunction to engage in justice in the process of interpretation – albeit within the parameters of the agreement.

1.3.3 Use of 'text', 'objects and purposes' and 'context' under Article 31 of the VC

The question of how the conditions 'text, context and objects and purposes' set out in Article 31 of the VC should be approached by an interpreter has arisen on a number of occasions in the WTO. Underlying this question are judgements as to what weight should be given to each of these conditions – particularly the text and the objects and purposes. Thus, Article 31 can be read either sequentially or holistically, masking a preference either for a textual/literal approach or for a more teleological approach to interpretation.

The overwhelming authority and weight in the WTO is given to the view that the correct approach is the holistic approach. Thus, the AB observed in EC–Chicken Classification:

> Interpretation pursuant to the customary rules codified in Article 31 of the *Vienna Convention* is ultimately a holistic exercise that should not be mechanically subdivided into rigid components.[40]

This pronouncement comes against the backdrop of some ambivalence, and possible soul-searching, within the WTO. Thus, there have been panel decisions wherein the sequential approach was taken,[41]

[40] EC–Chicken Classification (AB) para 176. See also US–Shrimp (AB) para 114; US–Section 301 of the Trade Act (Panel) para 7.22; Japan–Taxes on Alcoholic Beverages (AB) 11–12; EC–Bed Linen (21.5) (Panel) para 6.86; EC–Asbestos (Panel) para 8.46; Canada–Certain Measures Affecting the Automotive Industry (Panel) para 10.12; ILC Commentary to Article 31 of the VC [1966] 2 *YILC* 219–20 (A/CN.4/SER.A/1966/Add.1); I. Sinclair *The Vienna Convention on the Law of Treaties* (2nd edn Manchester UP, Manchester 1984) 116.

[41] The Panel in EC–Chicken Classification (later to be corrected by the AB on appeal) interpreted the AB statement in the US–Shrimp case at para 7.92 as follows: 'In other words, the AB indicated that the object and purpose should be considered after the treaty

sometimes as a consequence of a misinterpretation of the AB statement in the US–Shrimp case.[42] However, the holistic approach now arrived at comes arguably somewhat marred. This is because of the AB observation that Article 31 is 'ultimately' a holistic exercise. In addition, it is the case that as a matter of practice, a sequential approach (as opposed to a hierarchical approach in terms of text, context and objects and purposes) is tolerated. Although, at the risk of reading too much into the qualification 'ultimately', it is the case that the Panel in US–Section 301 of the Trade Act did not qualify 'holistic' in this fashion, neither did any of the previous panel and AB pronouncements.[43] Indeed, no such qualification is to be found in the relevant commentary of the ILC. In the same vein, ECJ and NAFTA practice does not qualify the role of objects and purposes in this manner.[44] Is this, then, a WTO interpretative gloss?

interpreter has determined the meaning of the words constituting the treaty obligation in question when read in their context.' The Panel in US–Carbon Steel interpreted the AB statement in US–Shrimp at para 8.46 as follows: 'With regard to the object and purpose of parties to a treaty and of the treaty, we note that the AB has stated, in *US–Shrimp*: A treaty interpreter must begin with, and focus upon, the text of the particular provision to be interpreted. It is in the words constituting that provision, read in their context, that the object and purpose of the states parties to the treaty must first be sought. Where the meaning imparted by the text itself is equivocal or inconclusive, or where confirmation of the correctness of the reading of the text itself is desired, light from the object and purpose of the treaty as a whole may usefully be sought. The context of a particular provision and the object and purpose of a treaty – or of the provision at issue – do not override the plain meaning of the text of the provision; rather, the text is to be read in its context and in light of the object and purpose of the treaty.' In US–Corrosion-Resistant Steel Sunset Review, the Panel stated at para 7.24: 'It is clear that interpretation must be based, first and foremost, on the text of the treaty, while context and object and purpose may also play a role.'

[42] US–Shrimp (AB) para 114. [43] Para 7.22.

[44] See for example Opinion of Advocate General Polares Maduro, Case C-327/02 (19 February 2004) para 24: 'According to well-established case-law, an international treaty must be interpreted not solely by reference to the terms in which it is worded but also in the light of its objectives. Article 31 of the Vienna Convention of 23 May 1969 on the Law of Treaties stipulates in that respect that a treaty must be interpreted in good faith in accordance with the ordinary meaning to be given to its terms in their context and in the light of its object and purpose.' See also NAFTA Arbitral Panel Established Pursuant to Chapter Twenty: In the Matter of Cross-Border Trucking Services (Secretariat File no. USA-MEX-98–2008–01) para 220 and footnote 242 therein; NAFTA Review of the Final Determination of Anti-Dumping Investigation In the Matter of Rolled Steel Plate Imports Originating in or Imported from Canada (Case MEX-9691904–02); and In the Matter of the Interpretation of and Canada's Compliance with Article 701.3 with Respect to DURUM Wheat Sales (CDA-92–1807–01) Final Report 8 February 8 1993.

1.3.3.1 'Text' under Article 31 of the VC

Text has primacy in the sense that interpretation 'must be based above all upon the text of the treaty'.[45] Furthermore, the construction of the text must be rooted in its ordinary meaning.[46] However, the absence of text does not exclude the possibility of implying it.[47]

The reference to text and ordinary meaning has led to the frequent use of the English dictionary. This in turn has led to the *Oxford English Dictionary* being referred to as one of the WTO Agreements! However, there is a more serious side to this almost knee-jerk recourse to the dictionary that calls for some reflection, because the language of international trade can be said in some measure to be informed by its own culture, as can the language of the negotiators. Not everyone is singing all the time from the same hymn sheet.[48] This is a point not so much about the 'context' as about the 'circumstances of the conclusion' of the agreement. Unthinking recourse to the dictionary may also displace or detract from the real meaning, given that a dictionary can open up a number of possible meanings. Language is not spoken or written from a dictionary. Rather, it is the dictionary which represents an effort at recording the meaning current at any given time. In short, what is not being asserted here is that the dictionary should not be used – merely that there ought to be some basis for resorting to its use, and, when doing so, for some caution.[49] Moreover, as has been pointed out,

> words should not be construed solely in the light of legal, logical and linguistic data, but also by reference to psychological data. Certain

[45] See Japan–Taxes on Alcoholic Beverages II (AB) 12. See also EC–Hormones (AB) para 181: 'The fundamental rule of treaty interpretation requires a treaty interpreter to read and interpret the words actually used by the agreement under examination not words the interpreter may feel should have been used.'

[46] US–Softwood Lumber IV (AB/R) paras 58–9.

[47] US–Carbon Steel (AB/R) para 65.

[48] See Mr Ago [1966] 1(Part II) *YILC* 56: 'no term has an inherent meaning. That was why it was essential to use terms as far as possible in the sense in which they were being customarily used, which was what was understood by the "ordinary meaning"'. See also Mr Bartos, 192 para 88: 'In his view the "ordinary meaning" was that which was understood inter parties – between the parties which had drafted the treaty.'

[49] This has been recognised in US–Gambling (AB) para 164, wherein the AB stated: 'In order to identify the ordinary meaning, a panel may start with the dictionary definitions of the terms to be interpreted. But dictionaries, alone, are not necessarily capable of resolving complex questions of interpretation, as they typically aim to catalogue all meanings of words – be those meanings common or rare, universal or specialized.'

dangers, threats and aspirations might compel the use or avoidance of certain words.[50]

1.3.3.2 'Objects and purposes' under Article 31 of the VC

The objects and purposes can be found in the preamble of the agreement and can also be discerned from the agreement as a whole. Thus, with respect to the locus of the objects and purposes under Article 31 of the VC, the AB has provided the following clarification:

> It is well accepted that the use of the singular word 'its' preceding the term 'object and purpose' in Article 31(1) of the *Vienna Convention* indicates that the term refers to the treaty as a whole; had the term 'object and purpose' been preceded by the word 'their', the use of the plural would have indicated a reference to particular 'treaty terms'. Thus, the term 'its object and purpose' makes it clear that the starting point for ascertaining 'object and purpose' is the treaty itself, in its entirety. At the same time, we do not believe that Article 31(1) excludes taking into account the object and purpose of particular treaty terms, if doing so assists the interpreter in determining the treaty's object and purpose on the whole. We do not see why it would be necessary to divorce a treaty's object and purpose from the object and purpose of specific treaty provisions, or *vice versa*. To the extent that one can speak of the 'object and purpose of a treaty provision', it will be informed by, and will be in consonance with, the object and purpose of the entire treaty of which it is but a component. (Footnotes omitted)[51]

[50] See Mr Bartos referring to François Geny, [1966] 1(Part II) *YILC* 201. See also Richard Brooks 'Agatha Christie's Grey Cells Mystery' *Sunday Times* December 2005 (http://www.timesonline.co.uk/article/0,,2087–1938204,00.html), which reports the conclusions of the Agatha Project, in which neurolinguists from certain Universities in the UK found that Agatha Christie's 'phrases act as a trigger to raise levels of serotonin and endorphins, the chemical messages in the brain that induce pleasure and satisfaction'.

[51] EC–Chicken Classification (AB) para 238. Contra US–'Zeroing' Dumping Margins (Panel) footnote 292, wherein the Panel stated: 'We note that Article 31 of the *Vienna Convention* provides that the object and purpose of a treaty must be taken into account in establishing the ordinary meaning of the terms used therein. Since Article 31 refers to "the object and purpose" of *the treaty* and not of its individual provisions, the argument of the European Communities regarding Article 9.3 might be better characterized as a further contextual argument rather than an argument relating to object and purpose. We further note that since the *AD [Anti-Dumping] Agreement* contains no discrete statement of objectives, one can only derive or deduce its objectives from the operational provisions of the Agreement. While it is perhaps possible at a very high level of generality to deduce from the operational provisions of the *AD Agreement* as a whole that for instance, one of the "objectives" of the *AD Agreement* is to provide a multilaterally agreed framework of rules governing actions against injurious dumping, claims of more specific objectives are

This is a welcome clarification. It gives the interpreter much scope in the determination of the objects and purposes. The AB, however, did not refer to Article 31 (3) (c) of the VC, which refers to taking into account 'any relevant rules of International Law'. Are the objects and purposes of the WTO Agreements augmented by the wider goals of the international legal system as a whole? There are dangers here of too much subjectivity and sophistry in the scope for both inductive and deductive reasoning that such an interpretation potentially allows.

In the context of the WTO, because the Marrakesh Agreement takes priority over other WTO Agreements,[52] its objects and purposes must stand at the apex of the configuration of objects and purposes set in the WTO Agreements.

1.3.3.3 'Context' under Article 31(2) of the VC

With respect to context under Article 31 (2) of the VC, the following general clarifications should be noted. First, the context comprises text, preamble and annexes. These are expressly referred to in Article 31 (2).[53] Preambles usually contain statements of the objects and purposes of agreements. Thus, Article 31 can refer to objects and purposes twice. Second, context requires reading the terms in the context of the treaty as a whole.[54] Third, an agreement or instrument forming part of the context of the agreement is not of mere evidential value, to be referred to in cases of ambiguity or obscurity, as when turning to supplementary material under Article 32.[55] Overall, the context requires an enquiry into the parameters of the agreement and directs that terms be interpreted in their context.

More particularly, in relation to the nature of the 'agreement' and 'instrument' forming part of the context (referred to in Article 31 (2) of the VC), the following points are to be noted. First, a unilateral

difficult to discern with any facility or compelling force due to the lack of anything that could properly be described as constituting a clear statement of the objectives of the *AD Agreement*. In this regard, we note that the European Communities refers to "the object and purpose of the *AD Agreement* regarding the consistent application of basic economic concepts" in the measurement of international price discrimination between two markets. The precise meaning the European Communities ascribes to these concepts and the manner in which the European Communities derived them from the text of the *AD Agreement* are unclear.'

[52] Article XVI (3) of the Marrakesh Agreement.

[53] EC–Chicken Classification (Panel) para 7.153.

[54] US–Copyright Act (Panel) footnote 49; US–Cotton Yarn (Panel) para 7.46.

[55] EC–Chicken Classification (Panel) para 7.153.

document does not qualify as part of the context, unless 'not only was it made in connection with the conclusion of the treaty, but its relation to the treaty was accepted in the same manner by the other parties'.[56] Second, for the agreement or instrument to be 'related' to the treaty, so as to form part of its context, it 'must be concerned with the substance of the treaty and clarify certain concepts in the treaty or limit its field of application. It must equally be drawn up on the occasion of the conclusion of the treaty.'[57] Third, the agreement or instrument must be accepted by the parties. Therefore, documents emanating from the GATT (General Agreement on Tariffs and Trade) or WTO Secretariat will not automatically suffice.[58] Nor will 'explanatory statements by members of a drafting committee in their personal capacity'.[59] However, 'interpretations given at a conference, e.g., by a chairman of a drafting committee, may constitute an "agreement" forming part of the "context"'.[60] Finally, an agreement or instrument that forms part of the context under Article 31 (2) does not *ipso facto* become integral to the treaty.[61] Thus, whether it should be characterised as a 'general rule' or an 'exception' is another matter.

The VC sets out a general adumbration of the material that could constitute the context. WTO jurisprudence has managed to clarify aspects of this adumbration. However, because of the addition of qualitative conditions, such as relationship to the substance of the treaty, and the function of clarification, some uncertainty may be said to have been added to the process of determining the context. After all, Article 31 (2) refers to 'any' agreement or instrument.

The process of judicial clarification of the context has its inherent limits.[62] Therefore, there is no reason that in the practice of WTO negotiations, at the time of the conclusion of an agreement, there

[56] EC–Chicken Classification (Panel) para 7.153. See also US–Copyright Act (Panel) para 6.45.

[57] EC–Chicken Classification (Panel) para 7.154. See also US–Gambling (Panel) para 6.76; US–Copyright Act (Panel) para 6.45.

[58] In US–Gambling (AB), the AB took a strict textual approach to defining 'agreement' to exclude instruments that evidenced mere consensus or understanding falling short of a formal agreement. See for a critique of this F. Ortino 'Treaty Interpretation and the Appellate Body Report in US–Gambling: A Critique' (2006) 9(1) *JIEL*, 117–48.

[59] US–Copyright Act (Panel) para 6.46. Although such statements could feature as part of the preparatory works.

[60] Ibid. [61] Ibid para 6.45.

[62] In US–Gambling, the Panel determined certain GATT documents to be 'context' under Article 31 (2), whereas the same documents were considered by the AB as 'supplementary material' under Article 32 of the VC.

cannot be an agreement on the precise parameters of its context. Indeed, this is an exercise that can even be managed post-agreement. The WTO Agreements are complex enough without added uncertainty over their precise contours.

1.3.4 'Subsequent practice' under Article 31 (3) (b) of the VC

Three particular points of focus have been identified with respect to subsequent practice under Article 31 (3) (b) of the VC:[63]

1. What constitutes practice?
2. How can the agreement of the parties not involved in the practice be established?
3. How can consistency in the practice be established?

The AB has shed light on the first of these questions:

> Generally, in international law, the essence of subsequent practice in interpreting a treaty has been recognized as a 'concordant, common and consistent' sequence of acts or pronouncements which is sufficient to establish a discernable pattern implying the agreement of the parties regarding its interpretation. An isolated act is generally not sufficient to establish subsequent practice; it is a sequence of acts establishing the agreement of the parties that is relevant. (Footnotes omitted)[64]

This was further clarified in US–Gambling as involving two elements:

1. 'there must be a common, consistent, discernable pattern of acts or pronouncements';
2. 'those acts or pronouncements must imply agreement on the interpretation of the relevant provision'.[65]

In EC–Chicken Classification the Panel had to consider

> whether 'common' and 'concordant' practice 'necessarily means that all WTO Members must have engaged in a particular practice in order for it to qualify as 'subsequent' practice . . . or whether the practice of a sub-set of the entire WTO-membership, including the practice of one Member only, may suffice.[66]

[63] EC–Chicken Classification (AB) para 54.

[64] Japan–Taxes on Alcoholic Beverages II (AB) 12–13. Subsequently cited in other cases, including EC–Chicken Classification (AB).

[65] See EC–Chicken Classification (AB) para 257, referring to the AB in US–Gambling.

[66] Ibid para 258.

The AB clarified this by stating:

> not each and every party must have engaged in a particular practice for it to qualify as a 'common' and 'concordant' practice. Nevertheless, practice by some, but *not all* parties is obviously not of the same order as practice by only one, or very few parties. To our mind, it would be difficult to establish a 'concordant, common and discernible pattern' on the basis of acts or pronouncements of one, or very few parties to a multilateral treaty, such as the *WTO Agreement.* We acknowledge, however, that, if only some WTO Members have actually traded or classified products under a given heading, this circumstance may reduce the availability of such 'acts and pronouncements' for purposes of determining the existence of 'subsequent practice' within the meaning of Article 31 (3) (b).[67]

As to the character of the agreement, the AB stated:

> in general, agreement may be deduced from the affirmative reaction of a treaty party. However, we have misgivings about deducing, *without further inquiry,* agreement with a practice from a party's 'lack of reaction'. We do not exclude that, in specific situations, the 'lack of reaction' or silence by a particular treaty party may, in the light of attendant circumstances, be understood as acceptance of the practice of other treaty parties. Such situations may occur when a party that has not engaged in a practice has become or has been made aware of the practice of other parties (for example, by means of notification or by virtue of participation in a forum where it is discussed), but does not react to it. However, we disagree with the Panel that 'lack of protest' against one Member's classification practice by other WTO Members may be understood, on its own, as establishing agreement with that practice by those other Members. (Footnotes omitted)[68]

This clarification raises a number of issues. First, there is in international relations a distinction between decision-making by consensus and decision-making through a more proactive form of agreement. I suggest that Article 31 (3) (b) has been interpreted more in line with the WTO practice of decision-making by consensus. Thus, not every party must engage in the actual practice, and silence (albeit under certain conditions) can be considered indicative of agreement. However, Article 31 (3) (b) refers to 'subsequent practice' which establishes the

[67] See EC–Chicken Classification (AB) para 257, referring to the AB in US–Gambling para 265.
[68] Ibid para 272.

'agreement'.[69] Second, by introducing the requirement of agreement of a party where that party is not engaging in the practice, has the AB not collapsed the distinction between Article 31 (3) (a) and (b), and thereby rendered Article 31 (3) (b) in part superfluous? Finally, by de-coupling the practice from the agreement of certain parties, the reference in Article 31 (3) (b) to the practice establishing the agreement is somewhat undermined. In brief, is this construction of 'subsequent practice' a legislative *modus operandi* for those more active members to lead the development of the agreement or merely the indicia of consensus in relation to an agreement already established?

1.3.5 'Relevant rules of international law applicable in the relations between the parties' under Article 31 of the VC

Article 31 (3) (c) of the VC[70] remains somewhat unclear, although the meaning of 'relevant rules' has been clarified by the AB to include general principles of international law.[71] What remains unclear is the meaning of 'parties'. In one case the Panel took note of the fact that the parties to the dispute alone were parties to certain relevant international agreements.[72] In the EC–Computer Equipment case,[73] the EC asserted that the Harmonised System and its Explanatory Note would be relevant in interpreting the obligations of the EC vis-à-vis WTO members who were also bound by it.

It would be an inappropriate interpretation of Article 31 (3) (c) if the analogous reasoning for the interpretation of Article 31 (3) (b), aligned to the practice of decision-making by consensus, were adopted here. In other words, members of the WTO should not be bound or affected by an international agreement through a consensus mode of decision-making when otherwise they would have had to engage in the agreement through express agreement. In addition, it needs to be stressed that Article 31 (3) (c) of the VC is about interpretation and not about amendment or modification.[74]

[69] See Mr Yasseen [1964] 1 *YILC* 286 para 52: 'subsequent practice meant the reference should be made to subsequent practice in so far as it helped to ascertain the intention of the parties. . . . Also it should not have the effect of modifying the treaty.'
[70] See also chapter 5 for the development perspective in the interpretation of this provision.
[71] US–Shrimp (AB) para 158.
[72] See US–Shrimp (Recourse to Article 21.5 by Malaysia) para 5.57. [73] (AB) para 13.
[74] See Mr Tunkin [1964] 1 *YILC* para 47 (ILC 767th Meeting A/CN.4/167/Add.3).

1.3.6 *Supplementary material under Article 32 of the VC*

Generally, in relation to Article 32, recourse to supplementary material can be made when the interpretation under Article 31 leaves the meaning of the treaty provision ambiguous or obscure or in order to confirm the meaning resulting from the application of Article 31.[75] Thus, recourse to supplementary material can be made only as an exception in specific circumstances,[76] and it is not mandatory. It is permissible if the conditions under Article 32 are satisfied.[77]

Furthermore, supplementary materials are not defined exhaustively. It has been pointed out that Article 32 states only

> that they *include* the preparatory work of the treaty and the circumstances of its conclusion. Thus, an interpreter has a certain flexibility in considering relevant supplementary means in a given case so as to assist in ascertaining the common intentions of the parties.[78]

In the circumstances, Article 32 is not limited to preparatory work. 'Supplementary materials' are not confined to preparatory work of the treaty and the circumstances of its conclusion.[79] Indeed, it has been noted that the principle of acquiescence could be considered relevant in the constitution of supplementary material.[80] At the same time, supplementary material does not have the same weight as the material of the agreement itself.[81]

[75] Article 32 of the VC. See also EC–Chicken Classification (AB) para 282.
[76] Japan–Taxes on Alcoholic Beverages (Panel) para 87.
[77] Canada–Measures Affecting the Importation of Milk and the Exportation of Dairy Products (AB) para 82.
[78] EC–Chicken Classification (AB) para 283. [79] US–Gambling (Panel) para 6.114.
[80] Ibid 6.122, referring to A. Aust *Modern Treaty Law and Practice* (Cambridge UP, Cambridge 2000) 200.
[81] Japan–Taxes on Alcoholic Beverages (Panel): '87. The Panel noted, in this respect, an interesting parallel with the legal status of "supplementary means" of interpretation of treaties – that comprise preparatory work – and their relevance for interpreting treaties. The Panel noted that according to Article 32 VCLT recourse to supplementary means of interpretation is required only as an exception in specific circumstances. The Panel noted in this respect the commentary of the International Law Commission: "The Commission considered that the exception must be strictly limited, if it is not to weaken unduly the authority of the ordinary meaning of the terms." The Panel further noted the statement of the International Law Commission that "the preparatory work... does not, in consequence, have the same authentic character as an element of interpretation, however valuable it may sometimes be in throwing light in the expression of the agreement in the text. Moreover, it is beyond question that the records of treaty negotiations are in many cases incomplete or misleading, so that considerable discretion has to be exercised in determining their value as an element of interpretation. D. Rauschning and R. G. Wetzel,

This analysis of the VC is, on the face of it, uncontroversial. However, it should be noted that with respect to the range of material included, the open-ended character of the provision has been pointed out. Certainly, no attempt at limiting the scope of such material is developed. On the other hand, this flexibility is constrained by ensuring that recourse to supplementary material in the WTO takes place only under the restrictive circumstances prescribed under Article 32.

However, there are persuasive arguments in favour of a liberal approach to the use of preparatory work under Article 32 of the VC. First, a restrictive approach is not universally followed in other international economic organisations, and even if it were, there is no evidence in WTO jurisprudence of following the practice of other international organisations in this respect. In relation to International Monetary Fund (IMF) practice, for example, it has been observed:

> *Travaux preparatoires* are almost always examined when interpretation is undertaken.[82]

> The IMF . . . does not consider the so-called supplementary means as either supplementary or confirmatory, and has recourse to them without observing the inhibitions of Article 31.[83]

In the IMF this is justified on the basis that such recourse reinforces the common intentions of the parties, and thus is in line with affirming the sovereignty of the members.

Second, there is some doubt whether under customary international law the restrictions on the use of the preparatory material actually exist.[84] Third, there was some dissent within the ILC in its preparatory

The Vienna Convention on the Law of Treaties, Travaux Preparatoires (Frankfurt: Metzner, 1978), pp. 255, 252. The Panel noted that considerable differences exist between preparatory work of international treaties and preparatory work of domestic legislation that preclude the automatic transposition of the reasoning of the International Law Commission to the case before it. Nevertheless, in the Panel's view, the analysis and reasoning of the International Law Commission could be relevant even in the context of preparatory work of domestic legislation.'

[82] J. Gold *Interpretation: The IMF and International Law* (Kluwer, London 1996) 184.

[83] Ibid 191. The reference by Gold to Article 31 must be a reference to Article 32.

[84] See Mr Rosenne [1964] 1 *YILC* 283 para 17: 'In the circumstances, to state that the travaux preparatoires had been used only to confirm an opinion already arrived at on the basis of the text of the treaty was coming close to a legal fiction. It was impossible to know by what processes judges reached their decisions and it was particularly difficult to accept the proposition that the travaux preparatoires had not actually contributed to form their opinion as to the meaning of a treaty which nevertheless, they stated to be clear from its text, but which, as the pleadings in fact showed, was not so. At all events, it

work in the drafting of the VC.[85] Fourth, Article 32 of the VC is in fact a compromise between two conflicting views as to the circumstances in which recourse can be had to preparatory work.[86] Fifth, it will be noted that the rule in Article 32 is 'inherently flexible',[87] given that the determination of what can be ambiguous can be subjective. Finally, in practice there is no bar to the use of the preparatory work when the terms are clear.[88] In the circumstances, there was ample opportunity in WTO dispute settlement to clarify the existence of flexibility in terms of recourse to the preparatory work.

1.3.7 'Circumstances of conclusion' under Article 32 of the VC

The circumstances of conclusion include a member's legislation, its practices,[89] court decisions[90] and the 'historical background against which the treaty was negotiated'.[91] The particular conditions under which an event, act or instrument can constitute circumstances of the conclusion of a treaty can be explained as follows. The particular event, act or other instrument must be relevant.[92] The AB clarified how the determination of relevance should be made:

> In our view, the relevance of a circumstance for interpretation should be determined on the basis of objective factors, and not subjective intent. We can conceive of a number of objective factors that may be useful in determining the degree of relevance of particular circumstances for interpreting a specific treaty provision. These include the type of event, document, or instrument and its legal nature; temporal relation of the circumstance to the conclusion of the treaty; actual knowledge or mere access to a published act or instrument; subject matter of the document, instrument, or event in relation to the treaty provision to be interpreted;

could be supposed that all practitioners of international law were free in their use of travaux preparatoires.'

85 See for example Yasseen [1964] 1 *YILC* para 56; Rosenne [1964] 1 *YILC* 317 para 38; US [1966] 2 *YILC* 93.

86 See Chairman of the ILC [1966] 1(Part II) *YILC* 203 (statement on the ILC 873rd Meeting).

87 See Special Rapporteur [1966] 2 *YILC* 99–100.

88 Ibid 58.

89 EC–Computer Equipment (AB) paras 92, 94.

90 EC–Chicken Classification (AB) para 309.

91 EC–Computer Equipment (AB) para 86; US–Gambling (Panel) para 6.113; Canada–Measures Affecting the Importation of Milk and the Exportation of Dairy Products (AB) para 132.

92 EC–Chicken Classification (AB) para 290.

> and whether or how it was used or influenced the negotiations of the treaty. (Footnotes omitted)[93]

Furthermore, the event, act or instrument may be relevant when there is a relationship of cause and effect between it and the text of the treaty and also when it sheds light on the common intentions of the parties.[94] In this context, both multilateral and unilateral sources can be relevant in discerning the common intentions of the parties.[95]

With respect to the necessary knowledge of the event, act or instrument constituting the circumstances of the conclusion of the treaty, the AB pointed out that 'constructive knowledge' can be imputed to the parties to the agreement when it stated:

> We understand the Panel's notion of 'constructive knowledge' to mean that 'parties have deemed notice of a particular event, act or instrument through publication'. We note the European Communities' view that 'deemed knowledge' on the basis of general 'access' to a publication cannot substitute the need for demonstrating a direct link between a circumstance and the common intentions of the parties. However, we consider that the European Communities conflates the preliminary question of what may qualify as a 'circumstance' of a treaty's conclusion with the separate question of ascertaining the degree of relevance that may be ascribed to a given circumstance, for purposes of interpretation under Article 32. As far as an act or instrument originating from an individual party may be considered to be a circumstance under Article 32 for ascertaining the parties' intentions, we consider that the fact that this act or instrument was officially published, and has been publicly available so that any interested party could have acquired knowledge of it, appears to be enough. Of course, proof of actual knowledge will increase the degree of relevance of a circumstance for interpretation. (Footnotes omitted)[96]

With respect to the timing of the relevant act, event or instrument, it has been pointed out that there is no 'temporal limitation on what may qualify as "circumstances of conclusion"'.[97] However,

> there may be some correlation between the timing of an event, act or other instrument (i.e. how far back in the past they took place, were enacted or were adopted) and their relevance to the treaty in question. It would be fair to state that, generally speaking, the further back in time

[93] Ibid para 291. [94] Ibid para 289. [95] Ibid. [96] Ibid para 297.
[97] EC–Chicken Classification (Panel) para 7.344.

> that an event, act or other instrument took place, was enacted or was adopted relative to the conclusion of a treaty, it is less likely to have influenced the ultimate text of the treaty and, therefore, it is less likely that it is relevant to the interpretation of that treaty. Furthermore, the fact that Article 32 of the *Vienna Convention* refers to 'circumstances of *conclusion*' indicates to us that the event, act or other instrument should be temporally proximate to the conclusion of a treaty in order for it to be taken into account for the interpretation of that treaty under Article 32 as 'circumstances of conclusion'. In our view, what is considered temporally proximate will vary from treaty provision to treaty provision.[98]

Indeed, the AB has added:

> In our view, it is possible that documents published, events occurring, or practice followed *subsequent to* the conclusion of the treaty may give an indication of what were, and what were not, the 'common intentions of the parties' *at the time* of the conclusion. The relevance of such documents, events or practice would have to be determined on a case-by-case basis. (Footnotes omitted)[99]

It will be observed here that the AB's conception of circumstances of conclusion is somewhat non-judgemental. The AB refrains from alluding to the fact that imbalance in negotiating strengths, abuse of negotiating powers and complexity in the negotiating processes can comprise the relevant circumstances of the conclusion of a treaty. These can impact the text and the common intentions of the parties. By the same token, being subject to 'constructive knowledge', without further ado, implies almost a disregard for the uneven burden on parties resulting from the process of negotiations and the added burden in the light of that constructive knowledge.

1.4 Conclusion

There has been much clarification and gloss – indeed, there have been many opportunities taken and missed. Above all, however, the interpretation of the principles of treaty interpretation in the VC has been characteristically oblivious to the possible underlying inequities in the process of multilateral trade negotiations, and to the impact that principles of treaty interpretation can further have on these underlying

[98] EC–Chicken Classification (Panel) para 7.344.
[99] EC–Chicken Classification (AB) para 305.

conditions. Indeed, the members of the WTO in their rush to conclude the Uruguay Round borrowed the customary rules of treaty interpretation without much reflection as to how they could be refined and better adapted for the WTO Agreements. It has also been in the same, somewhat blinkered, vein that interpretation of the VC has taken place on occasions in the WTO.

How will some of these interpretations be re-interpreted in the future and what lessons are there outside the WTO with respect to these interpretations? These are difficult questions. There is a case for caution in automatically adopting the WTO gloss, given that the interpretation arises from the particular exigencies and peculiarities of the WTO – in particular as an organisation concerned with international trade.

There is, indeed, a case for re-visiting the relevant interpretation provisions of the DSU, as there is an argument in matters of trade negotiations for some stock-taking on interpretative issues at the time of the conclusion of the agreement. There is also a case for a greater role for the objects and purposes in the interpretative process, along with inculcation of some measure of fairness into the canons of interpretation drawn upon. Interpreters are custodians of agreements. This places them under an obligation to ensure fairness within the scope that the interpretative process allows.

The principles of treaty interpretation established under the VC form a construct within which interpreters function as gate-keepers. This gate-keeping function can be effectively performed only if the VC principles are made clearer and injected with a greater degree of fairness. The VC principles are, in parts, unclear; they take a mechanical, blinkered view of the medium of language and allow for uncertainty in the very construct of the 'agreement' to be interpreted – and for still further uncertainty in the precise set of external factors that can be taken into account in the process of interpretation. Above all, the principles have generally been understood as being on the whole neutral in relation to questions of fairness/equity and justice in the process of interpretation.

2

Interpreting institutional aspects of the WTO Agreements

2.1 Introduction

In the now-substantial literature on WTO law, the legal focus has traditionally been oriented towards the substantive law aspects of the WTO Agreements – with the important exception of the dispute settlement system. The dispute settlement system is an important institutional pillar of the WTO, but it is not its only institution. In some senses, research and analysis have responded to the disputes developing around international trade liberalisation. Further explanations for this orientation lie in the institutional character of the WTO, namely, the relative age of the institution, the pace of its institutional development compared with the pace of development in its substantive law, and the non-controversial nature of a number of the institutional aspects of the WTO Agreements. In addition, it can be generally, albeit somewhat impressionistically, observed that a large number of the new breed of international trade lawyers – both academic and practising – have more of a substantive law interest in WTO law, often approaching the subject with the baggage of environmental law, general international trade law, European law and economic analysis of law. Indeed, those with expertise tend to be relatively less steeped in public international law, and consequently in the institutional aspects of the WTO Agreements.[1] Thus, in the short time during which the WTO has been in existence

I am grateful to Valerie Hughes, former Director of the AB, for her valuable comments on an earlier draft of this chapter. The errors that remain and the opinions expressed are mine.

[1] Of 83 professors in the field listed on the www.worldtradelaw.net site in 2004, only 34 were also listed with a teaching and/or research interest in public international law. The number of professors listed as being involved in international trade law had grown to 141 by July 2006. However, the proportion with a teaching and/or research interest in public international law had not grown by as much. This assessment is necessarily impressionistic, as not all the public international law interests are clearly set out.

there have been few[2] exhaustive monographs[3] exclusively on the institutional aspects of the WTO. Generally, legal treatises on the WTO, after historical and general institutional introductions, rapidly go on to focus at length on the substantive law aspects of the WTO and the dispute settlement system. More specifically, there has been little focus on the context of interpretation of the institutional aspects of the WTO.[4]

The various aspects of any international organisation can lead to the characterisation 'Janus faced', partaking of both constitutional and treaty aspects[5] – corresponding to the substantive and institutional provisions of the WTO Agreements. In general terms, the international institutional law focus is described as being the equivalent of domestic constitutional and administrative law.[6] The institutional aspect of the WTO is to be found particularly in the Marrakesh Agreement and the DSU, but it is found to varying degrees in all the WTO Agreements. The provisions are concerned with the administrative, procedural, institutional and constitutional aspects of the WTO. The substantive provisions of the WTO Agreements, in contrast, are concerned mainly with the liberalisation of international trade.

Thus far, the disputes among members of the WTO that have been referred to the dispute settlement system have tended to involve differences of interpretation of the substantive provisions of the WTO Agreements. However, in some measure there have also been disputes involving the institutional aspects of the WTO Agreements. For example, of particular note has been the consideration of the system of legal representation in the WTO dispute settlement system,[7] as well as the consideration of the respective functions of certain organs of the WTO.[8] The interpretative questions pertaining to the institutional

[2] See for example J. H. Jackson *The World Trade Organization: Constitution and Jurisprudence* (RIIA, London 1998); K. Kufuor *World Trade Governance and Developing Countries: The GATT/WTO Code Committee System* (RIIA, London 2004).

[3] In the English language.

[4] However, see for example L. Bartels 'The Separation of Powers in the WTO: How to Avoid Judicial Activism' (2004) 53 *ICLQ* 861–95; C.-D. Ehlermann and L. Ehring 'The Authoritative Interpretation under Article IX:2 of the Agreement Establishing the World Trade Organization: Current Law, Practice and Possible Improvements' (2005) 8(4) *JIEL* 803–24.

[5] H. G. Schermers *International Institutional Law* (3rd edn Martinus Nijhoff, The Hague 1995) 709. See also 4th edn.

[6] Schermers *International Institutional Law* (3rd edn) 7.

[7] See for example EC–Bananas (AB); Indonesia–Automobiles (Panel).

[8] See for example India–Quantitative Restrictions on Imports of Agricultural, Textile, and Industrial Products (AB).

aspects of the WTO Agreements are no less important than the substantive provisions.

There are important reasons to focus specifically on the institutional aspects of the WTO Agreements in terms of the processes involved in their interpretation. First, this importance flows from the role of interpretation in the context of institutional norms. Thus, interpretation can

- clarify the functional scope of the powers of different organs of the WTO;
- clarify the appropriate allocation of competences to the WTO and to its members, respectively;
- facilitate institutional support in the administration of the WTO Agreements generally;
- reinforce the dispute settlement system in particular;
- facilitate appropriate external relations.

Second, interpretation can contribute to the clarification of the interpretative process itself. Thus, interpretation can shed light on which interpretative principles are relevant, which interpretative approaches are appropriate and which materials may be relevant to the interpretative process. Third, a focus on interpretation in the institutional context assists in unravelling the underlying institutional forces that influence different interpretations. Finally, an interpretative perspective enables delineation of the institutional and substantive provisions of the WTO. This facilitates the application of the appropriate approach to interpreting the institutional provisions of the WTO Agreements – for example, whether a literal or purposive approach should be followed. Each institutional or substantive aspect involves and evokes different considerations in the interpretative process.

All the organs of the WTO and its membership are engaged in comprehending and applying the institutional elements of the normative framework of the WTO Agreements, and in that process interpreting this framework. Thus, not only is interpretation a process to be found in formal pronouncements and engaged in during the process of adjudication; it is also implicit in the actions of the organs of the WTO and its membership – where this involves the implementation of the WTO Agreements. This latter aspect of the process of interpretation is validated in the VC, although in a prescribed fashion.[9] This wider sense of interpretation, implicit in the practice of the

[9] See Article 31 (3) (b) of the VC.

implementation of the WTO Agreements, is in reality equivalent to a live picture of the WTO law and its institutions, and therefore legally significant. Thus not only the Panels and the AB but also the various committees and working groups in the WTO are relevant – as indeed are the actions of every member applying the WTO Agreements. Interpretation is thus a multifaceted process.

An examination of the institutional aspects of the WTO Agreements in the context of interpretation involves focusing on the agreements establishing the main institutions of the WTO, particularly from the standpoint of the institution of interpretation in the WTO and the role of interpretation in the clarification of institutional problems. A focus on the institution of interpretation involves considering inter alia the mandate to interpret, the aids to interpretation and the approaches to interpretation taken. On the other hand, the principal institutional problems in the WTO are essentially symptoms of jurisdictional tensions between different organs of the WTO, including its membership – real or imputed. The manner in which such institutional issues have been clarified through the process of interpretation is the context of interpretation.

The aim here is not an institutional study of the WTO. Rather, the object is to rehearse some of the principal institutional issues facing the WTO in the context of interpretation. The context of interpretation is not easy to define. It revolves around the central query underlying this focus – namely, what are the principal issues in terms of the institutional aspects of the WTO, including the institution of interpretation itself, that interface with the processes of interpretation? More particularly, what sense should those involved in interpreting an institutional issue be armed with? All of this, of course, is premised on the assumption that the institutional aspects of the WTO Agreements are self-evident and can be distinguished clearly at all times from the substantive law of the WTO.

2.2 The formal mandate to interpret the WTO Agreements

The general authority to interpret WTO Agreements is set out in Article IX (2) of the Marrakesh Agreement (hereinafter referred to as legislative interpretation).[10] Under this provision, a number of conditions have to be satisfied for the exercise of such authority. First, the authority to

[10] See Zhang N. 'Dispute Settlement under the TRIPS Agreement from the Perspective of Treaty Interpretation' 17(1) *Temp Int'l & Comp LJ* 206. It is referred to by Ehlermann and Ehring ('Authoritative Interpretation') as 'authoritative interpretation'.

interpret rests exclusively with the Ministerial Conference and the General Council.[11] Second, the adoption of an interpretation requires a three-quarters majority vote of the members. A decision by consensus could satisfy this requirement – although consensus decision-making is not the same as decision-making through formal votes. Indeed, the practice of consensus decision-making applies to Article IX of the Marrakesh Agreement, and the application of this practice has been attributed to Article IX being invoked infrequently, if at all.[12] Third, the authority to interpret is to be exercised 'on the basis of a recommendation by the Council[13] overseeing the functioning of that agreement'. Since each of the councils in the different spheres of WTO activities is empowered to set up subsidiary bodies as required,[14] the input of such subsidiary bodies[15] can also become relevant. However, as has been pointed out, where these organs cannot arrive through consensus at a decision, they need to refer the matter to the General Council.[16] Finally, the authority to interpret is not to be exercised in a way that undermines the amendment provision of the Marrakesh Agreement.

However, the interpretative process under Article IX of the Marrakesh Agreement is not very clear. First, there are open questions as to the form and procedure that the mandate to interpret under Article IX prescribes for a valid interpretation under its terms. For example, at least one pronouncement[17] by the Ministerial Conference has generated controversy as to whether it is in fact an interpretative decision under Article IX.[18] This is because of the form it took and the procedures

[11] Article IX of the Marrakesh Agreement.

[12] See Bartels 'Separation of Powers' 872. However, Ehlermann and Ehring ('Authoritative Interpretation') clarify that consensus decision-making is not the only reason for the infrequent use of this provision.

[13] That is, the Council for Trade in Goods, the Council for Trade in Services, and the Council for TRIPS.

[14] Article IV para 6 of the Marrakesh Agreement.

[15] Committees on Market Access, Agriculture, Sanitary and Phytosanitary Measures, Technical Barriers to Trade, Subsidies and Countervailing Measures, Anti-Dumping Practices, Import Licensing, Trade-Related Investment Measures, Safeguards; the Textile Monitoring Body and the Working Party on State Enterprises.

[16] See Ehlermann and Ehring 'Authoritative Interpretation'. See also for example WTO Rules of Procedure for Meetings of the Council for Trade in Goods WT/L/79 (7 August 1995).

[17] See the Declaration on the TRIPS Agreement and Public Health WT/MIN(01)/Dec/W/2 (14 November 2001).

[18] See for example S. Charnovitz 'The Legal Status of the Doha Declaration' (2002) 5(1) *JIEL* 207–11; F. M. Abbott 'The Doha Declaration on the TRIPS Agreement and Public Health: Lighting a Dark Corner at the WTO' (2002) 5(2) *JIEL* 469–505.

adopted in its formulation. At one extreme, the Doha Ministerial Declaration on the TRIPS Agreement and Public Health[19] has been described as a mere political declaration;[20] on the other hand, it has been described categorically as an interpretative decision under Article IX of the Marrakesh Agreement.[21] A middle-ground characterisation is that it is not an authoritative interpretation, mainly because it does not expressly refer to Article IX.[22] It is described as a declaration and not a decision, and it is not based on the recommendation of the TRIPS Council. However, it is considered to be a subsequent agreement between the members of the WTO regarding the application of the TRIPS (Trade-Related Aspects of Intellectual Property Rights) Agreement.[23] One point is clear: a Ministerial Declaration must first be interpreted on its own terms to discern its contents.[24] According to the WTO *Analytical Index*, Article IX (2) has never been used. However, this particular Doha Declaration came after June 2001, and the *Analytical Index* covers material only up to 30 June 2001. Even if the *Analytical Index* did extend to after June 2001, this point would simply be persuasive. Under the circumstances, should an interpretative pronouncement under Article IX be specifically termed a 'decision' and be clearly based on a recommendation by the council overseeing the functioning of that agreement?

Second, the assignment of 'exclusive authority' to the Ministerial Conference or the General Council on questions of interpretation does not, at first glance, fit comfortably with the interpretative deliberations of Panels and the AB (hereinafter referred to as judicial interpretation).[25] The Panels and the AB also have the authority to interpret the WTO Agreements. Thus, a Panel is required to make 'an objective assessment of . . . the applicability of and conformity with the relevant

[19] WT/MIN(01)/Dec/W/2 (14 November 2001).

[20] Robert Zoellick, cited in Charnovitz 'Legal Status of the Doha Declaration'.

[21] D. Shankar 'The Vienna Convention on the Law of Treaties, the Dispute Settlement System of the WTO and the Doha Declaration on the TRIPS Agreement' (2002) 36(4) *JWT* 721–72.

[22] See Charnovitz 'Legal Status of the Doha Declaration'; Abbott 'The Doha Declaration on the TRIPS Agreement and Public Health'.

[23] Via Article 31 (3) (a) of the VC.

[24] For example in US–Countervailing Duties on Certain Hot-Rolled Lead and Bismuth Carbon Steel Products (AB) para 49, the AB concluded that on its terms the Ministerial Declaration on Dispute Settlement Pursuant to the Agreement on Implementation of Article VI of GATT 1994 or Part V of the Agreement on Subsidies and Countervailing Measures was not binding as it was couched in hortatory language.

[25] See Zhang 'Dispute Settlement under TRIPS'.

covered agreements, and make such other findings as will assist the DSB [Dispute Settlement Body] in making recommendations or in giving rulings provided for in the covered agreements'.[26] Similarly, the AB is charged with considering 'issues of law covered in the panel report and legal interpretations developed by the Panel'.[27] These respective functions are reinforced by the fact that the dispute settlement system is recognised by the membership as an apparatus for the clarification of 'existing provisions' of the WTO Agreements.[28] This role in clarifying existing provisions has also been affirmed by the AB.[29] By the same token, the DSU expressly stipulates that deliberations by the Panel and the AB are not to prejudice the rights of members to seek authoritative interpretations under the covered agreement – a reference to legislative interpretation.[30]

There are three important differences between the legislative and judicial interpretative processes – leaving aside purely procedural ones. First, the Panel and AB can engage in interpretation only in the context of dispute resolution between parties, whereas the General Council and the Ministerial Conference have a wider scope for interpretation: they have the jurisdiction to interpret regardless of whether there is a dispute between members of the WTO. However, there is some evidence to suggest that this mandate for judicial interpretation in the DSU has itself been interpreted somewhat liberally – despite its limited scope. Thus, although the Panel's functions include an objective assessment of the applicability of the relevant covered agreements and their conformity with the facts,[31] and the AB's jurisdiction is limited to 'issues of law covered in the Panel report and legal interpretations developed by the panel',[32] the AB appears to have given guidance even when the clarification was no longer relevant to the case in hand. For example, at the request of the United States, the AB in US–Steel Products[33] gave general guidance to members about applying safeguard measures in the future with respect to the issue of 'causation' under the Agreement on Safeguards.[34] One explanation for this indulgence is that the AB is obliged to consider every issue that arises in a case.[35] However, the

[26] See Article 11 of the DSU. [27] See Article 17 para 6 of the DSU.
[28] See Article 3 (2) of the DSU. [29] See US–Shirts and Blouses (AB).
[30] Article 3 (9) of the DSU. [31] Article 11 of the DSU. [32] Article 17 (6) of the DSU.
[33] AB (2003) para 484.
[34] It is the case, though, that the advice given was based on previous cases. In this way, however, the AB reinforced and clarified its previous conclusions with respect to future matters.
[35] Valerie Hughes, e-mail dated 17 October 2004 to the author.

merits of this explanation rest on what constitutes an issue in any given case. In contrast, on the grounds of 'judicial economy', the AB did not clarify China's contention that it was entitled to the developing country status under the Agreement on Safeguards.[36] According to Valerie Hughes, the AB cannot engage in judicial economy because, unlike Panels, it is bound by Article 17.12 of the DSU.[37] However, the AB can address the issue and, having done so, decide that it is not necessary to resolve it.[38] There are conceptual similarities here, although there is a subtle difference. Be that as it may, although the doctrine of judicial economy (loosely speaking) echoes the exclusivity of the legislative interpretative process,[39] the process of judicial interpretation nevertheless carries with it scope for legislative development.

Second, there is no established doctrine of precedent in the WTO.[40] Consequently, the decisions of the AB and the Panels are limited in their scope to the parties in question – at least formally. In contrast, legislative interpretations are binding on the membership as a whole. It is this capacity to engage in legislative interpretation that is binding on the membership as a whole over which the General Council and the Ministerial Conference have exclusive authority;[41] this capacity does not exist 'by implication or by inadvertence elsewhere'.[42]

Third, the process of judicial interpretation is subject to two constraints not to be found in the context of legislative interpretation. First, recommendations and rulings of the DSB 'cannot add or diminish the rights and obligations provided in the covered agreements'.[43] In contrast, legislative interpretation is limited only by the requirement that it 'shall not be used in a manner that would undermine the amendment provisions in Article X'. The limitation here is not that the interpretation should not result in an amendment but that the specific

[36] Ibid.

[37] Ibid. Panels on the other hand are entitled to exercise judicial economy because their mandate is worded differently.

[38] Ibid.

[39] See for example US–Shirts and Blouses (AB); WTO *Analytical Index*: DSU paras 302–12; Article IX (2) of the Marrakesh Agreement.

[40] See for example Japan–Taxes on Alcoholic Beverages (AB) (1996); Jackson *The World Trade Organization*. See also for example Raj Bhala 'The Power of the Past: Towards *De Jure Stare Decisis* in WTO Adjudication' (2001) 33 *Geo Wash J Int'l L Rev* 873–978.

[41] See Article IX (2) of the Marrakesh Agreement.

[42] Japan–Taxes on Alcoholic Beverages (AB); US–Shirts and Blouses (AB); US–Certain EC Products (AB).

[43] See Article 3 (2) of the DSU.

provision on amendment in the Marrakesh Agreement should not be undermined.[44]

The amendment provision of the Marrakesh Agreement essentially covers procedural aspects of the amendment process – namely, the right to initiate an amendment, voting requirements for the amendment of different provisions and agreements of the WTO, and acceptance procedures for amendments. It is these procedures for amendment that must not be undermined. The focus is not amendment per se. In sum, therefore, undermining through the interpretation of procedural issues relating to amendments is equivalent to undermining through adding to or diminishing substantive rights and obligations.

In any event, even if the reference were to amendment per se, as opposed to the procedures involved in amendment – which it is not – the Marrakesh Agreement does not include a definition of 'amendment' as opposed to 'interpretation'. To the extent that there is any criterion by which to shed light on what constitutes an amendment, it is intended to differentiate between different types of amendments that call for different procedures for adoption.[45] The definition is not meant to distinguish between amendment and interpretation. Furthermore, as has been pointed, the notion of 'undermining' under Article IX (2) allows for some latitude.[46]

In addition, even in this context, the amendment criterion distinguishes between amendments that 'alter the rights and obligations of the Members' and those that do not.[47] The process of altering rights and obligations is of wider scope than the process of adding to or diminishing rights and obligations. Altering rights and obligations may or may not result in adding to or diminishing rights and obligations. In a sense, undermining the authority to alter rights and obligations through interpretation is more challenging than diminishing those rights and obligations – unless, of course, the interpretation is blatantly legislative and clearly sweepingly prohibitive of any exercise in alteration. In other words, it can be easier to diminish rights and obligations through interpretation than it is to affect the authority to alter those rights and obligations.

[44] Contra the view taken by Ehlermann and Ehring ('Authoritative Interpretation'), who interpret Article IX (2) as referring to amendment in the sense of 'revising trade rules'.

[45] See for example Article X (4) of the Marrakesh Agreement.

[46] Ehlermann and Ehring 'Authoritative Interpretation'. [47] Ibid.

The second constraint on judicial interpretation is that the AB and the Panel are to interpret the WTO Agreements in accordance with 'customary rules of interpretation of public international law' – a reference that has itself now been interpreted as referring to Articles 31–2 of the VC.[48] This requirement is not present insofar as the process of legislative interpretation is concerned. This noticeable absence suggests that the members have left themselves broad discretion over how they engage in the process of interpreting the WTO Agreements, and in particular that they are not confined by some of the disciplines relating to interpretation to be found in the VC. Indeed, the relating of restricted interpretation based on 'customary rules of interpretation of public international law' in the context of the DSU to Articles 31–2 of the VC – when, in fact, the former principles can be broader than those in Articles 31–2 of the VC[49] – is not applicable to the legislative interpretative process. Under international law it is open to the parties to establish a particular mode of interpreting the WTO Agreements.[50]

There are other differences in the rules for engaging in interpretation. In the case of the WTO Agreements relating to goods, services and intellectual property rights, the Ministerial Conference and the General Council are to engage in the interpretative process 'on the basis of a recommendation by the Council overseeing the functioning of that Agreement'. This injunction is not to be found in the DSU as such, which begs the question whether a similar input on the part of the respective councils is legitimate in the judicial interpretative process under the DSU. This question of legitimacy arises from the policy underpinning the legislative interpretative process – namely, that the political organs of the WTO have been charged with the process of interpreting the WTO Agreements. The range of material prescribed as being at the disposal of these organs for this purpose can include political and/or extra-legal input outside the strict range of aids to interpretation expressly set out in Articles 31–2 of the VC. Thus, built into the inclusion of materials for the process of interpretation is a good deal of discretion that accompanies the authority for interpretation under Article IX (2). The organs in the dispute settlement system, in

[48] See for example US–Gasoline (AB); Japan–Taxes on Alcoholic Beverages (AB).

[49] See for example Shankar 'Vienna Convention' 723. See also L. Bartels 'Applicable Law in WTO Dispute Settlement Proceedings' (2001) 35 *JWT* 499–519; C. P. Mavroidis 'Remedies in the WTO Legal System: Between a Rock and Hard Place' (2000) 2(4) *EJIL* 763–813.

[50] See for example Article 31 (4) of the VC.

contrast, are judicial or quasi-judicial organs with a mandate to clarify existing provisions of the WTO Agreements, under customary rules of international law, with the specific injunction that the interpretative process should 'not add to or diminish the rights and obligations' under the WTO Agreements.

However, the interpretations placed on the capacity of the judicial organs of the WTO under the DSU to avail themselves of information appear to put a gloss on the material that may be resorted to under the judicial interpretative process. Thus, Article 13 of the DSU accords the discretionary[51] right to a Panel to 'seek' information from any relevant source (individual or body)[52] it considers appropriate. This authority has been interpreted as being comprehensive[53] in order to enable the Panel to make an objective assessment of the facts and the applicability and conformity of the relevant agreements.[54] It has been interpreted thus to authorise the seeking of both factual and legal information and advice. Thus, in Japan–Agricultural Products,[55] the United States successfully argued that the 'information' that can be sought by Panels under Article 13 includes clarification of legal points from any relevant source.[56] In US–Copyright Act, the EC argued that Article 13 of the DSU is limited to factual information and technical advice, and therefore does not include provision for legal arguments or legal interpretations received from non-members.[57] This contention was not accepted by the Panel. In Chile–Agricultural Products (AB), the AB noted that the Panel in the process of interpreting the term 'variable import levies' sought documents under Article 13 of the DSU that formed part of the circumstances of the conclusion of the WTO Agreement.[58]

Article 13 has thus been construed as being wide enough to allow for resort to the deliberations of the various councils – including for the purposes of interpretation. Indeed, it would appear that even those organs of the WTO not mentioned under Article IX of the Marrakesh Agreement are included. Further, external sources – for example, the

[51] See EC–Bed Linen (AB) (21.5).

[52] See US–Lead Bars (Panel) para 6.6.

[53] US–Shrimp (AB); EC–Hormones (AB). 'Seek' can mean 'receive' also.

[54] US–Shrimp (AB); Japan–Agricultural Products (AB).

[55] Japan–Agricultural Products (AB) para 30. [56] Ibid; US–Shrimp (AB) para 106.

[57] (Panel) para 6.6. The EC has proposed, however, in the DSU reform that under Article 13 there should be authority to consider both factual and legal argumentation. See WTO Job [03] 69 Re 2, 29.

[58] Para 230 footnote 206.

IMF[59] and World Intellectual Property Organization (WIPO)[60] – have also been resorted to under this provision.

With respect to the powers of the AB to avail itself of information, the authority is set out in Article 17.9 of the DSU, and Rule 16 (1) of the Working Procedures in relation to a division of the AB. This mandate has been interpreted widely, similarly to Article 13 of the DSU. Thus, in US–Countervailing Duties on Certain Hot-Rolled Lead and Bismuth Carbon Steel Products,[61] the AB took the view that it had the legal authority to accept any information that was pertinent,[62] including an *amicus curiae* in an appeal.[63]

There is evidence that both Panels in their deliberations and members in the course of their arguments[64] have referred to the deliberations of relevant organs of the WTO – for example, the Council for Trade in Goods and subsidiary committees under that council. Thus, the Panel in Indonesia–Automobiles[65] took into account the 1997 Report to the WTO of the Council for Trade in Goods in relation to the work of the Trade-Related Investment Measures (TRIMs) Committee – in particular the fact that the TRIMs Committee stated that 'different views continued to be expressed' on the relationship of the provisions of the TRIMs . . . to those of the other WTO Agreements . . .'. Similarly, in US–Textiles Rules of Origin, the Panel relied on the harmonisation work by the WTO Committee on Rules of Origin.[66] The Panel asserted that it was not persuaded that the fabric formation rule was inherently unsound, in view of the 'substantial support within the framework of the harmonisation programme'. Further, the Panel observed that the Agreement on Rules of Origin 'clearly allows for differentiation of rules between products, as can be seen in the harmonization work programme . . .'.[67] In the same vein, the WTO *Analytical Index* itself refers to the decisions and recommendations of WTO bodies in charge of the operation of particular agreements.[68]

59 See India–Quantitative Restrictions on Imports of Agricultural, Textile and Industrial Products (AB) paras 147–8.

60 See US–Section 211 (Havana Club) (AB) paras 146, 189.

61 (AB) (2000) para 36. 62 Ibid para 39. 63 Ibid para 42.

64 See for example the Indian reference to criticism of US legislation in the WTO Committee on Rules of Origin in US–Textiles Rules of Origin (Panel) para 6.56.

65 See Indonesia–Automobiles (Panel) paras 6.36–7.

66 See US–Textiles Rules of Origin (Panel) para 6.74. 67 Ibid para 6.242.

68 See WTO *Analytical Index* Introduction. See also for example the WTO *Analytical Index* references to the Recommendations of the Committee on Anti-Dumping Practices in relation to Article 2 of the Agreement on Anti-Dumping with respect to the period of

However, this reference to the deliberations of relevant organs of the WTO in the dispute settlement system may not in fact result in engagement in interpretation on the basis of recommendations by the relevant council. First, it is the member and the organs of the DSU that seek to rely on deliberations of the work of the councils. It is well established that Panels have broad discretion over the sources from which they can seek information.[69] Second, the nature of the reliance needs to be considered in order to establish whether, on the facts, the material relied upon amounts to an actual 'recommendation'. Third, consideration should be given to the question whether the reliance stems from a mandate under the agreement in question or is consequential on the mandate of the relevant body. Finally, the reliance may result because the material constitutes evidence of subsequent agreement and practice in the WTO under the VC.

Furthermore, it needs to be noted that Articles 31–2 of the VC apply to the reception and factoring in of material through Article 13 of the DSU in the process of judicial interpretation. There is a danger, however, that the practice and construction of Article 13, if left unchecked, will conflate the legislative and judicial interpretative processes set out in the WTO (if it has not already done so). In particular, the arrogation of complete, unfettered control over the reception and evaluation of legal information from any source, as has been suggested,[70] is questionable. Panel and AB discretion to seek information cannot involve a capacity to receive the same information as the General Council and the Ministerial Conference under Article IX (2) of the Marrakesh Agreement – in particular the ability to receive and accept *de lege ferenda* advice, at least from a strictly legal perspective.

In conclusion, the 'exclusive authority' that rests under the Marrakesh Agreement with the General Council and the Ministerial Conference

data collection for dumping investigations. No express authority for such recommendations to the DSU is to be found in the AD Agreement generally or under Article 2 specifically. Nor is there any direct and express authority under the DSU for accepting such recommendations. However, authority for such organs of the WTO making recommendations may be implicit in the mandate of the organ or via Articles 31–2 of the VC as evidence of subsequent agreement or practice of the members of the WTO.

69 See Article 13 of the DSU; US–Shrimp (AB).

70 In Canada–Measures Affecting the Export of Civilian Aircraft (AB) para 184, the AB stated inter alia that it was 'within the province and the authority of a panel . . . to determine the need for information and advice in a specific case, to ascertain the acceptability and relevance of information or advice, and to decide what weight to ascribe to that information and advice'.

has a number of features that give the Article IX interpretative process a legislative character. Thus, the authority is legislative in that it exists in relation to matters that arise outside an actual dispute. The authority is legislative in that, when it is exercised, it may be said to prevail over any engagement in interpretation by other organs of the WTO – including Panels and the AB. Finally, the authority is legislative in that it is accompanied by broad discretion over the factors that can be taken into account in the interpretative process and the resulting interpretation. In contrast, the interpretative process under the dispute settlement system has rightly been characterised as judicial interpretation.[71] This is because such interpretation is engaged in by the judicial organs of the WTO, it is formally non-legislative in character, and the interpretative process is accompanied by certain disciplines.

The competition between the legislative and judicial processes of interpretation is not the only form of competition. In fact, although the Ministerial Conference and the General Council, as organs of the WTO, have exclusive authority in terms of legislative interpretation, this authority does not displace the capacity of the membership of the WTO as a whole to agree on matters of interpretation outside the remit of Article IX, via Article 31 (3) (a) and (b) of the VC, namely,

- through any subsequent agreement between the members of the WTO regarding the interpretation of the WTO Agreements or the application of particular provisions;
- through any subsequent practice in the application of the WTO Agreements that establishes the agreement of the members of the WTO regarding the interpretation of the WTO Agreements.

Both these VC processes of interpretation partake of the character of legislative interpretation. In this way, they exist in parallel with Article IX of the Marrakesh Agreement – somewhat in contrast to the judicial interpretative process, which does not carry with it the same democratic legitimacy when it strays into a legislative mode.

2.3 Approaches to interpreting the institutional aspects of the WTO under the Marrakesh Agreement

The Marrakesh Agreement is the principal agreement setting out the institutional framework of the WTO. As such it sets out the powers and

[71] Ibid.

functions of the various organs of the WTO. Until now, from an *institutional* perspective, there have been no significant interpretations of the provisions of the Marrakesh Agreement; nor have there been any notable disputes between members or between the WTO and a member directly involving the provisions of the Marrakesh Agreement. It is, however, possible that in future questions will need to be clarified involving, for example, the determination of the precise scope of the powers of the various organs of the WTO and the WTO Secretariat. Likewise, a dispute may arise between the WTO and a member involving, for example, Article VIII (2) of the agreement, dealing with the WTO's privileges and the immunities to be accorded by each member to the WTO in the discharge of its functions.

The provisions of the Marrakesh Agreement may be the subject of clarification through the legislative interpretative process. A dispute between members involving the agreement's provisions may benefit from panel or AB pronouncements. In the case of a dispute between the WTO and a member, the dispute settlement system is not available for this purpose.[72] Such disputes may be resolved through the General Council or the Ministerial Conference, for example, and further clarifications of the provisions may also be found in the decisions, declarations and acts of the General Council and Ministerial Conference.

From the perspective of interpretation, an important starting-point here is the Preamble of the Marrakesh Agreement, which sheds light on its provisions and the other WTO Agreements. At first sight, the Preamble appears to be concerned exclusively with substantive issues, focusing on the objects and purposes of the WTO. However, the Preamble has some relevance in informing the interpretation of the institutional provisions of the WTO Agreements. First and foremost, at a theoretical level, the objects and purposes of any international organisation cannot be completely separated from the shape of the institutional aspects of that organisation. In some measure, the objects and purposes of an international organisation must have a bearing on its institutional setting.

However, in practice, an organisation set up to eliminate racial discrimination in employment could well engage in discriminatory practices internally. An organisation set up to introduce democratic practices into nation-states might itself not be democratic in terms of

[72] Article 1 of the DSU read in conjunction with the remainder of the DSU seems to confine the availability of the dispute settlement system to disputes between members.

the participation of its membership within the organisation. Indeed, in this respect, not only may there be no concordance between the objects and purposes and the internal practices of the organisation, but an organisation may be institutionally hampered in achieving its goals because of the specific manner in which it has been structured. Here, the lack of concordance is between the legal structure and the legal mandate of the organisation as set out in its objects and purposes. Thus, practice may be de-coupled from ideals, and there may also be a dichotomy between the objects and purposes, on the one hand, and the express provisions relating to the institutional aspects of the organisation, on the other. Nevertheless, as a matter of logic, the objects and purposes of an organisation must to some degree shape its internal organisational framework. Thus, an organisation established to eliminate genocide cannot possibly authorise its secretariat to be staffed wholly by genocide contemplators! In the same vein, to the extent that there is no express displacement when it comes to interpretation, the objects and purposes of an organisation must inform and colour the interpretation of those provisions of the agreement concerned with the institutional aspects of the organisation. This must be taken to be the intention of the negotiators. In the case of the WTO, it is now well established that the Preamble, because it reflects the intentions of the negotiators, adds 'colour, texture and shading' to the interpretation of the WTO Agreements.[73] In the US–Shrimp case, notably in this context, the AB did not exclude from this relationship provisions in the WTO Agreements concerned with the institutional aspects of the WTO. Thus, there is a relationship not only in logic but also in law between the objects and purposes of an organisation and its institutional framework.

Second, the Preamble specifically refers to certain attributes that have a bearing on the institutional framework of the WTO – particularly Article III enumerating the functions of the WTO and Article IX setting out the decision-making processes in the WTO. Thus, the institutional framework of the WTO must be

- integrated;
- viable and durable;
- multilateral;

[73] US–Shrimp (AB) paras 152, 153, 155.

- sustainable in terms of making optimal use of the world's resources in accordance with the objective of sustainable development;
- imbued with the basic principles underpinning the multilateral trading system.[74]

'Integrated' implies that the various organs of the WTO are part of one system and therefore need to operate harmoniously with each other. 'Integrated' can also refer to the equal participation of all the members of the WTO in WTO affairs.[75] 'Viable and durable' refers to an acceptable, practical and efficacious institutional structure that will have a degree of permanence. Thus, an institution that responds only to the political expediencies of the day may well not be viable. 'Multilateral' is a reference not simply to membership but also to the nature of the institutional ethos. 'Sustainable development' involves inculcating good governance into the institution of the WTO. Finally, the basic principles underpinning the multilateral system embrace notions of fair competition, non-discrimination and efficiency. These principles can be said to have a bearing on the institutional aspects of the WTO.

In addition, certain basic policy grounds that underpin, or ought to underpin, the interpretative process pertaining to the institutional aspects of the WTO need to be outlined here:

- efficient disbursement of competences among organs;
- transparent, accountable, democratic and participatory allocation of competences between organs and members;
- efficient interfaces between the institutional and substantive objectives;
- fair, prompt and effective procedures.[76]

In line with some relevant international institutional practices (namely, those of the IMF and World Bank Group), the institutional provisions of the WTO Agreements, being of a constitutional nature, may well call for a teleological approach to interpretation rather than a strictly literal interpretation. This is confirmed by the view held by publicists.[77] Indeed, with respect to institutional matters in the

[74] See Preamble to the Marrakesh Agreement.
[75] See the *Concise Oxford Dictionary* (8th edn Oxford UP, Oxford 1990).
[76] US–FSC (AB) para 166.
[77] See for example R. Jennings and A. Watts *Oppenheim's International Law* (9th edn Longmans, London 1992) I: 1273 footnote 13; I. Brownlie *Principles of Public International Law* (5th edn Oxford UP, Oxford 2003) 658.

DSU, there is evidence of such an orientation in the jurisprudence of the WTO.[78]

2.4 Interpretation and the institutional aspects of the dispute settlement system

That the dispute settlement system of the WTO is an institution is axiomatic. In this context, its institutional framework has been the subject of much clarification through the jurisprudence of the WTO. However, there are sound reasons for treating the dispute settlement system in a disaggregated way because it has a number of facets. Each of these has different characteristics – and all of them combine to create the dispute settlement system. On closer examination, the disaggregated dispute settlement system focuses on such diverse issues as procedure, participatory rights, jurisdiction and implementation. Each of these may have its own dimensions for interpretation. In sum, this disaggregated form of the dispute settlement system can be reconstructed into four distinct aspects to facilitate analysis here:

- the system of interpretation;
- procedural and evidential issues;
- institutional aspects specific and internal to the dispute settlement system;
- institutional aspects of the dispute settlement system in relation to the WTO as a whole.

Only three of these partake of the character of institutional issues, and consequently they are more relevant to this chapter: (1) the mechanism of interpretation set out in Articles 3.2 and 11 of the DSU, the general aspects of which are discussed elsewhere[79] (here the focus is mainly on the mechanism of interpretation as it relates to the interpretation of the DSU itself); (2) the internal aspects of the system, involving its different organs (mainly the DSB, the Panel, and the AB); (3) those institutional aspects that focus on the relationship of the dispute settlement system to other organs of the WTO, and which are therefore constitutional in character.

[78] See below and for example US–Shrimp (AB) paras 107–10, quoted in WTO *Analytical Index* para 338: the AB castigated the Panel for reading the word 'seek' in an 'unnecessarily formal and technical' manner.

[79] See chapter 1.

2.4.1 *The system of interpreting the DSU*

Generally, the framework is no different for interpreting the DSU than for interpreting any other WTO Agreement. Thus, the provisions of the DSU are to be interpreted in accordance with 'customary rules of interpretation of public international law'.[80] In particular, the provisions of the DSU are to be interpreted against the background of its objects and purposes. These are similar to, though not necessarily the same as, the general objects and purposes of the WTO Agreements. The DSU itself does not have a Preamble as such, but its objects and purposes are set out in Article 3:

- security and predictability;
- the preservation of rights and obligations;
- clarification of existing provisions;
- prompt settlement;
- positive solutions.

To these need to be added

- the interests of developing members;[81]
- the interests of the least-developed members.[82]

In addition, the gloss placed by the jurisprudence of the WTO on these expressly stated objectives in the DSU needs to be considered: 'security and predictability of the multilateral trading system and through it that of the market-place and its different operators. DSU provisions must, thus, be interpreted in the light of this object and purpose and in a manner which would most effectively enhance it'.[83]

The procedural rules contained in the DSU have been described as designed to promote 'not the development of litigation techniques, but simply the fair, prompt and effective resolution of trade disputes'.[84] Moreover, it has been stated that the DSU is intended to ensure due process of law.[85]

It can be seen here that the jurisprudence of the WTO has indeed added to the objects and purposes of the DSU: the DSU itself does not refer to security and predictability in the market-place, nor does it refer

[80] Article 3 (2) of the DSU. [81] See Article 21 of the DSU. [82] See Article 24 of the DSU.
[83] See WTO *Analytical Index* on Article 3 (2); US–Section 301 of the Trade Act (Panel).
[84] See US–FSC (AB) para 166.
[85] See WTO *Analytical Index* in relation to Article 9; EC–Hormones (AB).

to the security and predictability of the different operators in the market-place. Similarly, there is no mention of 'fair' in the DSU.

Alongside the objects and purposes of the DSU, which feature in its interpretative process specifically, are other notable aspects of this process. The first is resorting to the practice of international tribunals for guidance in the operation of the dispute settlement system. Thus, in Turkey–Restrictions on Imports of Textile and Clothing Products (hereafter Turkey–Textile), the Panel decided that it did not have authority to direct a WTO member to act as a third party on the basis inter alia of the practice of international tribunals – specifically, the International Court of Justice (ICJ).[86] In US–Shirts and Blouses, the AB observed that 'various international tribunals, including the ICJ, have generally and consistently accepted and applied the rule that the party who asserts a fact, whether the claimant or the respondent, is responsible for providing proof thereof '.[87] In EC–Bananas III, the AB stated inter alia that there is nothing, in the 'prevailing practice of international tribunals, which prevents a WTO Member from determining the composition of its delegation in AB proceedings'.[88] The second noteworthy aspect is that the practice in the dispute settlement system has also been to resort in the interpretation of the provisions of the DSU to the common law and civil systems of law. Thus, in US–Shirts and Blouses, the AB relied on a 'generally accepted canon of evidence' in civil law and common law.[89]

The practices of international tribunals or the common law and civil systems are not in themselves sources of law or aids to interpreting the DSU. They do, however, constitute 'relevant rules of international law applicable' to the interpretation of the DSU.[90] The relevant rules of international law here would be from the corpus of general international law.

Finally, of note is what may be termed the 'nothing in the DSU doctrine' used in the interpretation of the DSU to justify a course of action. Thus, in EC–Hormones, the AB stated that 'nothing in the DSU limits the faculty of a Panel freely to use arguments submitted . . .'.[91] In Canada–Measures Affecting the Export of Civilian Aircraft, the Panel

[86] The Panel referred to the International Court of Justice in the *Military and Paramilitary Activities in and Against Nicaragua* case [1984] *ICJ Reports* 430–1 and the *Phosphate Lands in Nauru* case [1992] *ICJ Reports* 259–62 (preliminary objections). See WTO *Analytical Index* para 139.

[87] See US–Shirts and Blouses (AB) 14.

[88] EC–Bananas III (AB) para 10.

[89] US–Shirts and Blouses (AB) 14.

[90] See Article 31 (3) (c) of the VC.

[91] See EC–Hormones (AB) para 156.

observed that 'there is nothing in the DSU or in the Appendix 3 Working Procedures, to prevent a party submitting new evidence or allegations after the first substantive meeting'.[92] In US–Countervailing Duties on Certain Hot-Rolled Lead and Bismuth Carbon Steel Products, the AB stated: 'neither the DSU nor the Working Procedures explicitly prohibit acceptance or consideration of such briefs . . . we are of the opinion that as long as we act consistently with the provisions of the DSU and the covered agreements, we have the legal authority to decide whether or not to accept and consider any information . . .'.[93] In Thailand–Steel, the AB stated that 'nothing in the DSU prevents a defending party from requesting further clarification on the claims raised in a panel request from the complaining party, even before the filling of the first written submission'.[94]

According to Friedl Weiss, neither the Panel nor the AB can be described in these circumstances as relying on the doctrine of inherent powers.[95] Although there is a national court practice – and some evidence of such a practice in international courts and tribunals – of reliance on inherent powers for the necessary discharge of the judicial function or the maintenance of judicial integrity,[96] the WTO judicial organs cannot, Weiss claims, be said to exhibit this reliance. Inter alia this is because these are not circumstances that necessitate invoking inherent powers and because of the dependency of the Panels and the AB on the membership.[97] Thus, Weiss asserts that 'the AB is beset by a watchful if not vigilant Membership, guarding against the AB usurping judicial power through the exercise of its tools of interpretation'.[98]

Two points must be noted here, however. First, the existence and scope of 'necessity' in the context of the use of inherent powers by a judicial organ in discharging its functions is determined by the kind of judicial organ involved and the context in which it operates. Thus, whether a course of action is necessary can be a matter of judgement. Second, by the same token, whether the AB is 'too dependent upon the Members of the WTO for it to possess anything akin to inherent powers' is also a matter

[92] Canada–Measures Affecting the Export of Civilian Aircraft (Panel) para 9.77.

[93] US–Countervailing Duties on Certain Hot-Rolled Lead and Bismuth Carbon Steel Products (AB), para 39.

[94] Thailand–Steel (AB) para 97.

[95] See F. Weiss 'Inherent Powers of National and International Courts' in F. Ortino and E.-U. Petersmann (eds) *The WTO Dispute Settlement System 1995–2003* (Kluwer Law International, The Hague 2004) chapter 14.

[96] Ibid 178. [97] Ibid 189–90. [98] Ibid.

of judgement.[99] Furthermore, a distinction needs to be made between the membership acting as a check on the abusive use of inherent powers and the membership precluding the very use of such powers. There is, therefore, scope for arguing that at the very least the judicial organs of the WTO have at their disposal certain inherent powers to facilitate the judicial function, if not to subsume the already-articulated 'nothing in the DSU doctrine' into it. Indeed, a recent panel decision stated, albeit with reference to certain provisions of the DSU:

> The Panel nonetheless considers that, flowing from its terms of reference and from the requirement, in Article 11 of the DSU, to 'make an objective assessment of the matter before it . . . ', as well as the requirement, pursuant to Article 12 of the DSU, to determine and administer its Working Procedures, the Panel has the inherent authority – and, indeed, the duty – to manage the proceeding in a manner guaranteeing due process to all parties involved in the proceeding and to maintain the integrity of the dispute settlement system.[100]

However, given that the Panel did not draw on a sense of 'necessity' but grounded its decision in a sense of 'duty', this may still not be a good example of the arrogation of inherent powers by the Panel. That this is not a good example is reinforced by the fact that the Panel appears to have inferred from certain provisions of the DSU that it has 'inherent authority'. It is the case, though, as Weiss points out, that 'courts or tribunals often look either explicitly or implicitly to the intent of the legislature when contemplating using inherent powers'.[101] However, in this process, the Panel appears to have conflated implied powers and inherent powers. Insofar as implied powers are concerned, it must be observed here that in the jurisprudence of the WTO generally, the doctrine of implied terms – and consequently of implied judicial authority – is recognised and accepted,[102] although, under the doctrine of implied terms, 'necessity' is also an important factor.[103]

[99] Ibid.

[100] EC–Conditions for the Granting of Tariff Preferences to Developing Countries (Panel) para 7.8.

[101] Weiss 'Inherent Powers of National and International Courts' 178.

[102] See for example EC–Bananas (22.6) (US) para 3.7: 'If the Arbitrators were deprived of such an implied authority the principles and procedures of Article 22.3 of the DSU could clearly be circumvented.' See also for example EC–Bananas (22.6) (Ecuador) para 45; Australia–Automotive Leather I (Panel) para 6.21; Argentina–Footwear (AB) para 111; US–Lamb Safeguards (AB) para 126.

[103] See for example *Oppenheim's International Law* I: 1271 footnote 4.

If it is not possible to subsume the 'nothing in the DSU doctrine' into the doctrine of inherent powers or implied terms because of the possible absence of the 'necessity' factor, it is nonetheless there in the practice of the dispute settlement system. Furthermore, the manner of its formulation – echoing as it does the much criticised Lotus presumption of legitimacy of state action in the context of state jurisdiction[104] – could be cause for alarm were it not for the fact that it appears to be confined to the functioning of the dispute settlement system.

In addition to looking at the text of the DSU, it is also necessary to examine the secondary legal sources in the DSU[105] in any evaluation of its interpretative process – albeit as it relates to procedural aspects of the dispute settlement system. The process by which the organs within the dispute settlement system generate secondary legal sources itself involves a sub-set of an interpretative act, which in turn raises questions of conformity with the DSU and the WTO Agreements. Thus, Article 12.1 of the DSU enables Panels to craft their own procedures, if they so decide, on an ad hoc basis. Panels here have 'some discretion in establishing their own working procedures',[106] particularly in situations that are not 'explicitly regulated'.[107] One example is that of granting additional third-party rights.[108] Another example is the introduction of a requirement with respect to the timing of requests for preliminary determinations.[109] Such additional requirements need to be justified as being in accordance with the provisions of the DSU, including the edict that such working procedures 'should provide sufficient flexibility so as to ensure high-quality panel reports, while not unduly delaying the panel process'.[110] According to Petros Mavroidis, in US–Preliminary Determination with Respect to Certain Softwood Lumber from Canada (Panel), the additional requirement imposed was not inconsistent with Article 3.2 of the DSU in that because it was formulated on the basis of Article 12.2 of the DSU, it did not affect the balance of rights and

104 See the *Lotus* case (1927) 10 *PCIJ Reports Series A*. See also generally on jurisdiction D. J. Harris *Cases and Materials on International Law* (6th edn Thompsons, London 2004) chapter 6.

105 See for example P. C. Mavroidis 'Development of WTO Dispute Settlement Procedures through Case-Law (We Will Fix It)' in Ortino and Petersmann *WTO Dispute Settlement System* chapter 13, 155.

106 India–Patent (AB) paras 92–3.

107 EC–Hormones (AB) footnote 13.

108 EC–Hormones (AB) para 154.

109 US–Preliminary Determination with Respect to Certain Softwood Lumber from Canada (Panel), cited in Mavroidis 'Development of WTO Dispute Settlement' 154.

110 Article 12.1 of the DSU.

obligations of the parties as set out in the Uruguay Agreements.[111] Whether in that particular case the additional requirement was justified is, of course, arguable – and this Mavroidis concedes. However, the normative parameters provided in Article 12.2 immediately become apparent. There is clearly a fair degree of latitude here for Panels to interpret their authority in formulating additional procedural requirements. This discretion is limited by the requirement of due process and the prohibition on modifying the provisions of the DSU.[112] The parameters thus provide guidelines for the exercise of the Panel's authority and, at the same time, sufficient flexibility in the process.

Similarly, the AB is empowered to draw up its own working procedures under Article 17.9 of the DSU. In addition to the general Working Procedures drawn up under this authority, divisions of the AB are empowered on an ad hoc basis in an individual appeal to adopt appropriate procedures for that appeal 'where a procedural question arises that is not covered' by the Working Procedures.[113] These procedures, however, need to be consistent with the DSU, the other covered agreements and the Working Procedures.

Thus, the AB in EC–Asbestos created a system to enable the reception of *amicus curiae* briefs, under certain conditions, in the form of Additional Procedures under Rule 16 (1) of its Working Procedures.[114] Rule 16 (1) contains the 'nothing in the DSU doctrine', insofar as procedural questions are concerned. However, as has been pointed out, what constitutes a procedural question under Rule 16 (1) seems to have been interpreted widely to include the important question of who can make *amicus curiae* submissions to the AB.[115] Rule 16 (1) thus reserves to the AB some scope in interpreting what additional rules it enunciates.

2.4.2 Institutions within the dispute settlement system

At its core, the internal institutional dimension of the WTO dispute settlement system focuses on the configuration of the jurisdictional competences of its various organs and the members of the WTO. The process of interpretation in the dispute settlement system with respect to the DSU informs the configuration of the jurisdictional competences

[111] Mavroidis 'Development of WTO Dispute Settlement' 154.
[112] India–Patent (AB) paras 92–3.
[113] Rule 16 (1) of the Appellate Body Working Procedures.
[114] EC–Asbestos (AB) para 52. [115] See for example Weiss 'Inherent Powers' 180.

involved. This process of interpretation raises essential questions about the approach to interpretation and the locus of the authority to interpret. Underpinning this configuration are the power claims of various organs and entities.

2.4.2.1 The DSB

At the apex is the DSB – a political body whose remit is essentially to administer the rules and procedures set out in the DSU.[116] The DSB has a great amount of discretion because the manner in which it should administer the DSU is not spelled out. Nevertheless, its authority is confined to administering the rules and procedures set out in the DSU, except as otherwise provided. Thus, parties to a dispute can seek clarification of a panel request during a DSB meeting.[117] However, questions of interpretation relating to the authority of the DSB under the DSU appear to rest effectively with the General Council and the Ministerial Conference, under their authority to interpret.[118] In Australia–Automotive Leather II, the Panel, confronted with the question of evaluating the conduct of the DSB in establishing the Panel, stated:

> The establishment of a panel is the task of the DSB. It is by no means clear that, once the DSB has established a panel, as it did in this case at its meeting of 22 June 1998, the panel so established has the authority to rule on the propriety of its own establishment. Nothing in our terms of reference expressly authorizes us to consider whether the DSB acted correctly in establishing this Panel.[119]

A more confident AB subsequently clarified the circumstances in which a Panel has the authority to rule on the propriety of its own establishment. In Mexico–High-Fructose Corn Syrup, it identified two instances when a Panel was under a duty to consider this question:

> First, as a matter of due process and the proper exercise of the judicial function, panels are required to address issues that are put before them

[116] See Article 2 of the DSU.

[117] See Canada–Measures Relating to Exports of Wheat and Treatment of Imported Grain (AB) para 211.

[118] Article IX (2) of the Marrakesh Agreement.

[119] Australia–Automotive Leather II (Panel) paras 9.12, 9.14–15. See also Mavroidis 'Development of WTO Dispute Settlement' 160–7, wherein he points out a discrepancy in the case law. See also Korea–Measures Affecting Imports of Fresh, Chilled and Frozen Beef (Panel) para 6.2; Thailand–Antidumping Duties on Angles, Shapes and Sections of Iron or Non-Alloy Steel and H-Beams from Poland (AB) (hereafter Thailand–Antidumping Duties on Angles). Contra Korea–Dairy Safeguard (AB); Mexico–HFCS (AB) (21.5).

> by the parties to a dispute. Second, panels have to address and dispose of certain issues of a fundamental nature, even if the parties to the dispute remain silent on those issues. In this regard, we have previously observed that '[t]he vesting of jurisdiction in a panel is a fundamental requisite for lawful panel proceedings'. For this reason, panels cannot simply ignore issues which go to the root of their jurisdiction – that is, to their authority to deal with and dispose of matters. Rather, panels must deal with such issues – if necessary, on their own motion – in order to satisfy themselves that they have the authority to proceed.[120]

This clarification is consistent with a Panel's obligation to make an objective assessment of the facts and the applicability of the relevant covered agreements.[121] It is reinforced by the fact that no provision of the DSU is excluded from being invoked by a Panel – including Article 2. Also of note is the Panel's obligation to make 'such other finding as will assist the DSB in making its recommendations or rulings'.[122]

In relation to the propriety of the DSB in the establishment of a Panel, it is suggested that in principle here, too, a Panel should be able to address the conduct of the DSB, provided there is a legal basis for this. This legal basis rests on the fact that the conduct of the DSB touches on the very establishment and jurisdiction of the Panel – an issue of a fundamental nature that embraces the Panel's existence and function. However, in engaging in such a focus, the Panel may well need to 'maintain an astute sense of political awareness'.[123] Thus, the question of who has the power in applying to the DSB the WTO Agreements is grounded as much in politics as in law.

2.4.2.2 The dispute settlement system and the members

The relationship between the dispute settlement system and the membership is, in a sense, determined by the 'balance established' in the WTO Agreements (including the DSU) 'between the jurisdictional competences conceded by the Members to the WTO and the jurisdictional competence retained by the members for themselves'.[124] This balance has, however, been informed by the manner in which it has been interpreted in the jurisprudence of the WTO. The interpretation of this balance manifests itself through a number of discreet issues, which nevertheless are underpinned by the tensions arising from

[120] Mexico–HFCS (AB) (21.5) para 35. [121] Article 11 of the DSU. [122] Ibid.
[123] See Weiss 'Inherent Powers' 182 in relation to the AB and the membership.
[124] See EC–Hormones (AB) paras 115–17.

competing jurisdictional claims. Three examples are proffered here. First, members have been given broad discretion in bringing a dispute to the WTO; they do not have to demonstrate a legal interest.[125] On the face of it, this latitude relates to the circumstances under which members can bring a claim under the dispute settlement system. However, it also concerns the breadth of jurisdictional competence under the DSU. In short, by taking a broad-brush approach to the circumstances in which members can bring a claim, the organs in the dispute settlement system have reserved to themselves a wide scope of jurisdiction and business! The AB's reasoning in EC–Hormones echoed the 'nothing in the DSU doctrine'. It refused to find by implication the need for a 'legal interest' as a condition for bringing a claim.[126] Yet it was open to the AB to look at national and international judicial practice in this regard.

Second, the province of justiciable subject matter has been the subject of judicial determination in the WTO. This determination has been characterised by a generally extensive view of the province of the WTO judicial organs. Thus, the 'measure' under the terms of reference of a Panel[127] has been interpreted to include 'what appear on their face to be private actions' but 'may nonetheless be attributable to a government because of some governmental connection to or endorsement of those actions'.[128] Similarly, a 'measure' can be a 'practice' 'if it has an independent operational status as a measure'.[129] In the context of the traditional dichotomy between mandatory and discretionary legislation, whereby discretionary legislation was considered outside the province of judicial scrutiny under GATT, the scope of this exclusion has been under challenge. Thus, the discretion must be vested in the executive branch;[130] furthermore, the operation of the mandatory/discretionary dichotomy depends on the nature of the obligation – and in the substantive context of a given case, not in the abstract.[131]

[125] EC–Bananas III (AB) para 132. [126] Korea–Dairy Safeguard (Panel) para 7.13.

[127] See Article 6 (2) of the DSU; Article XXIII of GATT 1994.

[128] See Japan–Measures Affecting Consumer Photographic Film and Paper (Panel) para 10.52.

[129] Y. Naiki 'The Mandatory/Discretionary Doctrine in WTO Law' (2004) 7(1) *JIEL* 23–72, 70. See also Countervailing Measures on Certain EC Products (AB); US–Corrosion-Resistant Steel Sunset Review (AB) (2003) para 97.

[130] US–Anti-Dumping Act of 1916 (AB) paras 88–91.

[131] See US–Section 301 of the Trade Act (Panel) paras 7.53–4; US–Export Restraints (Panel) paras 8.10–13; US–Corrosion-Resistant Steel Sunset Review (AB) (2003) para 93; Naiki 'Mandatory/Discretionary Doctrine in WTO Law'.

Third, the level of deference to members has been under strain. Thus, the consistency of a national measure is to be evaluated against the relevant international agreement rather than against the national legislation implementing the international agreement.[132] This would appear to be the case even though there are occasions when international agreements leave a margin for national discretion in interpreting the international obligation, and when interpretation can be found in the national legislative formulation, which raises the question whether this is an indirect way of affecting the direct applicability of international obligations. In addition, a Panel may make its own determination of the national legislation,[133] and indeed weigh the national jurisprudence when there is uncertainty or division in the courts.[134] In the same vein, the 'manner in which municipal law classifies an item cannot, in itself, be determinative of the interpretation of provisions of the WTO covered agreements'[135] because 'it would be inappropriate to characterise, for purposes of applying any provisions of the WTO covered agreements, the same thing or transaction differently, depending on its legal categorization within the jurisdictions of different Members'.[136]

2.4.2.3 The Panel

As the judicial organ of first instance in the dispute settlement system, the Panel is involved in the interpretation of facts and law. However, before I consider the scope of this involvement, there is a prior question as to the very status of Panels in the WTO. Can Panels be equated with the WTO or contracting parties? The same question arises in the context of the AB. It arose in India–Quantitative Restrictions on Imports of Agricultural, Textile and Industrial Products, where the issue was whether the reference to 'Contracting Parties' in Article XV [2] of GATT 1994 included a Panel.[137] The Article states inter alia: 'In all cases in which the CONTRACTING PARTIES are called upon to consider or deal with problems concerning monetary reserves, balances

[132] See US–Underwear (Panel) paras 7.10, 7.12–13.

[133] See US–Anti-Dumping Act of 1916 (EC) (Panel) para 6.51.

[134] US–Anti-Dumping Act of 1916 (EC) (Panel) para 6.53.

[135] US–Final Countervailing Duty Determination with Respect to Certain Softwood Lumber from Canada (AB) para 65.

[136] Ibid para 56.

[137] See India–Quantitative Restrictions on Imports of Agricultural, Textile and Industrial Products (AB) para 5.12.

of payments or foreign exchange arrangements, they shall consult fully with the International Monetary Fund.'

In India–Quantitative Restrictions on Imports of Agricultural, Textile and Industrial Products, the United States argued that read in conjunction with paragraph 2 (b) of the Incorporation Clause of GATT 1994 in Annex 1 A of the WTO Agreement, the reference was to the WTO, and the WTO included the Panel.[138] India, however, argued otherwise, contending that 'to interpret the terms of Article XV to refer to panels meant to ignore the division of functions between the different bodies of the WTO'.[139] However, the Panel did not deliberate on the issue, because it had decided that it could consult the IMF under Article 13.1 of the DSU. Article 13.1 refers specifically to the powers of Panels in seeking information.[140] This point was not appealed, and so was not considered subsequently upon appeal.[141] This was unfortunate: the approach taken by the Panel to the question needed to be considered. The Panel simply took the view that it had another option available to it under Article 13.1 of the DSU, and so did not need to concern itself with the Article XV [2] point made by India. It can be argued, however, that the Panel needed to consider the relationship between Article XV of GATT 1994 and the DSU provision – in particular the question whether the greater powers of seeking information under the DSU were qualified by Article XV [2] of GATT,[142] following the interpretation by India, if that interpretation were indeed accepted. Setting aside the particular facts of this case, it nevertheless raises a general point about the status of a Panel, and specifically whether a Panel's personality can be assimilated to that of the WTO. The characteristics of the Panel must colour in some fashion the limits of its jurisdiction.

Although the general functions of a Panel are set out in the DSU, the precise scope of a Panel's mandate or jurisdiction in a particular case is determined by its terms of reference.[143] These are set by the DSB and cannot be unilaterally amended by the Panel.[144] The author of the terms of reference, however, is the complainant, which raises an important question surrounding the principles according to which the terms of

[138] See India–Quantitative Restrictions on Imports of Agricultural, Textile and Industrial Products (Panel) para 5.11.
[139] Ibid. [140] Ibid para 5.12. [141] Ibid (AB).
[142] Along with the subsequent gloss on how it should be interpreted.
[143] See Articles 6 and 7 of the DSU. See also for example Brazil–Desiccated Coconut (AB) para 21; India–Patent (AB) paras 92–3.
[144] India–Patent (AB) paras 92–3.

reference should be interpreted, and whether the exercise involves a question of fact or law. At first glance, the edict to interpret the provisions of the WTO Agreements in accordance with customary rules of interpretation of public international law would appear not to apply, as the text of the WTO Agreements is not directly implicated.[145] Nor could the terms of reference be readily characterised as secondary law of the WTO, given their initial authorship. In this characterisation, the fact that the terms of reference of the Panel are established by a decision of the DSB may well be ultimately significant. The following principles may be discerned from the WTO jurisprudence to date:

- The jurisdiction of the Panel derives from the terms of reference and cannot be assumed.[146] Therefore the terms of reference need to be interpreted strictly.
- The terms of reference have to be interpreted in good faith by the parties[147] and *a fortiori* by the Panel.
- The terms of reference have to be interpreted in the light of the 'attendant circumstances'.[148]
- The AB can review the interpretation placed on the terms of reference.[149] Consequently, the process of interpreting the terms of reference has been characterised as a legal question.

However, a distinction needs to be made between interpreting the terms of reference and applying the relevant provisions of the DSU – in particular Article 6.2 of the DSU,[150] which sets out what the terms of reference should contain. The former takes precedence over the latter.

Article 6.2 of the DSU (which sets out the requirements for the establishment of a Panel) has itself not been interpreted consistently.[151]

[145] Although the standard terms of reference essentially are implicated.

[146] See Articles 6 and 7 of the DSU; Brazil–Desiccated Coconut (AB) para 21; India–Patent (AB) paras 92–3.

[147] See Mavroidis 'Development of WTO Dispute Settlement' 164, interpreting Thailand–Antidumping Duties on Angles (AB).

[148] Korea–Dairy Safeguard (AB) para 124. Attendant circumstances include discussion at the relevant WTO committee level, the bilateral consultations and discussion at the DSB. See Mavroidis 'Development of WTO Dispute Settlement' 166; US–Safeguard Measures on Imports of Fresh, Chilled or Frozen Meat from New Zealand and Australia (Panel) paras 5.32ff.

[149] See Australia–Salmon (AB) paras 96, 102–3.

[150] For an excellent analysis of Article 6 (2), see Mavroidis 'Development of WTO Dispute Settlement' 160–7. See also Canada–Measures Relating to Exports of Wheat and Treatment of Imported Grain (AB).

[151] Mavroidis 'Development of WTO Dispute Settlement' 167.

This inconsistency reflects the fact that it defines the scope of a Panel's jurisdiction. The temptation therefore not to take too formalistic an approach to interpreting it must not be ruled out. Indeed, the case law seems to demonstrate a liberal approach to its interpretation, subject mainly to the constraint that no party should be prejudiced by a flexible interpretation.[152]

Finally, Panels have broad discretion in the way they focus on the factual aspects of a dispute – in the manner in which they consider evidence and in the credibility and weight they ascribe to it.[153] Furthermore, a Panel has broad and comprehensive authority to engage in fact finding under Article 13 of the DSU.[154] Insofar as involvement in legal interpretation is concerned, a Panel is free to 'use arguments submitted by any of the parties or to develop its own legal reasoning to support its own findings and conclusions on the matter under consideration'.[155] This discretion to consider legal arguments is limited by the requirement that a Panel need not 'examine all legal claims' – only those issues necessary to resolve the dispute.[156]

In sum, a Panel has a fair amount of discretion over the manner in which it functions. This degree of latitude is reinforced by the fact that a Panel's standard of assessment should generally be such that it does not commit 'an egregious error that calls into question its good faith'.[157] This standard set by the AB for the Panel seems unduly liberal.

2.4.2.4 The AB

The AB performs a two-tiered function through its powers of interpretation insofar as institutional matters are concerned – namely, clarifying its own jurisdiction and engaging in the supervision of the Panel system – through standard-setting and its appellate function. The

[152] Ibid; Thailand–Antidumping Duties on Angles (AB). See also Canada–Measures Relating to Exports of Wheat and Treatment of Imported Grain (AB), in which the AB again emphasised that the procedural rules were designed to promote fair, prompt and effective resolution of trade disputes (para 205) and that compliance with the requirements of Article 6 (2) of the DSU must be determined on the merits of each case (para 206).

[153] EC–Hormones (AB) paras 132–3, 135–8.

[154] Japan–Agricultural Products II (AB) paras 127–30. See also Canada–Measures Affecting the Export of Civilian Aircraft (AB) para 192.

[155] EC–Hormones (AB) para 156.

[156] See for example US–Countervailing Duties on Certain Hot-Rolled Lead and Bismuth Carbon Steel Products II; US–Shirts and Blouses (AB) 17.

[157] EC–Hormones (AB) paras 132–3, 135, 138.

AB's jurisdiction is limited in the DSU to 'issues of law covered in the panel report and legal interpretation developed by the panel'.[158] Furthermore, the AB can only 'uphold, modify or reverse the legal findings and conclusions of the panel'.[159] This express authority of the AB is, however, essentially subject to interpretation by the AB itself, and the AB has taken a broad approach to the interpretation of this authority, as set out in Article 17 of the DSU, such that it includes a supervisory and standard-setting role.

Thus, although factual questions are not within the remit of the AB, the AB has maintained an interest in questions of fact. For example:

- The question 'whether or not a panel has made an objective assessment of the facts before it as required by Article 11 of the DSU' is a question of fact.[160]
- The determination of national law is a question of fact,[161] but the criteria for and process of determining national law and mandatory law have been prescribed by the AB.[162]

Furthermore, owing to the AB's lack of remand authority, the AB has, with a view to settling a dispute, shown willingness to complete the analysis where 'there were sufficient factual findings made by the Panel' and the additional analysis was 'closely related' to the findings actually made by the Panel.[163] This is, in effect, an engagement in factual analysis or its receipt, albeit in very circumscribed circumstances.

Of particular note in the dynamics of the interpretative process in the AB is the practice of collegiality. This practice is set out in paragraph 4 of the Working Procedures for Appellate Review and was formulated by the AB in accordance with Article 17.9 of the DSU. Under the practice of collegiality the AB is required to 'convene on a regular basis to discuss matters of policy, practice and procedure' to ensure 'consistency and coherence in decision-making'.[164] Accordingly, each division of the AB is expected to exchange views with the other members before

[158] See Article 17 para 6 of the DSU. [159] Article 17 para 13 of the DSU.

[160] See EC–Hormones (AB) paras 132–3, 135, 138. In the same case the AB stated that 'Findings of fact . . . by a Panel are in principle, not subject to review by the Appellate Body.'

[161] See for example EC–Bananas III (AB) para 206.

[162] See US–Anti-Dumping Act of 1916 (AB) paras 84–102. For an excellent evaluation of the mandatory/discretionary doctrine see Naiki 'Mandatory/Discretionary Doctrine in WTO Law'.

[163] See EC–Asbestos (AB) paras 78–9; and WTO Analytical Index.

[164] See Working Procedures for Appellate Review para 4.

deciding on an appeal,[165] to draw on the individual and collective expertise of the AB members.[166] This practice, however, carries with it the proviso that it is not to be interpreted as 'interfering with a division's full authority and freedom to hear and decide an appeal assigned to it'.[167] According to Debra Steger, 'these exchanges of views have been extremely important in ensuring consistency and continuity in the numerous rulings of the AB, particularly in relation to procedural and general practice matters'.[168] Collegiality thus impacts the AB interpretative process, and is to that extent dependent upon the particular dynamics of the membership of the AB.

There are two important limits to the AB's province of interpretation, one legal and the other political. First, as Mavroidis points out, the 'WTO adjudicating bodies are limited by what has been pleaded before them . . . they cannot through their own legal reasoning affect the allocation of burden of proof to make the claim in place of the party carrying the burden of proof . . . because there is nothing like an "ex officio complaint" in the WTO law'.[169] Second, there is the political restraint, aptly highlighted by Weiss when he states: 'the AB is beset by a watchful if not vigilant Membership, guarding against the AB usurping judicial power through the exercise of its tools of interpretation'.[170]

2.4.2.5 The Legal Affairs Division of the WTO Secretariat and the AB Secretariat

The role of the lawyers from the WTO Secretariat Legal Affairs Division and the AB Secretariat in aiding Panels and the AB in the interpretative process needs to be mentioned. In the case of the Panels, the responsibility is to 'to assist panels'.[171] In the case of the AB, the availability of the legal assistance is formulated somewhat differently in terms of legal support as required.[172] The nature and quality of this legal assistance must in some measure depend not only on the background of the lawyers[173] but also on the chemistry and dynamics of their relationship with the Panels and AB members. The less professional and established the Panel, and in the same vein the members of the AB, the more

[165] Ibid para 4 (3). [166] Ibid para 4 (1). [167] Ibid para 4 (4).
[168] D. Steger 'Improvements and Reforms of the WTO Appellate Body' in Ortino and Petersmann *WTO Dispute Settlement System* chapter 4, 43.
[169] Mavroidis 'Development of WTO Dispute Settlement' 167.
[170] Weiss 'Inherent Powers' 190. [171] Article 27 of the DSU. [172] Article 17 para 7.
[173] Nationality, legal training and experience.

influence the lawyers' input is likely to have.[174] Thus Steger states, albeit in the context of the Panels: 'Anything that can be done to improve the "professionalism" of the panel process and to ensure that it is the panellists who adjudicate and decide cases, not the Secretariat, would be a major step forward.'[175]

2.4.3 Institutional aspects of the WTO and the WTO dispute settlement system

There have been a number of occasions when institutional issues have been the focus of judicial review. The most important of these has been the issue raised by India in India–Quantitative Restrictions on Imports of Agricultural, Textile and Industrial Products[176] – namely, whether there existed in the practice of the WTO a principle of institutional balance according to which the judicial organs of the WTO would defer to and take cognisance of the deliberations of the political organs charged with the same issue – in other words, whether the judicial organs of the WTO needed 'to exercise their power with due regard to the jurisdiction assigned to the other parts of [the WTO]'.[177]

At the outset, India's specific formulation of the principle of institutional balance needs to be considered, as the AB's conclusions are, it is suggested, limited to this. Throughout its consideration of the principle, the AB referred to it as the principle formulated by India or as a principle that dictates what India in the circumstances contends.[178] The AB formulated India's contention as follows:

> ...India argues that there is a principle of institutional balance which requires panels, in determining the scope of their competence, to take into account the competence conferred upon other organs of the WTO. According to India, the drafters of the WTO Agreement created a complex institutional structure under which various bodies are empowered to take binding decisions on related matters. These bodies must cooperate to achieve the objectives of the WTO, and can only do so

[174] Steger 'Improvements and Reforms' 48. [175] Ibid.
[176] AB. See also Turkey–Textile (AB).
[177] F. Roessler 'The Institutional Balance between the Judicial and the Political Organs of the WTO' www.ksg.harvard.edu/cbg/Conferences/trade/roessler.htm; also published in M. Bronckers and R. Quick (eds) *New Directions in International Economic Law* (Kluwer Law International, The Hague 2000). See also India–Quantitative Restrictions on Imports of Agricultural, Textile and Industrial Products (AB) para 8.
[178] India–Quantitative Restrictions (AB) paras 98–9, 105.

> if each exercises its competence with due regard to the competence of all other bodies. In order to preserve a proper institutional balance between the judicial and the political organs of the WTO with regard to matters relating to balance of payments restrictions, review of the justification of such matters must be left to the relevant political organs, i.e., the BOP [Balance of Payments] Committee and the General Council. In light of the powers attributed to these organs under Article XVIII; 12 of the GATT 1994 and the BOP Understanding, panels should, according to India, refrain from reviewing the justification of balance-of-payments measures under Article XVIII: B.[179]

The AB concluded that the constitutional principle of institutional balance, as formulated by India as a principle of international law, did not exist.[180] According to India, although there was no textual basis for the principle in the WTO Agreements, it was nevertheless a principle of WTO law.[181] However, the AB concluded that this was not borne out by the practice of GATT or the WTO.[182] In the circumstances, the AB based its decision on the scope of the competence of the Panel in considering trade restrictions arising from balance-of-payments problems on an interpretation of Article XXIII of GATT 1994, as elaborated and applied by the DSU, and of footnote 1 to the BOP Understanding.[183]

However, the question of the place of the principle of institutional balance in the WTO legal framework, in particular its role in the interpretative process in the DSU, has not been exhausted. The AB deliberated on a particular formulation of the principle by India and took into account the manner in which that principle was displaced by the actual words used in the footnote to the BOP Understanding. In short, the principle of institutional balance in the WTO was considered in the context of the particular legal and factual circumstances of the case, and India's formulation of it.

Furthermore, given that the principle of institutional balance calls for the 'taking into account' of the competence conferred upon other organs of the WTO, or the according of 'due regard' to the competence of other organs of the WTO, it is (to use a WTO analogy) similar to an accordion that can be stretched to different lengths according to the musician's composition.[184] In the case of India, the particular formulation involved essentially

[179] India–Quantitative Restrictions (AB) para 98.
[180] Ibid paras 99, 105. [181] Ibid para 99. [182] Ibid para 100. [183] Ibid para 83.
[184] See for example EC–Asbestos (Panel) para 3.426.

- a duty to cooperate to achieve WTO obligations;
- refraining from reviewing matters that have been the subject of consideration in another organ of the WTO – in this case the BOP Committee.[185]

It is this formulation that the AB ruled upon. However, it is the case that there are degrees to which 'account' can be taken of one organ of the WTO by another, and degrees to which 'due regard' can be accorded. The question of the role of the principle of institutional balance in the WTO remains, therefore, an open one and is not excluded.[186] The principle is to be found in the legal framework of the WTO through the interpretative process. Thus, F. Roessler states:

> Whatever the correct interpretation of the terms 'application of', the question remains whether the DSU provisions assigning competence to panels can be interpreted as overriding the provisions of other agreements assigning competence to the WTO's political bodies. It is recognised in international law that 'as a general rule, any body possessing jurisdictional powers has the right in the first place itself to determine the extent of its own jurisdiction'. When an organ of the WTO determines its own jurisdiction, it thus exercises its right to interpret the provision of the WTO Agreements conferring authority upon it. In doing so, it must pursuant to Article 31 of the Vienna Convention on the Law of Treaties take into account not only the terms of the provision attributing powers to it but also the context in which this provision appears. That context comprises those provisions of the WTO Agreement that attribute related powers to other bodies. An analysis of the terms of those jurisdictional provisions may lead the WTO organ to the conclusion that not only it but also other organs could claim jurisdiction over the matter at issue. Such a conflict must be resolved in good faith in the light of the institutional structure that the framers of the WTO have set up to realise the purposes of the WTO. The principles of interpretation of the Vienna Convention on the Law of Treaties thus suggest that the judicial organs of the WTO cannot determine their jurisdiction exclusively on the basis of the provisions of the DSU.[187]

[185] (AB) para 98.

[186] See also Bartels 'Separation of Powers' 882, where the author describes two situations in which it might be necessary for a tribunal to adopt this principle: first, when the tribunal in question has concurrent and also exclusive jurisdiction over a matter; second, when exercising jurisdiction would necessarily nullify the rights of a party. Bartels outlines three possible ways in which the principle could be effected: (1) refusal to establish a Panel; (2) declaration that the dispute is not properly before it; (3) suspension of proceedings.

[187] Ibid.

Thus, a principle of institutional balance can be discerned through the process of interpretation, and this is informed by the institutional framework of the WTO as a whole. The principle was again relied upon by India in EC–Tariff Preferences.[188] It highlights the fact that the DSU cannot be interpreted in isolation, particularly where a matter of the province of its jurisdiction is concerned. The judicial organ needs to be pictured by the interpreters in the context and against the background of the institutional framework of the WTO as a whole.

A form of the principle of institutional balance can be discerned in India–Quantitative Restrictions, where the AB specifically recognised that the judicial function was not 'unlimited'.[189] The elements of this form are

1. recognition that different organs have different functions – that is, that the BOP Committee and Panels have different functions;
2. recognition that judicial findings need to be without prejudice to the role of political organs – that is, panel findings need to be without prejudice to the role of the BOP Committee and the General Council;
3. recognition that the judicial organ cannot substitute itself for the political organ – that is, the finding that 'panels can review the justification of balance-of-payments measures' is not tantamount to the Panel substituting itself for the BOP Committee;
4. recognition that the judicial organs cannot ignore the determinations of the political organs – that is, Panels should not ignore the decisions of the BOP Committee and the General Council.[190]

In sum, the principle of institutional balance has a function in the interpretative process concerned with the determination of the limits of competence of the various organs of the WTO. It can inform and colour the interpretative process but can be displaced by express provisions.

* * *

To conclude here, the DSU is an important engine for the interpretation of the WTO Agreements. An examination of the institutions that take part in that process calls for particular attention to the objects and purposes of the DSU, the special sources of law pertinent to its

[188] EC–Tariff Preferences (Panel) para 4.199, wherein India submits: 'This uncertainty will have radical implications on the institutional balance between the political and judicial bodies of the WTO, and would engage the adjudicating bodies in a law-making process which is the exclusive prerogative of the membership.'

[189] India–Quantitative Restrictions (AB) paras 82, 104. [190] Ibid para 81.

interpretation, the manner in which gaps are filled, the scope of the authority to interpret and engage in the generation of secondary legislation, the institutions involved in the interpretative process and the manner in which jurisdictional conflicts are managed.

2.5 Interpretation and the Trade Policy Review Mechanism

The Trade Policy Review Mechanism (TPRM) of the WTO is an important and successful institution. There are essentially two questions that it raises from the point of view of interpretation. First, what is the precise scope of the review of a member's trade policies and practices that it authorises? This aspect of the TPRM has been analysed elsewhere.[191] Indeed, questions have been raised in individual trade policy reviews (TPRs) as to whether a matter is properly within or outside the scope of the review. However, the impact of the review in terms of consequences for the country under review is not serious enough to provoke it to call for clarification of the scope of the TPR under Article IX (2) of the Marrakesh Agreement or to raise it as a dispute through the dispute settlement system; therefore, the question of the precise scope of the reviews is somewhat academic. In any event, the DSU does not cover disputes arising from the Agreement establishing the TPRM in Annex 3 of the Marrakesh Agreement.[192] Therefore, the prospects for clarification of the provisions of the Agreement establishing the TPRM through interpretation in the DSU are limited.

Despite this limited scope of the DSU in the context of the TPRM, there remains the second question of the TPRM's relationship and relevance to dispute settlement proceedings, and consequentially to the interpretative process in the DSU. Information in TPRs can be factual, be indicative of state practice or attitude, comprise a legal conclusion on consistency with WTO obligations, and be proffered either to contradict or to support a position taken by a member. The Agreement establishing the TPRM, however, specifically states that the TPRM is not 'intended to serve as a basis for the enforcement of specific obligations under the Agreements or for dispute settlement procedures, or to impose new policy commitments on Members'.[193] Information

191 See for example A. H. Qureshi *International Economic Law* (Sweet and Maxwell, London 1999) chapter 13; A. H. Qureshi *The World Trade Organization: Implementing International Trade Norms* (Manchester UP, Manchester 1996) chapter 6.

192 See Article 1 of the DSU; Appendix 1 to the DSU.

193 See Annex 3 to the Marrakesh Agreement.

contained in TPRs has nevertheless been proffered in dispute settlement proceedings[194] – and frequently contested on the grounds that it is not supposed to be used in dispute settlement procedures. There is evidence of Panels disregarding the information derived from TPRs[195] but also of facts in TPRs sometimes being taken note of.[196]

Annex 3 establishing the TPRM has not been the subject of judicial clarification, despite its judicial application. It seems, however, that information contained in TPRs is used more as an evidential bar than as a prohibition on bringing proceedings with respect to matters already considered in TPRs. The practice of proffering TPR material in dispute settlement proceedings, despite the prohibition on doing so, must be a tactical attempt to prejudice the other party's case. Furthermore, on the one hand, this evidential bar is confined to the enforcement of specific obligations; therefore, the use of material from a TPR for a purpose other than enforcement – in particular, for example, as a defence or justification or to avail of an exception – does not seem to be precluded. This would include the use of material to assist in interpretation for this purpose. On the other hand, there is also an injunction that the TPRM is not intended to serve as a basis for dispute settlement procedures. It is not clear what is meant by this. Does it mean that material from TPRs cannot be used in dispute settlement procedures? This seems rather broad. Does it mean that the TPRM is not a substitute for dispute settlement procedures? Or does it mean that material from TPRs cannot be used to trigger dispute settlement procedures? It is suggested that the 'or for dispute settlement procedures' in Annex 3 cannot be read in isolation, but must be read in the context of the remainder of the sentence, including what precedes it. The 'not for dispute settlement

[194] See for example Korea–Polyacetal Resins (GATT) ADP/92,+Corr.1 (1993) paras 53, 58; Japan–Measures Affecting Consumer Photographic Film and Paper (Panel) para 5.62; India–Quantitative Restrictions on Imports of Agricultural, Textile and Industrial Products (Panel) para 3.10; Canada–Measures Affecting the Export of Civilian Aircraft (Panel) paras 6.153–4, 6.195, 6.198, 6.200, 6.325, 6.342, 8.14, 9.270, 9.274–5, 9.284, 9.290; India–Measures Affecting the Automotive Sector (Panel) paras 4.12–13; Turkey–Textile (Panel) 29 and para 6.117; Chile–Price Band System and Safeguard Measures Relating to Certain Agricultural Products (Panel) paras 4.47, 4.50, 4.108–9, 7.95; Canada–Export Credits and Loan Guarantees for Regional Aircraft (Panel) para 19; Chile–Agricultural Products (AB) para 18; EC–Conditions for the Granting of Tariff Preferences to Developing Countries (Panel) B-94–95, C-11, C-12.

[195] See for example Chile–Price Band System and Safeguard Measures Relating to Certain Agricultural Products; Canada–Measures Affecting the Export of Civilian Aircraft.

[196] See for example Chile–Agricultural Products (AB) footnote 27.

procedures' prohibition is coloured by the edict that the TPRM is not intended as a basis for the enforcement of specific obligations under the Agreements.

2.6 Conclusion

In this chapter the focus has been on the principal institutions established in the WTO Agreements, including the institution of interpretation in the WTO, in particular the intra-institutional tensions both within the dispute settlement system and within the WTO. The analysis has been from the perspective of identifying the issues and problems associated with interpreting these institutions and their relationships. One common undercurrent is the competition among the institutions for a greater stake in the authority and process of interpretation. Thus, there is competition in the process of interpretation between the judicial and legislative organs, between the judiciary and the adjudicated members, between the factual arbitrator and the legal arbitrator, and between the judicial organs and the political organs. Implicit in this competition is an acknowledgement that the process of interpretation partakes of the character of power. Whoever can interpret is the ultimate legislator, not the legislators! Another feature of the interpretative process is the general approach to the interpretation of institutional issues. This has generally been liberal rather than textual.

3

The national dimension to interpretation in the framework of the WTO

3.1 Introduction

Interpretation of international agreements by judicial organs in international organisations can have legislative characteristics.[1] Interpretation by States of their international commitments can equally spawn 'second-generation' norms reflecting the expression of national perspectives, within and outside the residual freedom that may accompany the international undertaking. Both national interpretations and domestic processes of interpretation interface with the WTO dispute settlement process and the implementation of the WTO Agreements. International agreements comprise a mix of 'agreements' and 'disagreements'. They harbour future discontent and opportunities. Once established, the agreements have to be interpreted at the international level with respect to domestic legislation, and in this manner enforced. By the same token, the agreements have to be interpreted at the national level in order to be implemented – as indeed do national trade measures that have an impact on international trade. However, implementation by a State of its international undertakings is a process organically removed from the agreement itself and from its constituent organisation. It is undertaken by the independent entity of the State, which has a momentum of its own. Domestic implementation by the State of an international agreement involves an internal process within the State of understanding and discourse with respect and in relation to the agreement, leading to an interpretation that is expressed both in words and in deeds.

Interpretation of the WTO Agreements at the national level is to be found in the way the WTO Agreements are translated into the national language, re-formulated in domestic legislation, interpreted in national

[1] See for example J.P. Trachtman and P.M. Moreman 'Costs and Benefits of Private Participation in WTO Dispute Settlement: Whose Right Is It Anyway?' (2003) 44 (Winter) *HJIL* 221–250.

tribunals and courts, and actually administered by agents of the State. Interpretation of domestic trade legislation as it affects international trade involves the implementation of the WTO Agreements; it is therefore set against the background of an understanding of the WTO Agreements and generally of international obligations within the domestic legal system. In the same vein, domestic court deliberations on the question of the direct applicability of the WTO Agreements are based on a certain understanding of the agreements, and thus involve interpretation. This direct and indirect understanding of the WTO Agreements is affected by the constitutional and legal system of the State, along with its cultural, historical and ideological background. It is also dependent on the resources available – including those made available by members of the WTO – to facilitate a proper understanding of the WTO Agreements by relevant decision-makers. Thus, just as the impartiality and standing of the judges at the international level in the WTO has a bearing on the manner and quality of interpretation of the WTO Agreements, so the manner and quality of interpretation of the WTO Agreements at the domestic level is informed by the calibre and the cultural and ideological orientations of the administrators and judges involved in considering questions related to the WTO Agreements – and by the resources at their disposal.

Given that this domestic apparatus for interpreting the WTO Agreements, broadly and narrowly defined, affects how they are implemented, the question arises whether the result can be nullification or impairment of a member's benefits.[2]

This chapter has two main objectives: first, to examine second-generation domestic WTO norms by shedding some light on the background and processes of the interpretation of national trade and WTO implementing legislation in national legal systems; second, to examine both generally and specifically national perspectives on the interpretation of WTO Agreements. In this manner, this chapter aims to discern and outline the theoretical and practical framework for the national interpretation of the WTO Agreements. At the domestic level, the objective of this exercise is to sharpen strategic thinking in the formulation of second-generation WTO norms and to assist in pre-empting departures from justiciable violations of WTO obligations. At the international level, the objective of this exercise is to outline the framework within which national second-generation WTO norms

[2] See Article XXIII of GATT 1994.

operate in order to facilitate a compliance appraisal. The main focus will be on the issues arising from domestic court interpretations and the process of translating WTO agreements into the native, non-official WTO language.

3.2 Theory

The national apparatus for interpretation of the WTO Agreements is expressed in national measures and deeds. The executive and administrative branches of government involved in trade or trade-related policy formulation and practice engage in the interpretative process through their executive and administrative actions. The process of interpretation is not only explicit and formal but also implicit in the consequent conduct of the agents of the State in administering the agreements. However, the inclusion of deeds as an aspect and manifestation of interpretation is not necessarily to conflate the process of implementation with the process of interpretation. Rather, it is to recognise that implementation found only in deeds (whatever form it may or may not take) is informed by and consequential upon an understanding of the WTO Agreements – including an appreciation of the different degrees of importance of the various obligations therein. Thus, there is an aspect of implementation that has the characteristics of an interpretative process – and that consequently is properly the focus of a study of interpretation at the domestic level. This aspect is empirically more difficult to discern from an external vantage-point, making it a challenge for research.

The national dimension to interpretation is informed by the degree of national appreciation of the domestic discretion left in the WTO Agreements, of the discretion left to interpret in different ways, and of the inherent scope of the interpretative process. This will inform the extent to which national trade policy is realised through the interpretative process. The scope for national perspectives to pass by osmosis into the parameters of the disciplines of the WTO Agreements is to be found, as is generally understood, in the WTO Agreements themselves. Thus, the WTO Agreements contain various exceptions that allow for domestic freedom in given conditions. Discretion is built into many of the provisions of the WTO Agreements – particularly where they are silent on specific issues. There is discretion inherent in the process of implementation. There is discretion in interpreting domestic legislation in the context of the WTO Agreements. There is cover available for some domestic decisions within certain WTO review processes – for example, the deferential standard of review in the WTO Anti-Dumping Agreement. Finally, there is the executive gamble on other members not challenging its 'grey' interpretations and its indiscretions.

The existence of a particular perspective on how the WTO Agreements should be generally or specifically interpreted is also pertinent. However, States differ in the degree to which they engage in strategic thinking on how the WTO Agreements might or should be interpreted. Often their approach is not proactive. In this respect, a member's practice of engagement in the dispute settlement process may provide valuable insights into its perspectives on questions of interpretation of the WTO Agreements, as well as into its particular sector preoccupations in international trade. In a sense, engagement in disputes is a discourse on questions of interpretation of the WTO Agreements – particularly given that the disputes taken up in the WTO tend to involve mainly questions of law or its application to facts. In this context, participation as a claimant reflects how one member's perception of the interpretation of the WTO Agreements differs from another member's perception; participation as a defendant reflects a member's original interpretation of the WTO Agreements, as set out in its national legislation. Generally, participation as a third party involves an engagement in the process of interpretation of the WTO Agreements on systemic issues of national concern.

Furthermore, the existence or otherwise of a coherent and well-formulated national trade policy will shape national interpretative outcomes. For this reason, domestic trade policy perspectives are an important component in understanding the influences that shape the interpretative processes at the domestic level.

This enquiry into the national dimension to the interpretation of the WTO Agreements leads first and foremost to a focus on the national WTO implementing legislation, and in particular the manner of its drafting. It is here that national trade policy is to be found.

Second, member States that do not share one of the official languages of the WTO engage in the process of interpretation of the WTO Agreements not merely through acts of legislative implementation but also through the very act of translating the WTO Agreements into their official language. This is because translation is a process of interpretation. In this respect, it is the national official translation that is pertinent. However, at the international level, this translated version does not change or displace the obligations of a WTO member.

Third, the national judicial apparatus touches upon questions of interpretation in various ways. The location and nature of the national authority charged with the interpretative process are significant. In some member States (e.g. China), only a designated organ can engage in authoritative interpretations. In addition, domestic principles for interpreting national legislation, set against the background of international commitments, provide insight into the domestic processes of interpreting the WTO Agreements. Thus, a purposive approach to interpreting domestic legislation that implements WTO commitments may not necessarily be consonant with the strict interpretation of the WTO obligation at the level of the WTO dispute settlement system. Indeed, it may well engage the member in a higher level of obligations than other members, and than its original executive intentions. National consciousness of approaches to interpreting the WTO Agreements at the level of the WTO need to be synchronised so that neither expansive interpretations of WTO obligations nor interpretations inconsistent with international commitments emerge from national interpretations. In addition, when and how the WTO jurisprudence is taken into account in the domestic engagement with trade policy informs the domestic interpretation of the WTO Agreements. Although this is in part a matter of source of law and hierarchy of norms, the absence of WTO jurisprudence in the process of engagement with the WTO Agreements nevertheless has a bearing on interpretative outcomes.

Fourth, the apparatus within the executive and administrative branches charged with administering the WTO Agreements can have a bearing on interpretative outcomes in different ways – for example, through administrative edicts, advice to the public and acts of implementation and enforcement. Although here the interpretation is primarily a matter of deed, it can be affected by executive and administrative measures consequent upon a particular understanding of the WTO Agreements. Thus, if panel and AB decisions are not translated into Japanese and Chinese in Japan and China, respectively, for their government agencies, these agencies will have an incomplete picture of the WTO Agreements.

Finally, national agents of interpretation of the WTO Agreements are conditioned by the political and ideological framework within which they are located. This national framework may be explicitly set out in the WTO implementing legislation. It has an impact in terms of the conditioning of the interpreters. This factor is as significant when law is viewed as a process of decision-making as when it is viewed as a set of rules. Although it is strictly more a matter of the sources of law drawn upon, this background factor can have an impact on the process of interpretation, and in particular the approaches taken to interpretation.

Broadly, therefore, the key factors in the interpretation of the WTO Agreements at the national level are

- domestic legislation implementing the WTO Agreements – in particular the manner in which the legislation has been drafted and the manner in which the WTO Agreements have been interpreted during the drafting process;
- in the case of members whose national language is not one of the official languages of the WTO, the manner of the translation of the WTO Agreements, reflecting a particular understanding of the WTO Agreements;
- the apparatus within the domestic legal system for interpreting WTO-implementing and related domestic trade legislation – in particular the mandate and authority to interpret, the approaches to interpretation and the way in which WTO jurisprudence relating to the WTO Agreements is received into the domestic system and affects the interpretative process;
- the apparatus at the level of the executive and administrative branches of government for the administration of the WTO Agreements through executive and administrative measures and deeds.

Actual national perspectives on how the WTO Agreements are and should be interpreted in domestic systems can be found in a range of sources, including

- statements made and positions taken during accession negotiations or multilateral negotiations;
- positions taken during litigation in the WTO, either as a party or as a third party;
- positions taken in the various organs of the WTO;
- official responses to allegations of violations of the WTO Agreements;
- statements made in TPRs, by the member on its own behalf and in response to the reviews of other members;
- official statements on national trade policy and practices;
- the national foreign trade regime.

The influences that shape these perspectives include the general orientation of the economy and the national historical and political background.

The national dimension to interpretation of the WTO Agreements centres ultimately on a set of second-generation norms. These follow the text of the first-generation, primary norms – namely, the WTO agreements. These second-generation norms are created not only at the level of the WTO dispute settlement system, through panel and AB decisions, but also in the domestic system. Indeed, the domestic second-generation norms can give rise to WTO second-generation norms through the WTO dispute settlement system. However, since not all disputes result in WTO conflict resolution clarification, there is a significant pool of domestic second-generation norms that need to be understood to obtain a clear view of national trade practices and policies in terms of the WTO agreements. How these domestic second-generation norms are, or might be, formulated is an aspect of this process of comprehension.

Insight into the domestic apparatus for interpreting the WTO Agreements is necessary for a number of reasons consequent upon WTO jurisprudence;[3] indeed, this domestic apparatus may even be said to be legitimised by WTO jurisprudence. First, the WTO Agreements are not directly applicable in most domestic systems, nor are first- and second-generation WTO norms treated similarly in domestic systems.[4] Second, the domestic law that implements the WTO Agreements and the domestic law that impinges upon them have been characterised as matters of fact – and because they are matters of fact, the interpretation placed on them by the domestic authorities is important, given that national authorities are presumed to be better informed about questions of fact within their jurisdiction.[5] Third, it is recognised that there

[3] See for example US–Section 301 of the Trade Act of 1974 (Panel) 12, 13, 15. The panel stated (para 7.24): 'When evaluating the conformity of national law with WTO obligations in accordance with Article XVI:4 of the WTO Agreement account must be taken of the wide-ranging diversity in the legal systems of the Members. Conformity can be ensured in different ways in different legal systems. It is the end result that counts, not the manner in which it is achieved. Only by understanding and respecting the specifications of each Member's legal system can a correct evaluation of conformity be established'. Further on, the Panel stated (para 7.27): 'even though the statutory language granting specific powers to a government agency may be prima facie consistent with the WTO rules, the agency responsible, within the discretion given to it, may adopt internal criteria or administrative procedures inconsistent with WTO obligations which would, as a result, render the overall law in violation. The opposite may be equally true: though the statutory language as such may be prima facie inconsistent, such inconsistency may be lawfully removed upon examination of other administrative or institutional elements of the same law.'

[4] Ibid para 7.24. [5] Ibid para 7.19.

is a wide-ranging diversity in the legal systems of the members of the WTO. This implies a certain, limited, degree of licence for national authorities in terms of the manner in which they adapt to the WTO Agreements and the manner in which the WTO agreements are adapted to their systems.[6] Finally, the domestic legislation should be evaluated in terms of its end result. It cannot be considered in terms of only a particular part of the apparatus of the national legal system – for example, a particular legislation on its own, without reference to how it would actually be interpreted in court or administered by agents of the State.[7] In sum, these factors necessitate focusing on a wide range of domestic materials that contribute to the implementation of WTO Agreements at the domestic level.

3.3 Issues arising from domestic interpretations

Domestic interpretations – usually national court interpretations of domestic trade legislation or WTO implementing legislation – can become significant in the WTO dispute settlement process in a number of ways. By the same token, the domestic interpretative apparatus can have significance in terms of the implementation of WTO agreements within the national system. There is therefore an interface between the domestic interpretative apparatus and compliance with WTO norms, at both the domestic and WTO levels: first, in determining domestic legislation that conforms to WTO law; second, in determining the significance of the domestic interpretations that eventuate into the WTO Agreements in the process of interpreting the WTO provisions, particularly the schedules of concessions of members; third, in determining the significance of domestic interpretation in the WTO dispute settlement system.

With respect to determining the compliance of domestic legislation with the WTO Agreements, the domestic law for this purpose is a matter of fact.[8] National measures need to be understood within the context of the national legal framework, and thus against the background of the interpretation placed on them and any administrative measures by domestic courts and other relevant agencies.[9] Thus, the use

6 Ibid.

7 Ibid. See also for example US–Shrimp (AB), wherein the AB took note of the rigidity and inflexibility of US officials in the determination of the certification process in question.

8 See for example India–Patent (AB) para 65.

9 US–Anti-Dumping Act of 1916 (Panel) paras 6.48, 6.50.

of terms from the WTO Agreements in domestic measures is no guarantee that their meaning remains the same.[10] In addition, to view a national measure in isolation, without reference to how it would be interpreted and implemented in the domestic system, would be contrary to Article 11 of the DSU, which calls for an objective examination of the facts by the judicial organs of the WTO. A national measure thus has to be considered in its historical, cultural, legal and economic context, as this context would be taken into account by the domestic courts.[11]

When there are several national interpretations – as a consequence, for example, of different, competing national court decisions within the jurisdiction of the member – it is necessary to weigh those different interpretations within the context of the national jurisprudence and legal system. Thus, in the US–Anti-Dumping Act of 1916 case, the Panel referred to the practice of international courts, quoting the Brazilian Loans case:

> Where the determination of a question of municipal law is essential to the Court's decision in a case, the Court will have to weigh the jurisprudence of the municipal courts, and 'if this is uncertain or divided, it will rest with the court to select the interpretation which it considers most in conformity with the law' (Brazilian Loans, PCIJ [Permanent Court of International Justice] Series A, nos.20/21, p. 124).[12]

Relying on this, the Panel went on to state:

> We are nevertheless of the view that there is nothing in the text of the DSU, nor in the practice of the Appellate Body, that prevents us from 'weigh[ing] the jurisprudence of municipal (US) courts' if it is 'uncertain or divided'. This would not require us to develop our own independent interpretation of US law, but simply to select among the relevant judgements the interpretation most in conformity with the US law, as necessary in order to resolve the matter before us.

The Panel in the US–Anti-Dumping Act of 1916 case also gave guidance on the factors to be considered in the process of selecting the correct municipal judgment.[13] It pointed out that such a selection would need to take into account the national court hierarchy, 'paying utmost regard to the decision of municipal courts'. Indeed, the Panel added that it

[10] US–Anti-Dumping Act of 1916 (Panel) paras 6.50, 6.59. [11] Ibid paras 6.41, 6.60.
[12] *Case Concerning Elettronica Sicula S.p.A [ELSI]* (US *v.* Italy) ICJ (1989).
[13] Paras 6.56–7.

'would not substitute its own judgment for that of the domestic court'. More particularly, the Panel considered the quality and detail of the decision, as well as whether the decision was final or interim, to be relevant. In addition, greater weight was to be given to the interpretations of relevant domestic courts than to that of the agency administering the relevant national measure.[14] However, this weight had to be informed by the hierarchy of sources within the domestic legal system.[15]

Finally, if all else failed, the Panel observed:

> If, after having applied the above methodology, we could not reach certainty as to the most appropriate court interpretation, i.e. if the evidence remains in equipoise, we shall follow the interpretation that favours the party against which the claim has been made, considering that the claimant did not convincingly support its claim.[16]

This raises a number of issues. First, there is here an arrogation of the role of a supreme court in relation to domestic legislation. Several questions of conflicts of norms arise within the context of the domestic system that are not effectively resolved. What would be the status of such a determination within the domestic system? This would be a matter of domestic constitutional law. What would be the consequence if later a domestic supreme court took a view that contradicted the WTO ruling? Again, this would be a matter for the domestic constitution. At the international level, if the domestic interpretation led to non-compliance, the member state could be held to account. Second, the tie-breaker suggested by the Panel – favouring the interpretation against which the claim is made (i.e. favouring the member whose legislation is in question) – does not sit well with the Panel's position that it will interpret the domestic legislation within the context of the domestic interpretative apparatus. In a sense, such a default interpretation is ultimately a step backwards from the initial methodology outlined, indeed sanctioned, by international court practice. Here there seems to be a conflation of the process of interpreting treaty provisions, including principles of treaty interpretation, and the process of constructing in effect an interpretation of the domestic legislation. Finally, what of an ambiguous national provision where there is no diversity of

[14] US–'Zeroing' of Dumping Margins (Panel) para 7.64.

[15] Ibid, where the Panel noted such a hierarchy in the US system in making a similar observation.

[16] Para 6.58.

court interpretations? Here a Panel would need to construct a possible domestic court interpretation. Accordingly, it would need to apprise itself of the principles of domestic statutory interpretation in order to construct an interpretation.

Domestic court decisions with respect to national measures also become important when they form the basis of the 'circumstances of the conclusion' of the WTO Agreements, as supplementary material under Article 32 of the VC.[17] Here the domestic court decisions relate to national legislation, against which background the multilateral trade negotiations take place. The AB has held that such court interpretations can indeed feature as the 'circumstances of the conclusion' of the treaty, and consequently can be material in the interpretation of treaty text. The conditions for the inclusion of such domestic court interpretations are stated as follows. First, there is no temporal limit on when the court decision was made, as long as it is 'relevant' in shedding light on the treaty text.[18] Thus, the court decision can predate the conclusion of the treaty. Second, 'relevance' can be determined with reference to the influence of the domestic decision on the treaty text – in particular how the decision assists in discerning the common intentions of the parties to the treaty.[19] Third, 'relevance' needs to be determined according to objective factors, such as 'type of event, document, or instrument and its legal nature; temporal relation of the circumstance to the conclusion of the treaty; actual knowledge or mere access to a published act or instrument; subject matter of the document, instrument, or event in relation to the treaty provision to be interpreted; and whether or how it was used or influenced the negotiations of the treaty'.[20] Fourth, it is enough that the domestic court interpretation has been officially published and is publicly available.[21] However, significantly, mere access to the decision is not the same as acceptance of the decision.[22]

Although the AB in the EC–Chicken Classification case was concerned with a member's schedule of concession, which might be said to be closely related to domestic legislation, in its remarks the AB did not in any way confine itself to the interpretation of a member's schedule of concessions. Either way, the decision is remarkable because it appears to be imputing a level of knowledge to negotiators about another member's domestic case law, when most trade negotiators lack such

[17] See EC–Chicken Classification (Panel) and (AB).

[18] EC–Chicken Classification (Panel) Para 7.392.

[19] EC–Chicken Classification (AB) para 289. [20] Ibid para 291. [21] Ibid para 297.

[22] Ibid para 334.

knowledge (even about their own domestic jurisprudence). The decision may also impose a burden on negotiators to ensure that the vernacular they use in the negotiations is divested of domestic baggage.

Domestic court interpretations can feature in other ways in the WTO dispute settlement process, in particular to support arguments by the parties to the litigation. Indeed, the more integrated into the domestic legal systems of members the WTO Agreements become, the more such second-generation norms will be available to the parties to engage with at the level of the WTO. Where, however, the interpretation of a member's domestic court is at variance with the interpretation that the member is proposing in the WTO dispute settlement system, that variance on its own cannot usurp the WTO Panel's function of interpreting the relevant provision of the WTO Agreements. Thus, to an argument of estoppel, a WTO Panel ruled:

> More fundamentally, we reject the assertion that a WTO dispute settlement panel should find a violation of a provision of a covered agreement, not on the basis of inconsistency of a Member's measure with a provision of a covered agreement, but rather on the basis that a provision of a covered agreement is 'being applied in bad faith'. Whatever may be the implications of national court decisions for the argument of Members before WTO dispute settlement panels, a question which we neither address not resolve here, 'estoppel' based on national court decisions interpreting municipal law does not limit the decisions of WTO panels interpreting a covered agreements. A WTO panel is obligated to interpret the terms of covered agreements in accordance with customary rules of interpretation of public international law. We know of no basis in international law, and India has not cited any, that would require us to conclude that a measure which is consistent with a Member's obligations under a provision of a covered agreement that we have interpreted in accordance with customary rules of interpretation of public international law could nonetheless be found to be in violation of that provision on the basis of alleged 'bad faith'.[23]

3.4 Issues arising from translations of the WTO Agreements

There have been various cases in the WTO when issues of interpretation have arisen as a result of differences of opinion with respect to the

[23] EC–Bed Linen (Panel) (21.5) para 6.91.

correct translation of the domestic measures. Most of these issues appear to have arisen at the level of the Panel. This may well be because, in the WTO, questions relating to national measures are usually characterised as being questions of fact, and an appeal to the AB can be made only on questions of law. Differences in translation may also in theory occur at the national level, where the WTO Agreements can be invoked in national courts. These differences would relate for the most part to translations into the national language or to the domestic legislation implementing the WTO Agreements. Compiling a comparative insight into the form of any differences that have occurred and how they have been resolved would be valuable. However, this exercise would face the challenge of finding the linguistic skills required to accumulate the necessary data and comparative insights. It may also for the moment be a somewhat premature exercise, as the evidence for such differences may take some time to emerge. Therefore, only a brief discussion follows here. (The WTO jurisprudence raises similar issues, as it relates mainly to differences over the correct translation of domestic measures, except that in this case it is the WTO judicial organs that are considering the issues in question.)

Differences with respect to the correct translation may not reflect simply a difference of opinion about the actual translation. Rather, the underlying translation positions advanced may well be interpretative stand-points that are supportive of the arguments proffered by the parties to a litigation. Indeed, differences over the correct translation are probably differences over interpretation – otherwise they would be readily conceded. This is borne out by practice when the parties agree to versions of a translation on which little of importance hinges.[24] Thus, most of the WTO jurisprudence points to differences of interpretation, couched in terms of differences of translation – in essence, differences of interpretation of national measures in the context of the WTO Agreements.

In addition, differences in terms of the availability of translated material may well reflect attempts to attain tactical advantages in the

[24] See for example Argentina–Peach Safeguards (Panel) para 7.100. In this case the Panel interpreted itself, and the parties did not object to the interpretation. See also Mexico–Telecommunications (Panel). In this case Japan, a third party, drew the Panel's attention to a particular interpretation. This interpretation was accepted by the Panel as being more correct, but the Panel ruled that since there was no disagreement over the interpretation between the parties to the dispute, the Panel would consider the different translations as being interchangeable.

process of litigation. Thus, in Korea–Commercial Vessels the Panel observed:

> During the course of the information gathering procedure . . . nearly half of all annexes submitted by Korea were provided, in whole or in part, in the Korean language. . . . Korea asserted that it was not required to provide all information in a WTO working language. Korea recognised, however, that it could be instructed, either by the Designated Representative or by the Panel, to undertake the necessary translation. . . . the EC asserted that provision of a document in a non-WTO language was tantamount to non-provision of the document, and therefore non-cooperation.[25]

By the same token, the proffering of 'corrections' to translations may reflect an attempt to rebut arguments based on the original translation. Thus, in Brazil–Desiccated Coconut the Panel observed:

> On the second day of Panel's first meeting . . . Brazil submitted a document setting forth corrections to its translation of Interministerial Ordinance No 11 and DTIC Opinion 006/95, indicating that the initial translation did not properly reflect the original Portuguese-language determinations. The Philippines objected to consideration of the corrected translations of the two texts, asserting that there were substantive differences between the initial and corrected translations. The Philippines subsequently submitted a letter objecting to the 'acceptance' of the corrected translations, objecting to Brazil's failure to provide advance warning of the pending corrections, and inferring that the corrections were made in response to arguments made during the oral presentations of the Philippines and third parties and/or to address some of the concerns expressed in our questions to Brazil. The Philippines indicated three instances in which it considered that Brazil had gone beyond translation corrections to change the substance of the documents.[26]

As has been noted, matters relating to domestic legislation are considered to be questions of fact in the WTO – and therefore subject to some of the uncertainty that can surround factual determinations. Equally, the VC deals with questions of translation, but only as they relate to international agreements. Similarly, the DSU does not offer much guidance on how conflicts in terms of the translation of domestic measures ought to be resolved, although the working language in the WTO dispute settlement process can be any of the three official

[25] Para 23. [26] Para 291.

languages of the WTO, namely, English, French or Spanish.[27] In these circumstances, Panels appear to have evolved their own strategy for dealing with differences of opinion as to the correct translation of domestic measures. The most notable and organised of these endeavours is to be found in the Japan–Measures Affecting Consumer Photographic Film and Paper case, where the Panel drew up procedures for the resolution of possible translation issues:

> 1. The party first relying on a Japanese-language document in a written submission or oral presentation shall provide copies of the full Japanese-language document and the relevant portions in English at the time that the party first makes reference to the document in the Panel proceedings.
> 2. If one party believes that additional portions of a previously submitted document are relevant, it shall then supply the additional translation at the time that that party first makes reference to the document in the Panel proceedings.
> 3. If one party disagrees with the other party's translation of a Japanese-language document or portion thereof, it shall prepare an alternative version of the contested portion of the translation. This shall be submitted to the Panel and to the other party with supporting written argumentation as needed. The other party may also submit its argumentation at this stage.
> 4. To the extent relevant for the resolution of the legal issues involved in this case, the Panel shall attempt to resolve any translation problem submitted to it, having recourse as necessary to independent experts appointed by the Panel, or to such other means as the Panel deems appropriate to the circumstances.[28]

Notable in this procedure is that the function of translation does not appear to have been delegated to the independent experts as such. Rather, the Panel retains control over translation issues by reserving to itself the function of resolving the translation issue. Moreover, the Panel retains discretion even over recourse to the independent experts. In other words, even after seeking the opinion of independent experts, the Panel reserves a residuary discretion to reject the advice given.

Also of note from Panel practice is that the Panel has generally placed a premium on the consensus of the parties to the dispute in resolving translation issues.[29] It has given weight to any translation provided by

[27] Korea–Commercial Vessels (Panel) para 24. [28] See para 1.9.
[29] See for example Mexico–Telecommunications (Panel) para 7.167.

the WTO Secretariat,[30] and where subsequent 'corrected' versions of translations have been provided as afterthoughts, it has given weight to the original translation provided.[31]

A number of conflict of norms issues can arise from translation resolutions at the WTO with respect to domestic legislation. First, when the domestic measure is translated differently from the translation proffered by the member as its own domestic law, does the new translation automatically result in an amendment of the domestic legislation? This is distinct from the question of the status of a WTO panel/AB ruling within the domestic system, when the decision involves an interpretation of the WTO Agreements in the context of the compatibility of the national measure with WTO law. Here it is the national measure and changes to it that are at issue. That said, it would seem that similar considerations pertain. If the domestic legislation is not amended according to the new translation, the member will not be conforming to its WTO obligations. Furthermore, the status of the translated amendment in the domestic legal system will depend on the national constitution with respect to international obligations.

Second, what of the situation when a member translates its own legislation into a WTO working language in a way that makes it different from its domestic legislation?[32] In this situation, at the level of the WTO it is the member itself that has introduced an alteration to its legislation. In the domestic legal system, which of the two versions of the legislation will prevail? As a matter of domestic law, this must depend on the domestic constitution. As a matter of international law, such a situation could amount to misrepresentation. If the translated version was WTO compatible, the member would be in breach of its WTO obligations if it continued using the untranslated version in its domestic system. However, the translation may not affect WTO compatibility but still result in a substantive change in the national legislation.

3.5 Conclusion

From the stand-point of compliance with the WTO Agreements, the interpretative apparatus of domestic systems calls for some attention. Interpretation as knowledge calls for comparative material on relevant

[30] Ibid para 6.6. [31] Brazil–Desiccated Coconut (Panel) para 292 (2).
[32] See for example Korea–Government Procurement (Panel) paragraphs 2.50, 7.40.

domestic case law, some form of domestic translation of or access to WTO case law and regular case law updates for relevant decision-makers. Interpretation as compliance calls for some focus on national interpretative processes, such as approaches to interpretation and aids to interpretation, to pre-empt non-compliance with WTO obligations. Interpretation as a strategic legislative tool calls for thinking about the interpretative process specifically as an apparatus for attention. Interpretation as a conflict resolution mechanism calls for accompanying procedures for resolving conflicts in translation and differences between domestic and WTO interpretations.

4

Interpreting exceptions in the WTO Agreements

4.1 Introduction

There has to be a theory for interpreting exceptions to a rule in international agreements – and in the WTO Agreements in particular, given that they are frequently invoked, encapsulate vital sovereign interests, and their characterisation, along with their interpretation, has serious consequences for the outcomes of decisions. The need for exceptions is grounded in reason, balance, measure, logic and coherence. Thus, rationality involves being open to exceptions, and the logic of a rule invites giving it clear boundaries as much as reinforcement from exceptions. It is this grounding of exceptions that calls for a theory of interpreting them – one that reflects their role in the scheme of a rule. By the same token, identifying exceptions and their scope through the interpretative process under international law must involve decision-makers in the judicial organs of the WTO in conceptions of justice compelling exceptions and economic analysis reinforcing WTO tenets. Similarly, democratic processes defined in terms of facilitating maximum participation and all-encompassing engagement with diverse interests push for a conscious approach to exceptions. If international agreements are the composite of the will of the majority, exceptions in some measure champion minority rights and divergent interests.

More particularly, in legal analysis there are a number of reasons for the importance of exceptions. First, the onus of proving an exception rests on the party invoking it. Second, in national practice exceptions are subject to a strict interpretation. Third, for an international agreement, the precise placement of a particular goal within a rule/exception model has a bearing on how the agreement is interpreted. Thus, the aims and objectives of an organisation inform the interpretation of all the provisions of the agreement, including exceptions. Consequently, goals that are set within the context of exceptions have a limited role in informing the interpretation of the agreement as a whole. Fourth, in the same vein, a goal that is encapsulated as an exception has a diminished value as an agent for mainstreaming. For example, if the development dimension is to be integrated fully into all spheres of trade policies within the WTO Agreements, then this mainstreaming objective is handicapped by its characterisation as an exception. Finally, the place of a goal within a rule/exception model has a bearing on how it can be sold in the national systems. The internal psychology of the parties to an agreement with respect to the significance of a goal, as mirrored by its place within a rule/exception model, can affect how it is perceived externally and nationally.

The need to develop a theory for interpreting exceptions is beginning to be recognised consciously within the WTO judicial organs. This is, in a sense, a reaction to the almost knee-jerk response in international practice to exceptions, based on the received wisdom that they need to be interpreted restrictively. In this manner, an effort is discernible to foster a more measured approach to exceptions. At the political level, the approach to exceptions in the WTO is both sub-conscious and practical – but nevertheless set against some sense of 'exceptions'. Thus, exception advocates in the Doha Round argue for the development objective to be integral to the functions of the WTO, thereby placing it in the mainstream of the WTO agreements. In contrast, exception deniers call for the integration of exceptions only so that they are overwhelmed and thereby diminished in the context of the general rules and principles. Thus, the significance given to a particular interest is an important ingredient in the theory at the political level.

Fair trade is defined and informed through the exceptions to liberal trade that it encapsulates. Free trade or liberal trade, on the other hand, prescribes no or few exceptions. An institution that is intended to engage in the process of liberalisation admits exceptions in order to facilitate liberal trade, or else it is established against the background of a series of existing exceptions or desired external policy goals. Therefore, approaches to exceptions in international trade law are determined according to whether the WTO embraces, or is seen as embracing, fair trade or liberal trade (or is viewed as an institution working towards the liberalisation of international trade). Each of these goals sets different parameters for the placement of exceptions. It follows from this that the nature and importance of exceptions presupposes clarity about not only the general goals of the WTO but also the exceptions to those general goals. In the framework of the WTO, this clarity is not always seen.

Similarly, the normative framework of the WTO is the construct of multilateral negotiations in which compromises, accommodations, necessity, as well as generally accepted policy goals, have determined and shaped exceptions. The manner and spirit in which exceptions have been fashioned has a bearing on the approach taken to them.

Finally, any normative system that is intended to endure must encapsulate exceptions; without the flexibility and latitude that exceptions provide to a legal system, the system will snap. The international trading system is no exception. From this stand-point, exceptions form the pillars of the international trading system rather than the foundations of the institution. Interpretative principles that do not take into account this basic fact will undermine the very fabric of the system.

In sum, the configuration of questions that centre on the nature of the WTO and the character of its exceptions has an important bearing on how the WTO exceptions are determined and interpreted. Much of the WTO litigation is indeed centred on the invocation of exceptions, which will probably be a centre of focus in the future.

4.2 What are exceptions in the WTO Agreements?

A focus on the nature of exceptions in the WTO raises two specific questions: How are they determined? What are the indicia of an exception? These two enquiries are connected.

Exceptions may be categorized in the following manner:

- exceptions expressly articulated as such – that is, a pre-set *de jure* category;
- exceptions that need to be determined, which usually constitute departures from the goals of liberal trade as set out in the WTO – that is, a *de facto* category.

4.2.1 Pre-set de jure *category*

Exceptions expressly articulated as such in the WTO Agreements are relatively infrequent. In GATT 1994, the words 'exception' and 'exceptional' are to be found only 16 times in a total of 2,854 words. Among these occurrences, the word 'exception' occurs as a label to a provision only 3 times (in Articles XIV, XX and XXI). In the General Agreement on Trade in Services (GATS), it is to be found only 4 times in 11,400 words. As a label to a provision it occurs only twice (in

Articles XIV and XV bis). In TRIPS, the words 'exception' and 'exceptional' are to be found 16 times in a total of 12,594 words. A number of these instances refer to exceptions in multilateral intellectual property rights agreements referred to in the TRIPS. Among these, five articles are expressly labelled as provisions dealing with exceptions. This is, of course, a crude measure based on word searches; nevertheless it can give some degree of insight into the framework of the agreements and the place of pre-set, expressly stated exceptions. The perceived number of exceptions in substance is also found to be wanting generally – or at any rate vociferously, in the various demonstrations that have accompanied many of the WTO Ministerial Conferences.

With respect to the pre-set *de jure* category of exceptions, the most celebrated example of which is Article XX of GATT 1994, the question that needs to be addressed at the outset is whether it is a given that the characterisation of a provision expressly as exceptional in an international agreement is conclusive of its nature as an exception. As a matter of treaty law, whether an exception so labelled is in substance an exception is a matter of construction. It needs to be discerned through the process of treaty interpretation whether a pre-set exception was in substance intended as an exception. Exceptions so called could be merely convenient labels for, say, parallel or competing objectives that need to be taken into account or a description of the parameters of the broader objectives of the agreement within which the general agreement operates. Indeed, the label 'exception' may simply have been deployed loosely, almost as a default category, without necessarily carrying any significance.

Furthermore, in the case of the WTO Agreements, the normative framework is dynamic and chronologically diverse. Consequently, conceptions of exceptions can be fluid. An exception in one time frame may take on a different dimension in another time frame. This may be borne out, in particular, by its subsequent treatment and elaboration. It is also the case that the trade liberalisation objective in the WTO is an ongoing goal, set alongside other objectives. The presence of these externalities can inform the characterisation of exceptions. The trade liberalisation objective is set against the background of existing trade and other practices, competing and conflicting objectives, and the need to take a balanced approach to the liberalisation of international trade. All of this can blur any formal distinction between general principles and exceptions.

In conclusion here, the AB's assertion in EC–Hormones, albeit in the context of a non-preset exception, is equally relevant with respect to pre-set exceptions: the mere characterisation of a treaty provision as an exception was not conclusive of its significance as an exception.[1]

4.2.2 *Undefined* de facto *category*

The *de facto* category of exceptions constitutes departures from general principles that are not expressed as exceptions as such. Thus, Articles XXIV (Regional Integration), VI (Anti-Dumping and Countervailing Measures), XVI (Subsidies) and XII (Restrictions to Safeguard the Balance of Payments) of GATT 1994 are not expressly labelled as exceptions. Does this fact make them any less exceptional? Judicial engagement in the interpretation of the agreements also involves consideration of claims for implied exceptions,[2] and indeed their determination.[3] How are such determinations made? A number of considerations shed light on these questions.

First, it is necessary to focus on the nature of an exception in the context of an international agreement. An international agreement is not necessarily a statement of a rule (and seldom only of a single rule). An international agreement can embody consensus on a variety of issues broadly pertaining to a subject or correlating to a theme. There is, in fact, no condition that an international agreement must conform to the rule/exception model. This is the case with the WTO Agreements, which do not fit well into the rule/exception strait-jacket. In legal analysis, therefore, the existence of exceptions has to be determined against this background. Second, an exception is not *any* departure from a general rule. The degree and nature of the departure, the temporal parameters and, indeed, the long-term objectives facilitated by the departure may have a bearing here. Thus, if a temporary departure from the prohibition of quantitative restrictions is intended in the long term to secure further trade liberalisation (and does so in fact), is such a departure an exception to a general rule or to an aspect of the general rule? The latter could be a plausible explanation. Third, the intention of the parties is also important in this

[1] (1998) para 104.

[2] See for example Canada–Certain Measures Affecting the Automotive Industry (Panel); US–Copyright Act (Panel) para 3; US–Steel Safeguards (AB) para 195.

[3] See for example Japan–Taxes on Alcoholic Beverages (AB) para 11, wherein the AB held that the *de minimis* exception applied to the application of Article III (2) of GATT 1994; Indonesia–Automobiles (Panel), wherein the Panel held that a developing member is not deprived of its S&D benefits as a consequence of non-compliance with procedural notifications requirements.

process of characterisation. There has to be an intention that the departure is considered an exception, and not merely something that is permitted or tolerated. This is to reflect the fact that the parties negotiate their interests into an agreement, including to a great extent the rule/exception status of their interests. It is also to recognise that the law of treaties gives the parties to an agreement control over the content, status and hierarchy of a norm within the framework of the agreement. Finally, an exception is informed by the general rule to which it is an exception. Therefore, both the general rule in question and its nature are significant. In this context, is the general rule to be found with reference to the stated aims and objectives of the WTO or the general principles underpinning the WTO? The former, being closer to the intentions of the parties, would appear to have a better claim to being the controlling rule.

There are, indeed, various provisions in the WTO Agreements – in fact, whole agreements – that are not expressly labelled as exceptions but have been variously argued to be exceptions, in both the judicial and the political organs of the WTO. These include certain trade remedies,[4] special and differential treatment (S&D) provisions and regimes, Articles XXIV and XV of GATT 1994 and, at the micro level, Articles 3.1 and 3.3 of the Agreement on Sanitary and Phytosanitary Measures (the SPS Agreement). Among these, the genre that has most tested the exception/rule dichotomy is S&D provisions. Therefore, it is appropriate to draw on S&D to provide some insight into the various issues involved in the process of characterising an exception.

4.2.3 *Lessons from the WTO political discourse in the characterisation of S&D provisions*

S&D provisions in the WTO operate both in a defensive fashion, facilitating a flexible application of WTO disciplines, and in an offensive manner, enabling improved access to international markets for goods and services from developing members of the WTO. Key elements of S&D include transitional periods for implementing obligations, temporary departures from WTO commitments, certain obligations on developed countries to accord preferential treatment to developing

[4] For example, in US–Corrosion-Resistant Steel Sunset Review, the AB characterised the continuation of an anti-dumping duty as an exception after five years (see para 178). Similarly, in US–Carbon Steel (paras 86–90) the AB held that the termination 'of a countervailing duty is the rule and its continuation is the exception'.

members and technical assistance. In brief, S&D involves departures from certain basic free-trade tenets set out in the WTO – in particular non-discrimination.

The concept of S&D has been enshrined in the multilateral trading system from the inception of GATT 1947 right up to the Uruguay Round. In between, in this respect GATT 1947 was subject to amendment and augmentation, with Part IV in 1964, the Enabling Clause in 1979, and the Tokyo Round Agreements. The July 2004 decision of the Doha Round reaffirmed S&D as an integral part of the WTO Agreements, and thus the development of S&D continues.[5]

The negotiations in the Doha Round in relation to S&D have been taking place in the Special Session of the WTO Committee on Trade and Development. This committee has been charged with incorporating S&D provisions into the architecture of the WTO rules. Although these are negotiations with respect to future changes, they nevertheless shed some interesting light on perceptions of such provisions in terms of whether they are to be regarded as exceptions.

The discussion on S&D among the membership of the WTO betrays a certain confusion in terms of the locus of S&D within the scheme of WTO norms. Thus, Paraguay considered S&D an integral part of the WTO but went on to characterise these provisions as exceptions.[6] A similar pronouncement was made by Kenya.[7] This characterisation of S&D as an exception could reduce it to a lesser genre of norm – a characterisation that a developing member fully informed about the principles of treaty interpretation might not want to concede in so hasty a manner. Further, such a categorisation might undermine the international endeavour to characterise S&D as integral to the WTO.

There are also differences over the importance and the locus of S&D within the WTO normative scheme. By some members, S&D provisions are elevated to great heights. Thus, the delegates of Pakistan and Malaysia referred to S&D as a 'right', in contra-distinction to a 'concession'.[8] The representative of Chile placed S&D on an even higher plane, describing it as being based not so much on rights as on 'need'.[9]

[5] '[T]he General Council reaffirms that provisions for special and differential (S&D) treatment are an integral part of the WTO Agreements . . . '. Earlier on in the Doha Ministerial Declaration 2001 (para 44) the WTO declared inter alia: 'We reaffirm that provisions for special and differential treatment are an integral part of the WTO Agreements.'

[6] TN/CTD/M/2.

[7] Kenya (TN/CTD/M/7): 'However, S&D treatment provisions were exemptions to the rule.'

[8] Ibid. [9] Ibid.

The representative of Senegal described it as a 'core principle in multilateral trade'.[10] The representative of Cuba took the view that as S&D provisions had been recognised since the creation of the Charter of Havana, and followed up in different rounds with various declarations and decisions, the S&D provisions in the WTO Agreements should 'not be interpreted as issues of concessions made to developing countries'.[11] The representative went on to state that the 'objectives included in the preamble to the Doha Ministerial Declaration were clear. One of them, as set out by the WTO Members, was to realise the greater participation of developing countries in international trade. So S&D was a right which developing countries had acquired in order to improve their effective participation in the multilateral trade system.' The representative of Kenya, on behalf of the African Group, stated that

> trade was not an end itself but something which was reflected in the objectives agreed to by the Members in setting up first the GATT and now the WTO. Trade should contribute to the improvement of living standards, especially in developing and least-developed country Members. It had to be a welfare generating activity. He said that, in this context, it was recognised that special measures would be necessary to assist developing and least-developed country Members to achieve a share in international trade that was commensurate with their development needs. He felt that this embodiment of special treatment in the core objectives and functions of the WTO recognised such treatment to be a basic right for developing and least-developed country Members as part of their overall right to economic development.[12]

There are three points to note here: first, the general view, mainly among the developing-country members, of the significance of S&D – in particular, its characterisation as an entitlement in the form of a right; second, the portrayal by developing members of S&D as an integral or core aspect of the WTO – a stand-point reinforced, of course, by paragraph 44 of the Doha Declaration; third, the identification of development as the primary goal of the WTO – resulting in the primacy of S&D within such a WTO order. This configuration of perspectives arguably provides a strong basis for not characterising S&D

[10] Kenya (TN/CTD/M/7): 'However, S&D treatment provisions were exemptions to the rule'.

[11] TN/CTD/M/3.

[12] TN/CTD/M/4. The identification of development as the primary objective of the WTO Agreements was an opinion shared by the LDCs. See Kenya (TN/CTD/M/5) para 11.

provisions as exceptions, or at any rate for not interpreting them strictly as exceptions.

Another school of thought, led mainly by the developed members, locates S&D on a lower plane.[13] This perception of S&D provisions uses different parameters, placing them in a different position within the WTO normative framework. Thus, the United States considered S&D provisions to be 'flexible provisions for developing countries', Japan regarded them as 'tools for developing countries and LDCs',[14] and the European Communities characterised them as a stepping stone.[15] All these members, together with Canada, took the view that S&D provisions were intended to ensure the full integration and effective participation of developing members in the multilateral trading system.[16] Furthermore, there was general consensus between the United States, the European Union, Japan and Canada[17] that S&D provisions were 'negotiated during the Uruguay Round as part of a single Undertaking in mind'.[18] The ultimate objective of S&D was 'to ensure a single set of rights and obligation to which all Members were accountable',[19] thus ensuring that recourse to S&D should take place without 'damaging the balance between the rights and obligations in the WTO Agreements', and thereby 'maintaining the integrity of those Agreements'.[20] The view was taken that S&D should not lead to 'two-tiered or multi-tiered structures of rights and obligations'.[21]

In conclusion, the perspective established here, led principally by the developed members, tends more towards a characterisation of S&D provisions as exceptions within a single normative framework – set firmly against the background of the multilateral trading system. There are thus two key related issues, perceptions of which might have coloured the nature of S&D provisions as exceptions:

1. whether S&D provisions are intended to facilitate development or the full and effective participation of developing members in the multilateral trading system;

[13] The perspective of the developed members set out here was shared by Paraguay, which stated that 'S&D was not an end to itself, but rather a means towards free and fair trade'. See TN/CTD/M/7 para 11.

[14] Ibid para 101. [15] TN/D/M/13 para 12 [b].

[16] See TN/CTD/M/7 para 101; TN/CTD/M/5 para 60; TN/D/M/13 para 12 [b]; TN/CTD/M/7 para 85.

[17] TN/CTD/M/7 para 101; TN/CTD/M/5 para 60; TN/D/M/13 para 12 [b]; TN/CTD/M/7 para 85.

[18] TN/CTD/M/5 para 60. [19] Ibid. [20] TN/CTD/M/7 para 101. [21] Ibid.

2. whether S&D provisions are to be part of a two-tiered system within a multilateral normative framework for the international trading system or part of a Single Undertaking.

At one level, analysis of the first issue will indeed shed light on whether S&D provisions are exceptions or are more integral to the multilateral trading system. Certainly, in the negotiations, some members considered the approach to S&D by other members to be placing 'undue emphasis on development being the end purpose of S&D, instead of helping developing countries integrate into the multilateral trading system, which they felt should be the main objective of S&D'.[22]

On the other hand, it needs to be noted that both objectives (i.e. trade and development) run along the same continuum. They are not parallel dimensions. Trade is not exclusive of the development goal, nor does development preclude trade. The nature of an exception is determined by the fact that it falls along another continuum. Therefore, it is not a given that the trade and development parameters will distinguish an S&D provision as an exception or as a mainstream goal of the multilateral trading system. Furthermore, the impression of the different trade and development objectives may be a matter of degree rather than of a clear choice informing the exception/general rule dichotomy. If the character of exceptions can be fluid in both time and nature, the different parameters within which exceptions might be conceived may position them closer to exceptions or closer to general rules. In this case what might be decisive is the individual nature of the S&D provision and the degree to which it is pitted against trade issues.

With respect to the second issue, this is in a sense part of the same argument as above. It is a different way of ensuring S&D provisions have the status of exceptions, by giving them the generic parameters of a multilateral trading system that is more trade oriented. In this manner, S&D provisions are made more sensitive to trade issues *stricto sensu*. However, it needs to be pointed out that the premise that S&D is a mechanism for facilitating greater and effective participation in the multilateral trading system, and therefore should be set in the context of a single normative tier, itself makes a number of assumptions:

1. that greater participation in the multilateral trading system will not be facilitated through a multi-tiered system of rights and obligations;

[22] TN/CTD/M/18 para 10.

2. that the balance of rights and obligations will necessarily be undermined through a multi-tiered system of rights and obligations;
3. that S&D is inconsistent with the existing unified normative framework;
4. that the goal of S&D can be determined artificially and limited to the easing of developing members into the multilateral trading system;
5. that S&D is a tool for the integration of the developing members into the multilateral trading system;
6. that integration is a realisable goal.

With respect to the second and third assumptions, the Indian delegate's reaction is highly pertinent; he pointed out that the existing normative framework already provided for differentiation within a unified system – for example, the Agreement on Agriculture, which provides differential treatment in favour of a set of members, the Agreement on Textiles and Clothing, and the Agreement on Subsidies and Countervailing Measures (ASCM), which provides differential treatment to those listed in its annex.[23] Furthermore, the Indian delegate

> asked Members to recognize the fact that under Article XXIV of GATT 1994, regional trade agreements [RTAs] had been sanctioned. RTAs provided differentiated treatment between parties to the RTA and non-parties to the RTA. All such differentiation derived legitimacy from existing agreements as did S&D treatment. There was no difference between S&D treatment and the differentiated treatment which had been referred to.[24]

The fourth assumption raises the question whether there are indeed some goals that in a sense defy being characterised as lesser norms. One might contend that once development permeates the trade framework, it has a dynamics of its own. Some colours mixed on a palette, to invoke an analogy, will leave a marked impression of their own. Furthermore, and importantly, development is a cardinal principle within international economic law. It trumps trade as a goal.

In relation to the final assumption, mechanisms constructed on a temporary basis to integrate developing members into the multilateral trading system assume that the goal of integration is achievable. The reality is that there will always be differences in development levels between nations that will call for multi-tiered normative structures.

[23] India (TN/CTD/M/7) para 112. [24] Ibid.

In sum, parallel and symbiotic goals, along with respective normative frameworks, within a continuum can co-exist, without one necessarily being subservient to the other.

One other aspect of the S&D debate concerns the question of the relationship of one exception to another. For example, under Article XX of GATT 1994 (in particular Article XX [b]), a member is entitled to depart from certain WTO obligations in order to protect human, animal or plant life or health. Article XX [b] has been further elaborated under the SPS Agreement. With respect to this exception, as elaborated in the SPS Agreement, the US representative questioned the role of S&D:

> At the heart of any discussion of SPS, however, was the Member's overarching concern for the protection of human health. Making mandatory S&D provisions which would delay the implementation of SPS measures would affect the overall balance of the Agreement, the good of which was the protection of human health. The provisions could not be considered out of context.[25]

According to the US representative, the Article XX [b] GATT exception in the form of the SPS Agreement would be undermined by the mandatory S&D provisions proposed. From the perspective of interpretation, the interesting question is, given the origins of the SPS Agreement and its stated objective of being the elaboration of Article XX [b] of GATT 1994, whether it retains its exceptional character – particularly for the purposes of interpretation. If it does (contrary to the US assertion) – and this is a matter of legal analysis and construction – then how is an exception to an exception to be interpreted, particularly one that at the least is intended to reinforce trade? Logic suggests it would be interpreted less strictly than the actual SPS measures, if exceptions are subject to strict interpretation. It is suggested here that the SPS Agreement partakes of an exception, as it is expressly rooted in Article XX, the general exceptions provision of GATT 1994.

4.2.4 Lessons from the legal discourse in the characterisation of S&D exceptions

The WTO judicial organs have witnessed on a number of occasions different parties arguing for and against the characterisation of an agreement, provision or regime as an exception or a general rule.

[25] TN/CTD/M/3.

EC–Tariff Preferences is a leading case that clarifies many of the issues that surround the characterisation of exceptions generally, and in particular S&D regimes. The case involved the so-called Enabling Clause, which gave the developed members authority to depart from the most-favoured-nation standard in GATT 1994 and thereby to accord preferential treatment to developing members.[26] However, the case needs to be considered against the background of other cases that also focus on the question of characterising exceptions in the WTO.

The following guidance may be discerned in terms of the establishment of an exception, in particular from this case and generally from the WTO jurisprudence. First, the determination of an exception is a matter of legal analysis – specifically, a matter of interpretation. Thus, in EC–Tariff Preferences the AB stated:

> Whatever its characterization, a provision of the covered agreements must be interpreted in accordance with the 'customary rules of interpretation of public international law', as required by Article 3.2 of the *Understanding on Rules and Procedures Governing the Settlement of Disputes* (the 'DSU').[27]

Second, an exception can encapsulate a WTO objective. Thus, the AB stated in EC–Tariff Preferences, with reference to the protection of the environment and S&D:

> We note, however, . . . that WTO objectives may well be pursued through measures taken under provisions characterized as exceptions. The Preamble to the *WTO Agreement* identifies certain objectives that may be pursued by Members through measures that would have to be justified under the 'General Exceptions' of Article XX. For instance, one such objective is reflected in the recognition by Members that the expansion of trade must be accompanied by:
>
> . . . the optimal use of the world's resources in accordance with the objective of sustainable development, [with Members] seeking both to protect and preserve the environment and to enhance the means for doing so in a manner consistent with their respective needs and concerns at different levels of economic development[.]
>
> 95. As the Appellate Body observed in *US–Shrimp*, WTO Members retained Article XX (g) from the *General Agreement on Tariffs and Trade*

[26] Decision on Differential and More Favourable Treatment, Reciprocity, and Fuller Participation of Developing Countries, GATT Document L/4903 (28 November 1979) BISD 26S/203 (attached as Annex 2 to this report).

[27] Para 98.

> *1947* (the 'GATT 1947') without alteration after the conclusion of the Uruguay Round, being 'fully aware of the importance and legitimacy of environmental protection as a goal of national and international policy'. Article XX (g) of the GATT 1994 permits Members, subject to certain conditions, to take measures 'relating to the conservation of exhaustible natural resources if such measures are made effective in conjunction with restrictions on domestic production or consumption'. It is well-established that Article XX (g) is an *exception* in relation to which the responding party bears the burden of proof. Thus, by authorizing in Article XX (g) measures for environmental conservation, an important objective referred to in the Preamble to the *WTO Agreement*, Members implicitly recognized that the implementation of such measures would not be discouraged simply because Article XX (g) constitutes a defence to otherwise WTO-inconsistent measures. Likewise, characterizing the Enabling Clause as an exception, in our view, does not undermine the importance of the Enabling Clause within the overall framework of the covered agreements and as a 'positive effort' to enhance economic development of developing country Members. Nor does it 'discourag[e]' developed countries from adopting measures in favour of developing countries under the Enabling Clause. (Footnotes omitted)[28]

Third, an exception need not be of a 'non-trade' character. In this context the AB stated:

> We do not consider it relevant, for the purposes of determining whether a provision is or is not in the nature of an exception, that the provision governs 'trade measures' rather than measures of a primarily 'non-trade' nature.[29]

Finally, there 'appears to be no overriding general principle' to distinguish between a 'provision of the WTO Agreement and an "exception" to a provision of the WTO Agreement'.[30] This is an assertion, however, which may well be re-visited in the WTO judicial discourse. It is, at any rate, intuitively at odds with the very concept of an exception in a general agreement on trade, despite the apparent blurring of the distinction between an exception and a general rule.

4.2.5 *Indicia of an exception*

Against this background it is possible *to construct* the indicia of an exception in the WTO, which derive inter alia from the various

[28] (AB) para 94. [29] Ibid para 97.
[30] Brazil–Export Financing Programmes for Aircraft (Panel) para 7.46.

arguments advanced by the parties in the WTO dispute settlement system, as well as from the deliberations of the Panel and the AB, especially in the EC–Tariff Preferences case.[31] None of these is conclusive in itself.

Positive indicators:

1. text of the provision(s);
2. position of the provision(s) within the framework of the WTO Agreements;
3. object and purpose of the provision(s);
4. intention underlying the provision(s);
5. proximity/closeness to the principal objectives;
6. presence of choice in drawing on the exception;
7. conditionality in the rights accorded in the provision(s);
8. function of the relevant provision(s);
9. similarity to/affinity with other exceptions;
10. nature of the exception;
11. pursuit of objectives not set out in the principal provision(s);
12. narrowness in a quantitative and qualitative sense: narrow scope and a distinct objective.[32]

Negative indicators:

1. exceptions do not provide for unconditional positive obligations;
2. exceptions do not partake of autonomous or special regimes;
3. an exception does not present a situation of conflict of norms;[33]
4. an exception is not an exemption;
5. exceptions do not apply to the *exclusion* of a general rule;
6. there is a lack of intent on the part of the parties, as evidenced by the text of the treaty;
7. exceptions do not partake of *lex specialis*;
8. an exception does not partake of a fundamental principle that displaces rather than excepts a general rule;
9. an exception does not conflict with other principles.

[31] See EC–Tariff Preferences (AB) paras 10–11, 13–15, 36–7, 64, 80–1, 86, 89–90, 91, 93–4, 97, 98; EC–Hormones (AB) para 104.

[32] US–Copyright Act (Panel) para 6.109.

[33] Joost Pauwelyn *Conflict of Norms in Public International law* (Cambridge UP, Cambridge 2003) 163, where he states: 'At first sight there is always an apparent conflict between a rule and an explicit exception to that rule. However, in case the exception explicitly provides that the rule does not apply in the exceptional circumstances, the apparent conflict disappears.'

Neutral indicators:

1. pursuit of WTO objectives through the exception provision(s);
2. exceptions need not be of a non-trade character.

In conclusion, an exception is understood as a 'limited derogation' from the application of a rule or general regime.[34] It excludes something from the application of a general rule while affirming the rule to which it is an exception.[35] An exception authorises a departure for a specific purpose under certain conditions. It is distinguishable from a genre of allied concepts, some with similar consequences, such as an 'affirmative defence',[36] waivers,[37] exemptions,[38] and provisos and limitations[39] to or qualifications in a provision. Some of these terms are occasionally used synonymously.[40] A proviso limits or qualifies the scope of the rule to which it is addressed.[41] An exemption, on the other hand, simply excludes a party or sphere from the operation of a rule or rules. Although technically different, both are subject to similar principles of interpretation.

4.2.6 *Who defines exceptions?*

Exceptions are determined in a variety of ways. However, the agencies for their determination are not specifically recognised as exceptions-creating ones, although they engage with exceptions in practice within their general remit. That said, the general law-creating and law-determining agencies of the WTO are necessarily the relevant agencies here.

De facto exceptions are discerned through the judicial process. They are determined through the establishment both of the limits of a general rule and of the limits of the scope of an exception – indeed, through the

34 US–Copyright Act (Panel) para 6.107; EC–Trade Marks (US) (Panel) para 7.650.
35 See for example Dominican Republic–Measures Affecting the Importation and Internal Sale of Cigarettes (Panel) para 7.131; Brazil–Export Financing Programmes for Aircraft (Panel) para 7.46.
36 Brazil–Export Financing Programmes for Aircraft (Panel) para 7.46; Dominican Republic–Measures Affecting the Importation and Internal Sale of Cigarettes (Panel) para 7.131.
37 US–Sugar Waiver (GATT) (Panel) (1990) paras 3.33, 5.9.
38 See argument of the EC in EC–Commercial Vessels (Panel) para 7.58.
39 US–Copyright Act (Panel) paras 6.107.
40 N.S. Bindra *Interpretation of Statutes* (8th edn The Law Book Company (P) Ltd, Allahabad, India 1997) 86, quoting Crawford.
41 Ibid.

very characterisation of a provision as an exception. There is thus an asymmetry between the legislative process involved in the formulation of general rules or principles and the legislative process involved in the formulation of exceptions. The creative processes involved in the generation of general rules are closer to democratic processes than are those that relate to exceptions.

Moreover, the methodology adopted by the AB (at any rate in one case) does leave some room for development. In Turkey–Textile, Turkey argued that the 'right under Article XXIV to establish a customs union is an autonomous right; it is not an "exception" from other GATT obligations'.[42] The AB did not directly and clearly address this. It considered Article XXIV as a possible 'defence' to a finding of inconsistency under GATT 1994.[43] However, the justification is to be found set out in a footnote:

> [13]We note that legal scholars have long considered Article XXIV to be an 'exception' or a possible 'defence' to claims of violation of GATT provisions. An early treatise on GATT law stated: '[Article XXIV] establishes an *exception to GATT obligations* for regional arrangements that meet a series of detailed and complex criteria.' (emphasis added) J. Jackson, *World Trade and the Law of GATT* (The Bobbs-Merrill Company, 1969), p. 576. See also J. Allen, *The European Common Market and the GATT* (The University Press of Washington, D.C., 1960), p. 2; K. Dam, 'Regional Economic Arrangements and the GATT: The Legacy of Misconception', *University of Chicago Law Review*, 1963, p. 616; and J. Huber, 'The Practice of GATT in Examining Regional Arrangements under Article XXIV', *Journal of Common Market Studies*, 1981, p. 281. We note also the following statement in the unadopted panel report in *EEC–Member States' Import Regimes for Bananas*, DS32/R, 3 June 1993, para. 358: 'The Panel noted that Article XXIV:5 to 8 permitted the contracting parties to *deviate from their obligations under other provisions of the General Agreement* for the purpose of forming a customs union . . . '. (Emphasis added)[44]

The decision of the AB may well be correct. However, its reasoning is not well elaborated. Nor is it forthright. Article XXIV is considered a 'defense' in quotes. The AB 'notes' legal writings, and even that by way of a footnote. Can so profound a question as the character of Article XXIV really be dealt with in such a manner? Ought such a question to be delegated to legal analysts outside the WTO? Should such a question be informed by statements from a time frame that

[42] AB. [43] Ibid para 45. [44] Footnote 13.

may not have much relevance now? Finally, is this the definitive statement on Article XXIV? The AB does not appear to have viewed the question of characterisation through the prism of the principles of treaty interpretation as set out in the VC itself. Instead, it jumps straight to publicists – placing a premium on legal analysts. This approach must be attributed to the fact that the AB did not itself have the requisite indicia of an exception.

4.3 Principles for interpreting exceptions in treaty law

Not much has been written specifically about the principles for interpreting exceptions in international agreements. Rather, the focus has usually been somewhat incidental to the general elucidation of the principles of treaty interpretation. Indeed, generally the principles involved seem to have been considered self-evident without much clear analysis of the subject.

The principles for interpreting exceptions in treaties are to be found in both general international law and the domestic practice of interpreting exceptions in statutes. The latter can be a source of general principles in international law. There is no specific reference in the VC to how exceptions are to be interpreted in a treaty once they are found to exist. However, as has been noted, the general principles for treaty interpretation as set out in the VC are relevant to the identification or characterisation of an exception. This is because this question is grounded in the intentions of the parties, as expressed in the text of the treaty, along with its object and purposes. Judicial pronouncements, therefore, cannot in principle result in the introduction of exceptions where these are not intended.

However, once an exception is found, certain canons of construction come into play. One that is often referred to in terms of exceptions is the principle expressed in Latin as *exceptio est strictissimae applicationis*. In accordance with this principle, exceptions to treaty obligations are interpreted restrictively. This has been explained to mean that 'any doubt will be resolved in favour of the general provision and against the exception'. Thus, calls for a liberal interpretation of exceptions involve stricter interpretation of the general rules.[45] This principle of strict interpretation has been applied also to provisos, exemptions[46] and waivers.[47]

[45] See Bindra *Interpretation of Statutes* 88, quoting Crawford.

[46] Ibid 86, 87. [47] US–Sugar Waiver (Panel) (1990) para 5.9.

Allied to this is the evidential rule that exceptions need to be proved. The onus of proving an exception falls on the party invoking it.[48] This is the case also in relation to domestic legislation.[49] Consequently, there are often hard-fought arguments by the different parties in litigation claiming or denying the existence of an exception.

There is some lack of clarity in general international practice over whether the application of the principle of interpreting exceptions strictly is mandatory or discretionary. Thus, according to the authors of *Oppenheim's International Law*:

> while international law permits recourse to many principles and maxims, it does not always require recourse to them. The appropriateness of applying many of them depends on a variety of considerations which will determine whether, although they are accepted in international law as potentially relevant, they are also suitable for application in all the circumstances of the particular case. In such cases the principle is not so much a rule for international law as a discretionary aid . . .[50]

Further on, the authors observe: 'it is usual for courts to interpret strictly exceptions to a principal provision imposing obligations on a State, notwithstanding that the principle *in dubio mitius* may suggest that the exception be given a liberal interpretation'.[51] This certainly is borne out by judicial practice.

However, much judicial practice indicates a mandatory understanding of this principle. Thus, in one NAFTA case, albeit in the context of reservations to a treaty, an Arbitral Panel observed as follows:

> the Panel recalls an old legal principle expressed in Latin as *exceptio est strictissimae applicationis* that has been utilized to signify that reservations to treaty obligations are to be construed restrictively.[52]

[48] See US–Shirts and Blouses (AB) 14: 'it is a generally accepted canon of evidence in civil law, common law, and in fact, most jurisdictions, that the burden of proof rests upon the party, whether complaining or defending, who asserts the affirmative of a particular claim or a defence. If that party adduces evidence sufficient to raise a presumption that what is claimed is true, the burden then shifts to the other party, who will fail unless it adduces sufficient evidence to rebut the presumption.'

[49] See for example Bindra *Interpretation of Statutes*.

[50] *Oppenheim's International Law* I: 1268, 1270. [51] Ibid 1279.

[52] NAFTA Arbitral Panel Established Pursuant to Chapter Twenty: In the Matter of Cross-Border Trucking Services (Secretariat File no. USA-MEX-98–2008–01).

Similar pronouncements have been made by the ECJ:

> 18 According to the Commission, the interpretation of the exception laid down in point 2 of Annex F to the Sixth Directive must be based on the wording of that provision. In addition, as it is an exception to the primary rule, the provision must be interpreted strictly . . .
>
> 33 It is settled case-law that the terms used to specify the exemptions which constitute exceptions to the general principle that VAT [value-added tax] is to be levied on all services supplied for consideration by a taxable person must be interpreted strictly (see, inter alia, to that effect Case 348/87 Stichting Uitvoering Financiele Acties 1989 ECR 1737, paragraph 13; Case C-453/93 Bulthuis-Griffioen 1995 ECR I-2341, paragraph 19; Case C-216/97 Gregg 1999 ECR I-4947, paragraph 12; and Case C-150/99 Stockholm Lindopark 2001 ECR 1–493, paragraph 25).[53]

Likewise, the ICJ has stated:

> 212. The Court observes that the method of straight baselines, which is an exception to the normal rules for the determination of baselines, may only be applied if a number of conditions are met. This method must be applied restrictively.[54]

The practice in the GATT and until recently in the WTO has mirrored these pronouncements.[55] These deliberations prescribe the application

[53] Judgment of the Court (Fifth Chamber) of 7 March 2002 *Commission of the European Communities* v. *Republic of Finland* Case C-169/00 (Court of Justice of the European Communities 2002 ECR I-02433). See also Judgment of the Court of First Instance (Fourth Chamber, extended composition) of 11 December 2001 Case T-191/99, wherein the Court held: '66. The exceptions to document access fall to be interpreted and applied restrictively so as not to frustrate application of the general principle of giving the public the widest possible access to documents held by the Commission (Case T-309/97 *Bavarian Lager* v. *Commission* 1999 ECR II-3217, paragraph 39 and the case-law there cited).' See also judgement of 9 October 1999 Case C-382/99 (Court of Justice of the European Communities 2002 ECR I-05163 [ECJ CELEX LEXIS 3581]): '100. But, as we have seen, it is the settled case-law of the Court that all exceptions to a general rule must be strictly construed. Were I to adopt the analysis of the Netherlands Government, I would have to conclude that the principle of strict interpretation of exceptions to a rule must be set aside in the case of just such an exception. The principle of strict construction of exceptions to a rule would therefore not be observed if the analysis of the Netherlands Government were adopted.'

[54] *Case Concerning Maritime Delimitation and Territorial Questions Between Qatar and Bahrain* Merits General List no. 87, 16 March 2001.

[55] See for example EC–Bananas I (GATT): '339. The Panel recalled that the burden of proof was on the party invoking an Article XI: 2 exception, and that such exceptions were to be interpreted narrowly'; Canada–Import Restrictions on Ice Cream and Yoghurt (GATT): '59. The Panel recalled that it had previously been concluded that a contracting party

of the principle of strict/restrictive/narrow interpretation of exceptions in a categorical manner and rely variously on the established practice in the GATT/WTO, on the principle itself and on the principles set out in the VC.

It is therefore somewhat surprising that against the background of international practice, including the practice of GATT 1947, the AB seems to have re-interpreted its previous application of the principle of

invoking an exception to the General Agreement bore the burden of proving that it had met all of the conditions of that exception. It also noted, as had previous panels, that exceptions were to be interpreted narrowly and considered that this argued against flexible interpretation of Article XI: 2(c) (i)' (footnotes omitted); US–Tuna I (GATT): '5.22. . . . the practice of panels has been to interpret Article XX narrowly'; US–Sugar Waiver (GATT): '5.9.. . . The Panel took into account in its examination that waivers are granted according to Article XXV: 5 only in "exceptional circumstances", that they waive obligations under the basic rules of the General Agreement and that their terms and conditions consequently have to be interpreted narrowly'; US–Pork (GATT): '4.4. . . . as an exception to basic principles of the General Agreement, had to be interpreted narrowly . . . '; US–Customs User Fee (GATT) (1987): '84. The exception stated in Article II: 2(c) requires particularly strict interpretation, however, because it does not conform to the policy justification normally given for such exceptions'; US–Shrimp (Panel), citing US–Tuna II (GATT): '7.46. We find support for our reasoning in the *Tuna II* case where the panel considered a similar issue and found as follows: 5.26. The Panel observed that Article XX provides for an exception to obligations under the General Agreement. The long-standing practice of panels has accordingly been to interpret this provision narrowly, in a manner that preserves the basic objectives and principles of the General Agreement.[84] ([84]Reports of the Panels in *Canada–Administration of the Foreign Investment Review Act*, adopted 7 February 1984, 30S/140, 64, para. 5.20; *United States–Section 337 of the Tariff Act of 1930*, adopted 7 November 1989, 36S/345, 393, para. 5.27)'; US–Underwear (Panel): '7.21. We conclude from the interpretation of these provisions in the light of Article 31 of the VCLT that recourse to transitional safeguards should be taken on an exceptional basis only. Consequently, in our view, Article 6 of the ATC should be interpreted narrowly. This conclusion is consistent with the past practice of GATT panels.[22] ([22]See the panel reports on "Canada–Administration of the Foreign Investment Review Act [FIRA])", adopted on 7 February 1984, BISD 30S/140; "United States–Customs User Fee", adopted on 2 February 1988, BISD 35S/245; "Japan–Restrictions on Imports of Certain Agricultural Products", adopted on 22 March 1988, BISD 35S/163; "European Economic Community–Restrictions on Imports of Dessert Apples", Complaint by Chile, adopted on 22 June 1989, BISD 36S/93; "Canada–Import Restrictions on Ice Cream and Yogurt", adopted on 5 December 1989, BISD 36S/68; "European Economic Community–Regulation on Imports of Parts and Components", adopted on 16 May 1990, BISD 37S/132; "United States–Countervailing Duties on Fresh, Chilled and Frozen Pork from Canada", adopted on 11 July 1991, BISD 38S/30; "United States–Definition of Industry Concerning Wine and Grape Products", adopted on 28 April 1992, BISD 39S/436; "United States–Measures Affecting Alcoholic and Malt Beverages", adopted on 19 June 1992, BISD 39S/206.)'

strict interpretation. The re-interpretation is to be found in the AB decision in EC–Hormones, wherein it stated:

> 104 . . . The general rule in a dispute settlement proceeding requiring a complaining party to establish a prima facie case of inconsistency with a provision of the SPS Agreement before the burden of showing consistency with that provision is taken on by the defending party, is not avoided by simply describing that same provision as an 'exception'. In much the same way, merely characterizing a treaty provision as an 'exception' does not by itself justify a 'stricter' or 'narrower' interpretation of that provision than would be warranted by examination of the ordinary meaning of the actual treaty words, viewed in context and in the light of the treaty's object and purpose, or, in other words, by applying the normal rules of treaty interpretation.[56]

This case has subsequently been cited on a number of occasions – including in EC–Tariff Preferences.[57] It has also been commented on

[56] AB.

[57] See for example US–Steel Safeguards (Panel): '10.13. Moreover, the Panel, when interpreting Article XIX of GATT 1994 and the Agreement on Safeguards, must bear in mind that exceptions under WTO law are not to be interpreted narrowly[4874] but rather in light of the ordinary meaning of the terms of such exception provisions taking into account the object and purpose of the Agreement on Safeguards, including the need to maintain a balance between market access and safeguards rights and obligations. Since the Agreement on Safeguards itself would have been drafted so as to recognize its exceptional nature and the emergency character of safeguard measures, the Agreement on Safeguards does not call for any especially restrictive interpretation. ([4874]This principle of interpretation in WTO law was first established by the Appellate Body in *EC–Hormones* (para. 104) for the SPS Agreement. It was reiterated recently in the Appellate Body Report in *EC–Sardines* (para. 271), when discussing Article 2.4 of the TBT Agreement; in the Panel Report in *US–Carbon Steel* (para. 8.45, upheld by the Appellate Body) when discussing Article 21.3 of the SCM Agreement; in the Article 21.5 Appellate Body Report in *US–FSC* (para. 127) when discussing the scope and meaning of footnote 59 of the SCM Agreement; and in the Appellate Body Report in *Brazil–Aircraft* (para. 137) when dealing with the scope of the provisions on developing countries)'. See also EC–Sardines (AB): '272. In much the same way, merely characterizing a treaty provision as an "exception" does not by itself justify a "stricter" or "narrower" interpretation of that provision than would be warranted by examination of the ordinary meaning of the actual treaty words, viewed in context and in the light of the treaty's object and purpose, or, in other words, by applying the normal rules of treaty interpretation'; EC–Tariff Preferences (AB): '98. Whatever its characterization, a provision of the covered agreements must be interpreted in accordance with the "customary rules of interpretation of public international law", as required by Article 3.2 of the Understanding on Rules and Procedures Governing the Settlement of Disputes (the "DSU") . . . .([212]In this regard, we recall the Appellate Body's statement in EC–Hormones that: . . . merely characterizing a treaty provision . . .).'

with approval (albeit somewhat in passing) by observers. Thus, Joost Pauwelyn states:

> Arts 31–2 of the Vienna Convention do not call for a restrictive interpretation of derogating norms or exceptions. Whereas under GATT 1947 panels stated that exceptions (in particular GATT Art. XX) are to be interpreted narrowly, the Appellate Body has rightly pointed out that 'merely characterizing a treaty provision as an "exception" does not by itself justify a "stricter" or "narrower" interpretation of that provision than would be warranted... by applying the normal rules of treaty interpretation'. (Footnotes omitted)[58]

One implication of the AB decision has been to render neutral in importance an exception vis-à-vis other principal objectives of the WTO and to recognise an exception as a vehicle to further equally both trade and non-trade objectives established in the WTO.[59] Thus, with reference to S&D, the AB has stated:

> In sum, in our view, the characterization of the Enabling Clause as an exception in no way diminishes the right of Members to provide or to receive 'differential and more favourable treatment'. The status and relative importance of a given provision does not depend on whether it is characterized, for the purpose of allocating the burden of proof, as a claim to be proven by the complaining party, or as a defence to be established by the responding party.[60]

The central question in relation to the EC–Hormones exceptions determination is whether the principle of strict interpretation of an exception has now been overruled in the WTO. There are a number of reasons why this should not be the conclusion drawn. First, the AB has not explicitly overruled this principle of interpreting exceptions. What the AB has said is that the mere characterisation of a provision as an exception does not by itself invoke the application of the principle. What the AB has not said is that an exception does not by reason of being an exception invoke the application of the strict interpretation rule. Second the reference to the text, context, object and purposes of the treaty in accordance with the international rules of treaty

[58] Pauwelyn *Conflict of Norms*.

[59] EC–Tariff Preferences (AB) para 94: 'We note, however, as did the Panel, that WTO objectives may well be pursued through measures taken under provisions characterized as exceptions.'

[60] Ibid para 98.

interpretation merely reinforces the principle of strict interpretation of exceptions, inasmuch as the principle is not independent of this treaty material but rather draws from it. The principle is intended to reflect the proposition that the parties intend their consensus not to be undermined by a liberal interpretation of exceptions and that exceptions agreed upon are indeed established and intended to operate within the parameters of the agreement as a whole. The principle of strict interpretation of exceptions is thus grounded in the fundamental principle of treaty law – *pacta sunt servanda.* That said, the text, context, and object and purposes of an agreement can well displace this presumed approach to interpreting exceptions. In sum, the statement that mere characterisation as an exception does not by itself trigger the application of the strict interpretation principle, and that the approach to interpretation of exceptions is in fact grounded in normal principles of treaty interpretation, is tautological. The principle of strict interpretation of exceptions must be informed by the nature of the exception and its setting, and not by whether a provision is formally described as an exception. The formal cloaking of a provision as an exception has a bearing on its nature but need not be conclusive. Given that the principle of strict interpretation is intended to re-enforce the rule aspect of the agreement in accordance with the intentions of the parties,[61] it must be the case that the principle is directed only at real exceptions or departures from the norm thus intended – and thus intended to be interpreted. If non-real exceptions or departures fall within the scope of the principle, its application will undermine the rule aspect of the agreement.

To complete the picture here, there are a number of other principles of interpretation whose interaction with and implications for interpretation of exceptions need to be highlighted. First, the principle of effective treaty interpretation (*ut res magis valeat quam pereat*) applies to exceptions.[62] According to this principle, the general rule 'must simply be carved out to the extent required to give effect to the exception (the exception can then even be considered as a conditional right, delinked from the general rule)'.[63] The principle of effective

[61] See for example EC–Chicken Classification (Panel) (Thailand), wherein the Panel observed at para 7.94: 'the primary purpose of treaty interpretation is to identify the common intentions of the parties and that the rules contained in Articles 31 and 32 of the Vienna Convention have been developed to help assessing in objective terms, what was or what could have been the common intention of the parties to a treaty'.

[62] Pauwelyn *Conflict of Norms* 163. [63] Ibid.

interpretation in particular assists by 'giving effect to the wording making clear that one provision . . . is derogated from another'.[64] The principle is 'embodied in (what is now Art.31(1)) which requires that a treaty shall be interpreted in *good faith* in accordance with the ordinary meaning to be given to its terms in the context of the treaty *and in the light of its objects and purposes*'.[65] However, the 'maxim does not call for an "extensive" or "liberal" interpretation in the sense of an interpretation going beyond what is expressed or necessarily to be implied in terms of the treaty'.[66]

Second, of note is the principle of *in dubio mitius*. In accordance with this principle, as explained by the AB in EC–Hormones, 'if the meaning of a term is ambiguous, that meaning is to be preferred which is less onerous to the party assuming an obligation, or which interferes less with the territorial and personal supremacy of a party, or involves less general restrictions upon a party'.[67] In this context, Joost Pauwelyn states: 'consistently to prefer obligations over and above explicit rights is at variance also with another principle of international law . . . namely *in dubio mitius*'.[68]

It may well be that when Pauwelyn was making this observation he did not intend to refer to its application to exceptions. This is not clear. However, there is some suggestion that the principle of *in dubio mitius* does not apply to exceptions. Thus, it has been observed: 'it is usual for courts to interpret strictly exceptions to a principal provision imposing obligations on a State, notwithstanding that the principle *in dubio mitius* may suggest that the exception be given a liberal interpretation'.[69] However, given the re-interpretation of the principle of strict interpretation of exceptions in the WTO, this observation may need to be considered afresh. The principle of *in dubio mitius* may well have a bearing on the manner in which exceptions are interpreted in the WTO within the remit of Articles 31–2 of the VC.

Finally, of note is the *lex specialis* principle of treaty interpretation, whereby the *lex specialis* must prevail over the *lex generalis*. This, according to Pauwelyn, 'coincides with the principle of effectiveness'.[70]

[64] Ibid 250.

[65] See commentary to ILC Draft in D. Rauschning *The Vienna Convention on the Law of Treaties, Travaux Preparatoires* (Metzner, Frankfurt 1978) 251, referred to by Pauwelyn *Conflicts of Norms* 248.

[66] Commentary to ILC Draft. [67] Quoted in Pauwelyn *Conflict of Norms* 186.

[68] Ibid. [69] *Oppenheim's International Law* I: 1268, 1270.

[70] Pauwelyn *Conflict of Norms* 414.

With reference to exceptions, he states: 'if one treaty norm states that it is an exception to another norm, i.e., that it is a specific carve-out from this other norm, this first treaty norm or *lex specialis* must be given effect and "prevail" over the general rule . . . '. As with the principle of effectiveness, however, this does not imply that a more liberal approach is to be taken to the actual interpretation of the *lex specialis.*

4.4 Conclusion

The legal discourse in the WTO in relation to S&D may well have clarified the process of characterising an exception and its interpretation. And it may well have taken the heat out of the debate on exceptions, in both the political and judicial organs. However, this blurring of the distinction between exceptions and rules raises the question whether it facilitates the attainment of certain critical communal goals, such as the development objective. In the context of the development dimension, where an S&D provision is an exception, it shifts the burden on to the developing member, exposes the S&D provision to a possible strict interpretation, relegates an S&D right or obligation to a conditional status, strips S&D of its capacity to mainstream the generality of the WTO and detracts from the intermediate concept of an autonomous regime advocated by some developing members with respect to S&D.

All this reinforces the need for a theory of exceptions. A theory of interpreting exceptions must be open to their recognition and open to giving effect to them. The basis for being open to their recognition must rest on

- the intentions of the parties;
- compatibility with the objects and purposes of the agreement;
- the significance of the goals in question in the contemporary international setting.

Equally, there may be a category of exceptions that are self-evident and/or inherent in a rule – in other words, not necessarily a function of legal analysis and treaty construction. This category may not be so directly a consequence of intentions.

The basis for giving effect to exceptions through the interpretative process, on the other hand, needs to be weighed against their impact on the general rules and principles, as well as the societal goal in question. One suggestion made by Frank Garcia is that the degree to which the goal has a democratic imprint at the national level ought to have a bearing on the interpretative approach.[71] However, this is perhaps more a matter of implementation than of interpretation. How an exception is implemented or availed of by members of the WTO is a question independent of the existence of an exception and its interpretation. Nevertheless, the point may have a bearing on the interpretation of the national measure and the application of the WTO exception once it has been interpreted.

There is, of course, a prior question whether indeed there should be a theory of exceptions, or whether this should be left in the realms of judicial discretion. A theory of exceptions should not thwart judicial discretion, since the process of recognising and interpreting exceptions calls also for latitude, given that the circumstances when exceptions need to be recognised are varied and potentially infinite. Equally, one hallmark of a civilised society and an enduring legal system is a conscious approach and openness to recognising and interpreting exceptions. Therefore, there is a strong case for a theory of exceptions, but one that at the same time does not unduly hinder judicial discretion.

[71] Observations made by Frank Garcia at a workshop on 'Trade Governance, Democracy, and Inequality' held at the University of Bremen, Germany, 7–8 October 2005.

5

Interpreting the WTO Agreements for the development objective

5.1 Introduction

Of late, there has been considerable general focus among legal analysts on the processes involved in the interpretation of the WTO Agreements.[1] This focus has been direct and also rooted in the continuing appraisal of the WTO dispute settlement system and an exploration of the relationship between the WTO and international law. Yet the methods of interpreting international agreements have been the subject of consideration for almost as long as treaties have been in existence – with established international rules and practices having been in

This chapter is based on papers delivered on 14 June 2002 at the Annual General Meeting of the British Institute of International and Comparative Law, in a session on the WTO entitled 'Doha Proposals and Objectives'; at a workshop organised by Center for Trade Law and Development Policy (CTLD) in Geneva on the 8 January 2003; and at a conference organised by the International Centre for Trade and Sustainable Development (ICTSD) titled 'Making the WTO Dispute Settlement System Work for Developing and Least Developed Countries' held in Geneva on 7 February 2003. This chapter is also based on a substantially shorter paper published in ICTSD Resource Paper no. 6, 'Fostering the Development Interests of Developing and Least Developed Countries through the WTO Dispute Settlement System' (Geneva 2003), and the article 'Interpreting WTO Agreements for the Development Objective' (2003) 37(5) *JWT* 847–82.

1 See for example M. Lennard 'Navigating by the Stars: Interpreting the WTO Agreements' (2002) 5 *JIEL* 17–89; D. Palmeter and P.C. Mavroidis 'The WTO Legal System: Sources of Law' (1998) 92 *AJIL* 398–413; J. Pauwelyn 'The Role of Public International Law in the WTO: How Far Can We Go?' (2001) 95 *AJIL* 535–78; J. Pauwelyn 'Cross-Agreement Complaints before the Appellate Body: A Case Study of the EC–Asbestos Dispute' (2002) 1(1) *World Trade Rev* 63–87; G. Marceau 'Conflicts of Norms and Conflicts of Jurisdictions: The Relationship between the WTO Agreement and MEAs and Other Treaties' (2001) 35(6) *JWT* 1081–1131; M. Footer 'Developing Country Practice in the Matter of WTO Dispute Settlement' (2001) 35(1) *JWT* 55–98; G. Marceau 'WTO Dispute Settlement and Human Rights' (2002) 13 *EJIL* 753–814; Shankar, 'Vienna Convention'; M.M. Slotboom 'Do the Different Treaty Purposes Matter for Treaty Interpretation? The Elimination of Discriminatory Internal Taxes in EC and the WTO Law' (2001) 4(3) *JIEL* 557–79.

existence for some time now.[2] By the same token, despite the increasing participation of developing members in the WTO and its dispute settlement system, a significant number of developing members have expressed concerns about the manner in which the interpretation and application of the WTO Agreements has advanced the development objective. Thus, it has been asserted:

> A careful reading of the accumulated jurisprudence of the [dispute settlement] system thus far reveals that the interests and perceptions of developing countries have not been adequately taken into account. The panels and the Appellate Body have displayed an excessively sanitized concern with legalisms, often to the detriment of the evolution of a development-friendly jurisprudence.[3]

This general focus by jurists on the WTO interpretative process, together with the particular concerns of developing members of the WTO in relation to the development dimension in that process, arises mainly because (as Sinclair stated as long ago as 1973) the apparently established international rules on treaty interpretation

> are expressed at a level of generality sufficient to ensure that questions of treaty interpretation will still give rise to serious divisions of opinion as among the members of international tribunals and indeed as among international jurists in general. If the topic of treaty interpretation has generated passions among jurists in the past, it will, notwithstanding the Convention rules, continue to generate similar passions in the future.[4]

[2] See the VC. Essentially, there are three approaches to interpretation, based on the text, the intention, and the object and purposes of the agreement.

[3] Zambia on behalf of the LDC Group (TN/DS/W/17, 9 October 2002). See also Kenya on behalf of the African Group (TN/DS/W/15, 25 September 2002), wherein it is stated: 'In their interpretation and application of the provisions, the panels and the Appellate Body have in several instances exceeded their mandate and fundamentally prejudiced the interests and rights of developing-country Members as enshrined in the WTO Agreement; The panel and Appellate Body composition and operation have not been conducive to ensuring the achievement of the development objectives of the WTO and of equity in geographical distribution; and The core development and equity concerns of African Members have not been taken into account in assessing the operation and the need for improvement of the DS.... Conflicts between Agreements or provisions have been conveniently interpreted away, to the prejudice or potential prejudice of development prospects. For instance, the flexibility developing-country Members may have under transition periods and exceptions could be subject to what the panels and Appellate Body might consider over-riding or cumulative obligations.' See also India on behalf of Cuba, Honduras, India, Malaysia, Pakistan, Sri Lanka, Tanzania and Zimbabwe (TN/DS/W/18, 7 October 2002).

[4] See I. Sinclair *The Vienna Convention on the Law of Treaties* (2nd edn Manchester UP, Manchester 1984) 154.

For example, is sequencing or a holistic approach to the operation of Article 31 (1) of the VC the appropriate methodology under international law? Is a textual approach to the interpretation of the WTO Agreements the only approach sanctioned under international rules of interpretation? What exactly is meant by 'relevant rules of international law applicable in the relations between the parties' under Article 31 (3) of the VC?

More particularly, the significance of the process of interpretation to development is two-fold. First, there is a development dimension to interpretation. This development dimension in the interpretation of the WTO Agreements has hitherto been neither sufficiently articulated nor coherently structured in the architecture of international trade agreements. Developing members of the WTO, however, have sensed its existence and consequently have expressed dissatisfaction with the record of interpretation thus far in the jurisprudence of the WTO. The dissatisfaction has focused on the approaches to interpretation and the methodology and materials involved in interpretation, along with the participants engaged in interpretation.

Second, as negotiators become more skilled, and as developing countries mature their skills in terms of engaging in international economic relations, the value of foresight of future interpretative issues and outcomes becomes increasingly apparent at the time of negotiations. Thus, the Doha Declaration on the TRIPS Agreement,[5] which emphasises the role of the object and purposes of the TRIPS Agreement in the process of interpreting it, perhaps might not have been so necessary if the interpretative approach that was taken to the agreement could have been foreseen.

This focus on the interpretative process, including the focus on the interface between interpretation of the WTO Agreements and development, can be underpinned or clouded by vested economic, political and national concerns. These concerns need to be noted at the outset. Thus, some of the preferences for particular approaches and methods of interpretation of the WTO agreements may in fact reflect perceived economic advantages and the desire to preserve advantages gained. Although no economic analysis has been conducted in the interpretation sphere in this particular context, the subject may in fact provide some useful pointers, or at any rate a focal point for analysis. Among the lines of enquiry that economic analysis can offer, the effects of the

[5] WT/MIN(01)/Dec/W/2, 14 November 2001.

approaches to interpretation on market access costs and benefits to individual members and the membership of the WTO as a whole is the most central.[6] Second, enquiries into the motivation of members (through game theory) in the sphere of interpretation may also provide useful insights into strategies that have been adopted or need to be adopted. Finally, normative economic analysis is also relevant in the sphere of interpretation. This is because the process of interpretation can indeed involve creating or extending goals. Normative economic analysis would thus suggest interpretations that enhance efficiency.

Impressionistically, therefore, drawing from economic analysis, the initial individual approaches to interpretation one might assume are informed inter alia by a preference for those approaches that are least likely to undermine or jeopardise the market access gains represented in the WTO Agreements. The post-agreement strategy here for the immediate 'winners' may be more one of preservation rather one of further gains. On the other hand, for the initial 'losers' or long-term 'winners', the initial rational strategy would be further cost reduction, increasing the gains secured and drawing on the gains set in the long-term objectives. The strategy here is not so much one of preservation following agreement as a dynamic and legislative one. In conclusion, the strategy for the immediate winners will be a textual approach, with a greater stake in the policing of the agreement by the winners of the bargain. In contrast, those whose gains in the WTO system will materialise in the longer term (the long-term winners) will emphasise the objects and purposes of the agreement (i.e. the teleological approach), which facilitate future gains.

Similarly, there are political concerns, mainly rooted in nationalism, that influence the methodology of interpretation to be adopted. The WTO Agreements are not static, normative frameworks: they are and have set in motion a dynamic, evolving system. This characteristic of the agreements calls for greater attention to and scrutiny of the interpretative process on a continuing basis to ensure that national sovereignty negotiated away is not further interpreted away. Furthermore, national perspectives can contribute scepticism about the capacity of the WTO, as an organisation, to engage impartially in the interpretative

[6] See for example R.A. Cass 'Economic Perspectives on International Economic Law' in A.H. Qureshi (ed) *Perspectives in International Economic Law* (Kluwer, The Hague 2002) chapter 15, 280.

process and/or to have the maturity to deliver desirable interpretative outcomes.

In the circumstances a number of questions are raised, particularly in the context of the development dimension:

- Why should the process of interpreting the WTO Agreements engender such a specific focus, particularly given that the internationally recognised rules of treaty interpretation do not appear to distinguish between treaties dealing with different subjects?[7] Do the WTO Agreements call for a re-invention of the wheel of treaty interpretation?
- Is there a development dimension to the interpretation of the WTO Agreements that needs to be further developed? Is development an objective that calls for a special interpretative approach? Are there in practice differences in interpretative processes according to the sphere of international economic relations covered? If so, are there lessons to be drawn for the interpretation of the WTO Agreements – particularly to enhance the development dimension? Does the WTO practice in terms of interpretation facilitate development?
- Are there strategic policy questions that underpin issues relating to the different processes of treaty interpretation that trade negotiators should also bear in mind at the time of negotiating multilateral trade agreements?
- What types of reform can be brought to bear in the interpretative process?

The remainder of this chapter is divided into three sections. Section 5.2 focuses generally on the interface between development and interpretation – emphasising materials that facilitate the development dimension of the international trading system, along with those that inhibit it. Section 5.3 focuses on the relationship between the textual and teleological approaches as they relate to the development dimension. Here the argument is not so much about any dichotomy between the textual and teleological approaches in terms of development, but rather one of the relative weight and emphasis to be given to the two approaches. Section 5.4 is a brief review of the Doha Round and possible reforms. This chapter is not intended to be an exhaustive study of all the issues involved here; rather, its primary objective is to identify the parameters of the subject and to highlight some of the principal issues.

[7] See Lennard 'Navigating by the Stars' 85, where he quotes US–Steel from Japan (AB).

5.2 The development dimension to the interpretation of the WTO Agreements

The development dimension to the interpretation of the WTO Agreements essentially involves a focus on those aspects of the interpretative process that lend themselves (as far as they can within the framework of the text of the WTO Agreements) to

- reducing or alleviating some of the burdens that accompany trade liberalisation;
- facilitating fair play between the differing memberships of the WTO;
- facilitating those aspects of the development objective that are enshrined in the WTO Agreements or that are established in the relevant international law that the interpretative process is informed by.

The interpretative processes that lend themselves to such an objective comprise the canons of interpretation and materials for inclusion in the interpretative process, along with the general procedures and the participants involved in the process of interpretation. The development dimension to interpretation can be further elucidated by identifying the specific considerations in the interpretative process that need to be factored in to facilitate the development objective. Thus, the development dimension in interpreting the WTO Agreements involves

- factoring in the development dimension objectives;
- factoring the condition of development into the interpretation and application of the WTO Agreements;
- factoring in the special characteristics of development;
- factoring good governance into the process of interpretation;
- factoring in relevant rules of international law that facilitate development;
- factoring in an appropriate approach to interpreting S&D terms;[8]
- factoring in the textual approach *in rem*;
- factoring in the rehabilitation of the teleological approach for the development dimension.

This development dimension to interpreting the WTO Agreements not only needs to be considered by the membership of the WTO at the time of negotiating trade agreements and thereafter but also needs institutionalising into the architecture of the WTO system. There has to be

[8] i.e. special/differential and more favourable treatment terms.

oversight and foresight of interpretative issues and outcomes at the time of negotiations, as well as outside the negotiations.

5.2.1 Factoring in the development dimension objectives

The development dimension as an objective needs to be factored in at the time of drafting the WTO Agreements, institutionalised in the very process of interpreting the WTO Agreements, engineered into actual interpretations of the WTO Agreements and facilitated through the introduction of development-friendly material into the judicial process.

The principles of interpretation applied in the jurisprudence of the WTO and set out in Articles 31–2 of the VC allow for the development dimension to be factored in – particularly through reference to the text, context, and objects and purposes of the WTO Agreements. First, where development considerations are expressly set out in the text, there is relatively little issue – although even here the scope of the text can be informed by the objects and purposes of the agreement. Where the text does not expressly mention development, the role of the objects and purposes (as these refer to development) in interpreting the text becomes more significant in facilitating the development dimension.

The objects and purposes of an agreement are generally expressly set out and are often found in the preamble to the agreement. However, although such express statements are the normal source for discerning the expressed objects and purposes of an agreement, they are not the only source. The objects and purposes of an agreement need not be only explicitly expressed; they can also be discerned from the operative clauses of the agreement taken as a whole.[9] In this respect, I take issue with M. Lennard when he seems to suggest that only the explicitly expressed objects and purposes are relevant.[10]

The importance of the objects and purposes of an agreement in influencing the outcome of the interpretative process is generally acknowledged. Thus, in the jurisprudence of the WTO there is evidence of frequent reliance on the objects and purposes of the particular agreement in question. Furthermore, the significance of the Preamble to

[9] See Sinclair *Vienna Convention* 128, quoting G. Fitzmaurice 'Law and Procedure of the International Court of Justice 1951–4: Treaty Interpretation and Other Points' (1957) 33 *BYIL* 228.

[10] Lennard 'Navigating the Stars' 29.

the Marrakesh Agreement is noted, as is any heading to a particular provision.[11]

Indeed, the impact of the objects and purposes is even acknowledged by one of the most pessimistic of analysts of the role of the objects and purposes in the interpretative process: Marco Slotboom, through a comparison of provisions dealing with discriminatory internal taxes in the EC and WTO Agreements that are similarly worded but have different objects and purposes, concedes that the interpretative outcome in terms of the scope of the similarly worded provisions may be different and that other legal provisions, although similarly worded, may lead to different interpretations as a consequence of the different objectives of the two agreements.[12]

[11] For example, in Brazil–Export Financing Programmes for Aircraft, the AB (para 65) arrived at its determination on the question of onus of proof by noting that the title of Article 27 is 'Special and Differential Treatment of Developing Country Members' and that para 1 of that article provided that 'Members recognize that subsidies may play an important role in economic development programmes of developing country Members'. In EC–Bed Linen, the Panel (para 6.232) held: 'We do not consider that an interpretation of Article 15 which could, in some cases, have negative effects on the very parties it is intended to benefit, producers and exporters in developing countries, is required.' In US–Shrimp, the AB (para 156) noted: 'It is proper for us to take into account, as part of the context of the chapeau, the specific language of the preamble to the *WTO Agreement*, which, we have said, gives colour, texture and shading to the rights and obligations of Members under the *WTO Agreement*, generally, and under the GATT 1994, in particular.' Earlier in the same case the Panel (para 7.52) stated: 'we note that the Preamble acknowledges that the optimal use of the world's resources must be pursued "in accordance with the objective of sustainable development, seeking both to protect and preserve the environment and to enhance the means of doing so in a manner consistent with [Members'] respective needs and concerns at different levels of economic development". Thus the Preamble endorses the fact that environmental policies must be designed taking into account the situation of each Member, both in terms of its actual needs and in terms of its economic means'. In Indonesia–Automobiles, the Panel stated (paras 5.194, 5.196, 8.210): 'Special and differential treatment of developing country Members is one of the objects and purposes of the Subsidies Agreement as evidenced by Article 27, which details that treatment, and by the language of Article 27.1 ("Members recognize that subsidies may play an important role in economic development programmes of developing country Members").' 'Furthermore,' the Panel noted, 'the DSU not only prohibits the nullification or impairment of Indonesia's benefits, it prohibits the impedance of an objective of the Subsidies Agreement expressed in Article 27.1 .... In other words, the universe of benefits extended to developing countries under the Subsidies Agreement includes the right (albeit conditional) to provide subsidies. Therefore, because an affirmative finding of the threat of serious prejudice to a "like product" would operate to deprive a developing country Member of this generally available right, "like product" must be narrowly construed ...'.

[12] Slotboom 'Do the Different Treaty Purposes Matter' 578. It is contended here that even in terms of the similarly worded provisions in the GATT and the EC treaty on

Second, this range of material (i.e. text, context and objects and purposes, as indicated in Article 31 of the VC) is intended to facilitate a holistic approach to interpretation, and may even be characterised as a description of one. Thus, sequencing between the text, context, and objects and purposes as a *modus operandi* in interpretation, if it involves exclusion and hierarchy among these materials, is controversial.[13] Sequencing has the consequence of detracting from the role of the objects and purposes of the agreement.[14] In fact, the consideration of these materials is a neutral process[15] and involves a holistic approach.[16] Because the convenience of sequencing can result in an intellectual lapse, it does indeed need to be checked.

discriminatory internal taxes, the comparisons are not well founded given that the objects and purposes of the two agreements are not very substantially different.

[13] See for example statement of India on behalf of Cuba, Honduras, India, Malaysia, Pakistan, Sri Lanka, Tanzania and Zimbabwe (TN/DS/W/18, 7 October 2002): 'Though there was no hierarchy between "ordinary meaning" i.e., "text" and "context", "object and purpose", the practice of the Appellate Body and the panels to date has been to begin their clarifications with textual interpretation by referring to the dictionary meaning of the provisions of the covered agreements.'

[14] See Shankar 'Vienna Convention' 726.

[15] See for example Lennard 'Navigating by the Stars' 28.

[16] See Sections 301–310 of US Trade Act 1974 (Panel) para 176; Argentina–Footwear (AB) para 81; Canada–Certain Measures Affecting the Automotive Industry (Panel) paras 3 and 10.12, wherein it was observed: 'Our understanding of these rules of interpretation is that, even though the text of a term is the starting-point for any interpretation, the meaning of a term cannot be found exclusively in that text; in seeking the meaning of a term, we also have to take account of its context and to consider the text of the term in light of the object and purpose of the treaty. Article 31 of the Vienna Convention explicitly refers to the "ordinary meaning to be given to the terms of the treaty in their [the terms'] context and in the light of its [the treaty's] object and purpose".[805] The three elements referred to in Article 31 – text, context and object and purpose – are to be viewed as one integrated rule of interpretation rather than a sequence of separate tests to be applied in a hierarchical order.[806] Of course, context and object and purpose may simply confirm the textual meaning of a term. In many cases, however, it is impossible to give meaning, even "ordinary meaning", without looking also at the context and/or object and purpose. ([806]"The Commission by heading the article 'General rule of interpretation' in the singular and by underlining the connection between paragraphs 1 and 2 and again between paragraph 3 and the two previous paragraphs, intended to indicate that the application of the means of interpretation in the article would be a single combined operation. All the various elements, as they were present in any given case, would be thrown into the crucible and their interaction would give the legally relevant interpretation." *Yearbook of the International Law Commission* (1966) Vol. II, A/CN.4/SER.A/1966/Add.1, 219 and 220.)' (footnote 805 omitted). See also Shankar 'Vienna Convention' 726; Slotboom 'Do the Different Treaty Purposes Matter' 577; *Golder* v. *United Kingdom* [1975] 14 *ECHR* Ser para 30; M. Dixon and R. McCorquodale *Cases and Materials on International Law* (Oxford UP, Oxford 2003) 87; Brownlie

Third, this multi-dimensional technique of interpretation (i.e. using text, context, objects and purposes), as every international lawyer is aware, is not a precise but a malleable tool. It allows for a margin of appreciation. Where there is such a margin of appreciation, questions may need to be asked about why development factors were not allowed to trump other considerations. Therefore, DSU provisions that invite an explanation of how development has been taken into account facilitate the inculcation of the development objective and need to be strengthened where necessary, as has indeed been suggested by some developing members.

Fourth, the objects and purposes of the WTO, along with certain specific provisions and instruments in the WTO, actually do call for development-supportive interpretations.[17] This needs to be emphasised, and strategies and arguments reinforcing this need to be further probed. Thus, development, sustainable development and S&D are all concepts set out in the Preamble to the Marrakesh Agreement (and are also found elsewhere in the WTO Agreements). These concepts are said to inform the interpretation of the WTO Agreements.[18] Although development and differential treatment as objectives are to be found in the Preamble and elsewhere in the WTO Agreements, if any lingering

Principles of Public International Law 634: 'A corollary of the principle of ordinary meaning is the principle of integration: the meaning must emerge in the context of the treaty as a whole and in the light of its objects and purposes.' See also ILC Commentary to Article 31 of the VC [1966] 2 *YILC* 219–20; UN Conference on the Law of Treaties (First Session, Vienna 26 March–24 May 1968) Official Records – Summary Records of the Plenary Meetings of the Committee of the Whole UN 184, statement by Expert Consultant Sir Humphrey Waldock: 'with regard to the question of hierarchy, he must emphasize that the arrangements of the elements set forth in article 27 was not intended to establish any order of priority among them; the Commission had simply adopted what seemed a logical arrangement.... As far as article 27 was concerned, the intention had been to place on the same footing all the elements of interpretation therein mentioned.' See also section 5.3 of this chapter. Contra EC–Chicken Classification (Panel) (Thailand), wherein the Panel, in interpreting AB observations in the US–Shrimp case relating to Article 31, observed at para 7.92: 'In other words, the Appellate Body indicated that the object and purpose should be considered after the treaty interpreter has determined the meaning of the words constituting the treaty obligation in question when read in their context.' I dispute this statement. See, however, EC–Chicken Classification (AB) para 176: 'Interpretation pursuant to the customary rules codified in Article 31 of the Vienna Convention is ultimately a holistic exercise that should not be mechanically subdivided into rigid components.'

[17] See the Preamble to the Marrakesh Agreement; US–Shrimp (AB); Articles 12.11 and 24 of the DSU; the 1993 Ministerial Decision on Measures in Favour of Least-Developed Countries.

[18] US–Shrimp (AB).

doubts remain in this respect, given the essentially trade character of the WTO as an institution, this goal needs to be more clearly spelt out.

Similarly, on at least two occasions special reference is to be found to least-developed members in relation to the question of interpretation. Thus, in the December 1993 Ministerial Decision on Measures in Favour of Least-Developed Countries, it is stated:

> The rules set out in the various agreements and instruments and the transitional provisions in the Uruguay Round should be applied in a flexible and supportive manner for the least-developed countries.

Article 24 of the DSU states:

> At all stages of the determination of the causes of a dispute and of dispute settlement procedures involving a least-developed country Member, particular consideration shall be given to the special situation of least-developed country Members.

Article 24 of the DSU can be read as an articulation of a liberal approach to interpreting the WTO Agreements to support LDCs, but since WTO provisions need to be interpreted uniformly for all members, the benefits of such an interpretation must trickle down to all other members when the provisions involved are of a general character. Indeed, it would appear that even when only developed members are involved in a dispute, the interpretation of the WTO provisions must not undermine the injunction that the interpretation should not be rigid and unsupportive in terms of the least-developed members to the extent that they may be affected by the interpretation in question.

In the same vein, Article 12.11 of the DSU stipulates that when a developing-country member is involved in a dispute, the Panel Report is to indicate how S&D provisions raised by that member have been taken into account. This provision, although apparently dependent upon S&D provisions being raised by the developing member, arguably contains elements of an invitation to the Panel to factor in the development dimension.

5.2.2 Factoring the condition of development into the interpretation and application of the WTO Agreements

In the practice of WTO dispute settlement, developing members have invoked the developing condition on a number of occasions, particularly as a shield when they have been respondents. Similarly, developed members have not refrained from actually policing or challenging the use by developing members of the developing condition as a basis for departures from normal WTO obligations. The developing condition has been proffered, first, as a relevant factual condition and, second, as a justification for preferential implementation of obligations. The normative framework of the WTO allows for the development condition to be a justiciable issue in certain circumstances.

Generally, the developing condition of a member in the dispute settlement process can become relevant where any of the WTO Agreements expressly accords the S&D standard to developing members. However, in the absence of express WTO reference to S&D, there have also been occasions when the judicial apparatus of the WTO has had to grapple with the question of the extent to which the developing condition of a member is relevant either to the interpretation or to the application of a particular WTO provision to a national measure or practice.

The WTO Agreements contain a category of obligations that are overtly neutral (in the sense that they do not make any express distinction between developed and developing members) but that nevertheless potentially allow for the developing condition to be factored into their application. These neutral rules are, in their application, receptive to the incorporation of all development levels, where relevant. In an interdependent world in which the WTO order is prevalent, the circumstances in which a developing member's conduct can become subject to WTO concerns are numerous. Equally, the explanations and justifications for the measures and actions of developing members can be multiple – and they can include the developing condition. Furthermore, neither the language nor the obligations expressed in the WTO Agreements are overtly averse to the factoring in of the developing condition. Indeed, in the WTO there is no principle of uniformity, as was claimed to exist by Joseph Gold in his numerous writings on the IMF.[19] Any such suggestion would now be negated somewhat by the Preamble to the Marrakesh Agreement, which calls for countries to make 'optimal use of the world's resources in accordance with the objective of sustainable development, seeking both to protect and preserve the environment and to enhance the means for doing so in a manner consistent with their respective needs and concerns at different levels of economic development'. The Preamble continues in this vein, referring to 'the need for positive efforts' to assist developing

[19] See for example publications by J. Gold in the IMF Pamphlet series.

countries. The room for factoring in the development condition, which the neutral rules do not exclude, is reinforced inter alia by the contents of the Preamble. Examples of such neutral rules are 'unjustifiable discrimination' (Article XX of GATT 1994), where the developing condition may provide justification, and measures 'necessary' (Article XX of GATT 1994, Article XIV of GATS and Article 27 [2] of TRIPS[20]), where the developing condition might inform what is necessary.[21]

Developing-country members have pointed to their developing condition on a number of occasions in relation to circumstances involving the neutral rules or in circumstances related to an S&D provision but not directly based upon it. Cases where the developing condition has been proffered as a relevant factual condition in the application of WTO provisions include the following.

- In Argentina–Measures Affecting the Export of Bovine Hides, Argentina argued that 'if the criterion of reasonableness' was relevant in the application of each of the sub-paragraphs of Article XX of GATT 1994, then it would be 'reasonable for a developing country such as Argentina' to establish 'a payment on account mechanism to improve' upon its tax collection given that tax evasion was an acute problem in Argentina.[22] In Argentina's view, tax evasion was a particularly acute problem that developing countries faced when economic conditions lent themselves to tax evasion – 'e.g., an informal economy, inflation, an inequitable tax system, tolerance of failure to comply with regulations, lack of simple and precise rules, inefficient tax administration, corruption, low levels of education, a disregard for tax-paying obligations, etc.'
- In Brazil–Export Financing Programmes for Aircraft, Brazil argued that it needed to adjust the level of its export subsidies, which exceptionally it had been allowed to maintain under Article 27 of the Agreement on Subsidies and Countervailing Measures in order to accommodate inflation. According to Brazil, the AB needed to take 'judicial notice' that 'currencies tend to depreciate over time because

[20] I am grateful to Dr Mohamed Abou El Farag Balat for pointing out a previous typing error here.

[21] Other examples: 'when it is administratively practicable'; 'administer . . . in a reasonable manner'; 'as soon as practicable' (Article X of GATT 1994); 'reasonable having regard to the conditions of traffic' (Article V [4] of GATT 1994); 'administer laws . . . in a reasonable manner' (Art XVIII of GATT 1994); 'necessary to the enforcement of governmental measures' (Article XI of GATT 1994).

[22] Panel.

of inflationary pressures, and these pressures are greatest in developing countries.[23]

The relevance of the developing condition to the application of the neutral rules, including where S&D provisions are involved, is also endorsed by developed members. Thus, in India–Quantitative Restrictions on Imports of Agricultural, Textile and Industrial Products, the United States pointed out that 'India's restrictions' under Article XVIII [11] of GATT 1994

> had caused particularly severe damage to the trade of developing countries. The *de facto* ban on consumer goods imports hurt developing country exports most severely, since it was developing country products that would be most competitive in many consumer-goods sectors. Restricted items included many agricultural goods and among them many tropical products; since the licensing system was operated so as to protect domestic producers, these restrictions were most severe on their developing-country competitors.[24]

Cases where the developing condition has been proffered as a justification for differential burdens in the implementation of WTO obligations include the following.

- In India–Measures Affecting the Automotive Sector, India argued that developing members should not be made to implement their WTO obligations through the WTO dispute settlement system in order to coerce such countries 'into making concessions in policy areas not covered by WTO law'.[25]
- In India–Quantitative Restrictions on Imports of Agricultural, Textile and Industrial Products, India explained in relation to Article XIII [2] (a) of GATT 1994 that as 'a developing country with a low standard of living, India simply did not have the financial and administrative resources to identify and administer the quotas for nearly 2,300 tariff lines'.[26]
- In India–Patent, India argued that patent 'protection for pharmaceutical and agricultural chemical products is the most sensitive TRIPS issue in many developing countries. To India, the Panel's interpretation of Article 70.9 has the consequence that the transitional arrangements would allow developing countries to postpone legislative changes in all fields of technology except in the most sensitive

[23] AB. [24] Panel. [25] Panel. [26] Panel.

ones'.[27] The European Communities responded that 'India's reference to the sensitivity of the question of exclusive rights for the marketing of pharmaceuticals and agricultural chemical products in developing countries is not relevant. The European Communities contends that the basic rule of international treaty law is "pacta sunt servanda", that is, that treaties must be observed'.

- In Indonesia–Automobiles, Indonesia argued that 'the burden of proof on complainants is higher in this case because Indonesia is a developing country' and that 'like product' must be interpreted differently because of Indonesia's status as a developing country.[28]
- In US–Shrimp, the United States argued that it had shown 'that its measures were consistent with the objective of respecting the "needs and concerns [of countries] at different levels of economic development" '.[29] In particular, the United States had shown that turtle excluder devices were relatively inexpensive, could be fabricated from indigenous materials and had been successfully adopted by many countries, including developing countries.

In both panel and AB decisions, there is evidence of an acknowledgement and acceptance of the relevance of the developing condition in the context of the neutral rules as well as in consideration of issues related to S&D provisions. Indeed, in relation to measures related to the environment, requirements for implementation by developing members take into account their developing condition. In addition, unilateral trade measures are considered inappropriate as instruments of national trade policy to deal with transboundary or global environmental problems, particularly in the case of developing members.

- In Argentina–Measures Affecting the Export of Bovine Hides, the Panel held that it had 'taken due account of the statements referred to by Argentina, including the fact that Argentina is a developing country Member' in its assessment of whether the relevant Argentinean measures fell within the terms of Article XX (d). The Panel took the view, however, that the fact that Argentina was a 'developing country Member which has to contend with low levels of compliance with its tax laws' did not 'provide a justification for discriminating against imported products under the facts of the present case'.[30]

[27] AB. [28] Panel. [29] Panel. [30] Panel.

- In Brazil–Export Financing Programmes for Aircraft, the AB confirmed the earlier Panel conclusion relating to the Brazilian adjustment for inflation of its export subsidies and added that in its view 'to take no account of inflation in assessing the level of export subsidies granted by a developing country Member would render the special and differential treatment provisions of Article 27 meaningless'.[31]
- In Indonesia–Automobiles, the Panel noted with respect to the question of representation that there were no provisions in the Marrakesh Agreement, in the DSU or in the Working Procedures that shed light on who can represent a government in making its representations in an oral hearing of the AB or Panel proceedings.[32] Nor was there any GATT practice of assistance. Nevertheless, the Panel concluded that representation by counsel of a government's own choice was 'a matter of particular significance – especially for developing-country Members – to enable them to participate fully in dispute settlement proceedings'. Developing members did not 'have at their disposal specially trained and highly experienced corps of WTO legal experts'. In addition, the Panel relied on the AB decision in EC–Bananas. Furthermore, with respect to Indonesia's failure to comply with its procedural notification obligations in time, the Panel stated 'we would like to strongly state our position that delay in notifying a measure, no matter under which provision, cannot in any way be construed as diminishing the benefits that any Member may have by virtue of it being in a special category, such as a developing country. While we agree that delay in notifying measures should ideally not occur, it must at the same time also be realized that small delegations often have constraints of resources which at times leads to an unintended delay in the notification of their measures. It is for this reason that we believe that any such procedural delays should not mitigate the benefits which any member may otherwise be eligible for, under a covered agreement.'
- In US–Shrimp, the Panel made two important determinations involving the development condition.[33] First, it stated that the Preamble to the WTO Agreements and the record before it endorsed the fact that environmental policies must be designed taking into account the situation of each member in terms of its actual needs, its economic means and its local and regional conditions. Second, the

[31] AB. [32] Panel. [33] Panel.

Panel determined that 'the diversity of the environmental and development situations underlined by the Preamble can best be taken into account through international cooperation'. The Preamble and general international law also implied 'that attempts to generalize standards of environmental protection' required multilateral discussion and negotiation, especially when developing countries were involved.

It may be that the circumstances in which the developing condition of a member is relevant need further clarification – for example, in terms of the relationship of the developing condition to the obligation, the necessary levels of development that justly call for recognition and the implicit recognition in the obligation in question of the developing condition.

5.2.3 Factoring in the special characteristics of development

As has been noted, for example, in a recent report from the United Nations Conference on Trade and Development (UNCTAD), albeit in the context of international investment agreements (IIAs), development is an objective that is 'flexible' and is coloured by time and circumstances.[34] Therefore, the means to achieve it are similarly unfixed. In particular, because of this flexibility, it calls for adjustments – through, for example, interpretation – 'to link the conceptual and practical levels effectively'.[35] Thus, development-related provisions 'that are vague or ineffective or are expressed in "best endeavour" terms'[36] require 'a more precise and action oriented interpretation'.[37] They need to be made operational, as developing members have repeatedly asserted.

5.2.4 Factoring good governance into the process of interpretation

Good governance in the interpretation process relates mainly to questions of transparency and participation in the judicial process, and it can be of particular concern to developing countries. If governance here is oriented in favour of developed countries and is lacking in transparency, then this orientation can affect the interpretative process and the perception of developing members in that process.

[34] UNCTAD *International Investment Agreements: Flexibility for Development* (UNCTAD/ITI/IIT/18, 2000) 128.
[35] Ibid. [36] Ibid. [37] Ibid.

The participants involved in interpreting WTO Agreements need to be representative of the membership of the WTO as a whole – particularly if the development objective is to be transparently facilitated. This consideration operates at all levels. Thus, it is as pertinent at the level of the legal advisors from the Legal Affairs Division and the AB who service the AB and Panels (and can also have an influence on the composition of a Panel) as it is relevant at the level of panellists and AB judges. Appointments of lawyers in the WTO may be on merit, but they are also subject to a level of political process. Certainly, the chief lawyers in both the Legal Affairs Division and the AB have always thus far been Canadian, US or EU nationals.

Similarly, there is no specific requirement in the DSU that Panels should have at any given time a panellist from a developing country. Certainly, when there is a dispute involving a developing-country member, that member may require one panellist to be from a developing member state and generally has an input into the selection of the Panel. Furthermore, the panellists should be selected from diverse backgrounds.[38] However, the development dimension does not necessarily feature in the WTO jurisprudence only when a dispute involves a developed and a developing member. Similar concerns may also be raised in relation to the AB.

By the same token, the need for transparency in terms of the materials and advice given by lawyers from the respective legal divisions to the Panel and the AB is also relevant, as has been pointed out by a number of developing members. Parties to litigation have an interest in being able to scrutinise the communication flows between the advisors and the judicial decision-makers.

5.2.5 *Factoring in relevant rules of international law applicable in the relations between the parties*

There has been much ado about the precise scope of Article 31 (3) (c) of the VC, which calls for 'any relevant rules of international law applicable in the relations between the parties' to be taken into account in the interpretative process.[39] In particular, there are some differences of opinion as to what is meant by the 'parties'.[40] Is the reference to all

[38] Article 8 [2] of the DSU.

[39] See chapter 1. See also for example Marceau 'WTO Dispute Settlement'.

[40] Ibid 778, 781–2.

the WTO members?[41] Is the reference to the parties to the dispute as accepted by the other members of the WTO?[42] Is the reference to treaties that are open to all members of the WTO? Is the reference to norms agreed and tolerated by all WTO members?[43]

For developing members, two concerns in particular arise in the determination of the precise scope of this provision. First, it is likely that many developing members may not be parties to as many relevant international agreements as developed members may be. There may be a number of reasons for this, including deliberate choice. In such circumstances, albeit in the context of interpretation, being subject to the influence of such international agreements may be of concern. Second, it needs to be emphasised that relevant rules of international law need not merely be 'obligations'; they may also partake of rights. Furthermore, they are not confined to human rights or environmental norms but include development-oriented norms. Development is an imperative of the international economic order. It is also an aspect of the function of 'achieving greater coherence in global economic policy-making' that the WTO is charged with in cooperation with the World Bank and the IMF.[44]

5.2.6 Factoring in an appropriate approach to interpreting S&D provisions

In relation to interpretation, there is a general tendency on the part of developed members to argue for limiting the scope of S&D provisions, whereas the developing members have had to argue for a liberal interpretation, often emphasising the Preamble and the objects and purposes of relevant agreements, as well as invoking presumptions in favour of developing members. Moreover, developing members have not only acted in concert in advancing their points but have also relied on the general practice of developing members, including their negotiating stance during the Uruguay Round of trade negotiations.

- In Brazil–Export Financing Programmes for Aircraft, Brazil pointed out that the Article 27 exemption from the Article 3 requirements

[41] See chapter 1. See also for example Marceau 'WTO Dispute Settlement'. US–Tuna EEC GATT (unadopted).

[42] See chapter 1; Marceau 'WTO Dispute Settlement' referring to US–Shrimp (AB).

[43] Marceau 'WTO Dispute Settlement' referring to Pauwelyn 'Role of Public International Law' 595.

[44] Article III [5] of the Marrakesh Agreement.

under the ASCM was titled 'Special and Differential Treatment of Developing Country Members'.[45] Brazil argued that it was in no way subordinate to Article 3 or any other article of the ASCM, and it was not to be narrowly interpreted in favour of any other provision: Article 27 was a transitional arrangement on its own terms. In Brazil's view, the temporary legitimacy of a developing-country member's export subsidies is presumed. Furthermore, 'both the context and the object and purpose of Article 27' supported the Panel's conclusion. The context was provided by the title of Article 27, which indicated the nature of the provision and expressed a concern for the well-being of developing-country members. Thus, a high degree of liberality in interpretation was required. Similarly, the object and purpose of the provision was stated in the first paragraph of Article 27, which read: 'Members recognize that subsidies may play an important role in economic development programmes of developing country Members.' Furthermore, according to Brazil, Canada's arguments for placing the burden of proof under Article 27 on developing-country members ignored the context and the object and purpose of the article. In addition, Brazil disagreed with Canada's argument that 'the temporary exemption provided for developing countries in Article 27.2 is the legal equivalent of the permanent exception from *GATT 1994* obligations for all Members provided by Article XX of *GATT 1994*'.

- In EC–Bed Linen, India (and Egypt as third party) asserted that the second sentence of Article 15 of the ADA (the Agreement on Implementation of Article VI of the General Agreement on Tariffs and Trade 1994) imposed a specific legal obligation to 'explore possibilities'.[46] That required 'a determination (or assessment) whether the essential interests of the developing country concerned' were involved. The investigating authorities were required to explore possibilities of constructive remedies provided for by the ADA, including 'the non-imposition of anti-dumping measures'. In addition, India rejected the notion that any procedural mechanisms could satisfy the requirements of the second sentence of Article 15. On the other hand, the United States submitted as third party that Article 15 of the ADA did not impose anything other than a procedural obligation to explore possibilities of constructive remedies. The word

[45] AB. [46] Panel.

'explore' did not imply an obligation to reach a particular substantive outcome; it merely required consideration of such possibilities.

- In India–Patent, India argued on several occasions, relying particularly on the object and purpose of the relevant provisions, that the 'rationale of Articles 65 and 70 was clearly to permit developing country Members to postpone changes in their law that other Members were required to make under Article 27 of the TRIPS Agreement'.[47] India further contended that to 'the knowledge of India, no developing country had acted under Article 70 on the basis of the interpretations proposed by the United States. Examination of the notifications submitted to the TRIPS Council under Article 63.2 of the TRIPS Agreement relating to Article 70.8 showed that not one of these notifications provided for a procedure to be established under which patents for pharmaceutical and agricultural chemical products would be made available as from 2005'.

In the circumstances, a frequent focus of determinations when the Panel and AB have been confronted with S&D provisions has been to address how the S&D provisions need to be interpreted. In this process, there has been frequent reference to the object and purpose of the agreement in question.[48] Thus, the significance of the Preamble to the Marrakesh Agreement has been noted, as has any heading of a particular provision.[49] Furthermore, it appears that procedural non-compliance cannot preclude the enjoyment of the benefit of an S&D provision.[50] In addition, there is evidence that apparently exhortatory provisions have been interpreted to give them some binding force.[51] On

[47] Panel.

[48] Brazil–Export Financing Programmes for Aircraft (AB); EC–Bed Linen (Panel); Indonesia–Automobiles (Panel).

[49] See extracts from US–Shrimp (AB) in note 11 above.

[50] See Indonesia–Automobiles (Panel).

[51] In EC–Bed Linen (para 6.233), the Panel held: 'We consider next the term "explore", which is defined, inter alia, as "investigate; examine; scrutinise" . . .. In our view, while the exact parameters of the term are difficult to establish, the concept of "explore" clearly does not imply any particular outcome. We recall that Article 15 does not require that "constructive remedies" must be explored, but rather that the "possibilities" of such remedies must be explored, which further suggests that the exploration may conclude that no possibilities exist, or that no constructive remedies are possible, in the particular circumstances of a given case. Taken in its context, however, and in light of the object and purpose of Article 15, we do consider that the "exploration" of possibilities must be actively undertaken by the developed country authorities with a willingness to reach a positive outcome. Thus, in our view, Article 15 imposes no obligation to actually provide or accept any constructive remedy that may be identified and/or offered . . .. It does,

the other hand, the subsequent practice of developing members alone does not constitute 'subsequent practice' under Article 31 (3) of the VC,[52] and the purposive approach may be affected by the principle that waivers and exceptions can be interpreted narrowly, where S&D provisions are appropriately characterised as 'waivers and exceptions'.[53]

In relation to this state of play, it has been suggested that despite the frequent references to objects and purposes in the jurisprudence of the WTO, there is a trend towards a stricter interpretation of S&D provisions.[54] This observation, however, needs to be evaluated against the number of cases the assessment of a trend is based on and against whether it distinguishes between outcomes that are a consequence of strict interpretations and outcomes that inevitably reflect the language of the provisions as negotiated. Certainly, no doctrine of strict interpretation of S&D provisions has been expressly articulated.

however, impose an obligation to actively consider, with an open mind, the possibility of such a remedy prior to imposition of an anti-dumping measure that would affect the essential interests of a developing country . . .'.

52 In India–Patent, the Panel (para 7.57) dealt with India's contention 'that no other developing country had notified the creation of a system for the grant of exclusive marketing rights under its domestic law and that this indicated that Article 70.9 was not understood by the developing country Members concerned as a provision that entailed the obligation to make changes in their domestic law as from the entry into force of the TRIPS Agreement. India requested the Panel to address this argument, given the importance of subsequent practice in treaty interpretation. . . . In the Panel's view, however, India had failed to demonstrate that the "subsequent practice" by developing country Members in fact established the agreement of all WTO Members regarding the interpretation of Article 70.9. On the contrary, the record showed that there had been no agreement on this issue in the Council for TRIPS; at most meetings of the Council, concern had been expressed by some Members about the absence of notifications or the limited information content of notifications related to the implementation of Article 70.9.'

53 See EC–Tariff Preferences (AB); chapter 4. Contra the previous decision in Indonesia–Automobiles, the Panel stated (paras 5.238, 5.305) that given 'that under the WTO system, waivers and exceptions "have to be interpreted narrowly", the waiver of the prohibition under Article 3.1(b) of the SCM Agreement cannot reasonably be interpreted as a license to violate any and all other obligations under the WTO agreements . . .. By its own words, Article 27.3 of the SCM Agreement is limited to stipulate a temporary exception to the prohibition contained in Article 3.1 (b) of the same agreement in favour of developing Members. It does not "authorise explicitly" developing Members to deviate from any other obligation, either in the SCM Agreement, such as Article 5, or in other agreements, such as GATT Articles III: 2 . . .'.

54 See Footer 'Developing Country Practice' 84, where she relies on India–Quantitative Restrictions on Imports of Agricultural, Textile and Industrial Products, Indonesia–Automobiles, Brazil–Export Financing Programmes for Aircraft, and an Egyptian communication to this effect.

In the same vein, a significant number of developing members of the WTO maintain that the record of the WTO jurisprudence shows that development issues have not been taken sufficiently into account.[55] This is a claim and an observation that has been made at a political level. As with any observation made in any context, however, this claim needs to be substantiated and examined for its accuracy. It is the case that such claims made in the context of the Doha review of the DSU have not been accompanied by sufficient evidence to justify a sweeping indictment. This is not necessarily to question the merits of such claims, however; after all, perceptions of whether the development objective is being facilitated are as important as the actual record.

In conclusion, in the jurisprudence of the WTO there is no coherent and expressly articulated development-friendly approach to interpreting the WTO Agreements. There is, however, some evidence of neutrality in terms of their interpretation.[56] The need for a development-friendly approach – in particular, one that tends to operationalise the normally hortatory S&D provisions and displaces the notion that S&D provisions are akin to exceptions – is apparent.

5.2.7 Foresight of interpretative issues and outcomes

There are two stages at which the interpretative process becomes relevant, namely, during negotiations[57] and after or outside the framework of negotiations. During negotiations, negotiators need to be aware of a number of considerations. First, after they reach preliminary conclusions in the negotiations, it is always advisable to engage in some form of 'foresight in interpretation' through legal advice. This involves engaging in legal analysis – in particular, posing the question 'Given the likely composition of Panels and the AB, if any of the terms agreed upon were the subject of interpretation in the DSU, what possible interpretations might be put on them?' Second, negotiators should pose the question 'Is there any possible advantage in promoting the development objective or leaving a possible ambiguity as it is?' Third, negotiators should engage in documented consensus-building on

[55] See footnote 3 above. [56] See EC–Tariff Preferences (AB).

[57] For some insights into treaty interpretation from a negotiator's perspective see K.J. Vandevelde 'Treaty Interpretation from a Negotiator's Perspective' (1988) 21 *Vand J Transnat'l L* 281–312.

desirable interpretations (Article 31 (2) (a) and (b) of the VC). Fourth, they should ensure the creation of a paper trail showing an adequate history of a development-friendly interpretation (Article 32 of the VC). Fifth, the agreement should be drafted in such as way that sufficient flexibility is built in to promote development. In this respect, a recent UNCTAD study in the context of investment agreements is very relevant in terms of identifying particular areas of focus at this stage.[58] Thus, negotiators need to focus first on the preamble (including the headings of particular parts and provisions), ensuring that firm language concerning the promotion of development is used. This should be reinforced by ensuring that the development provisions are not relegated to an exceptions category.[59] The agreements also need to distinguish between different levels of development, and the overall structure of the agreement needs to be crafted in such a manner that there are appropriate development-related exceptions, special provisions, derogations, safeguards and negative/positive lists. Care must be taken to facilitate the inclusion of fair, equitable and just provisions to reinforce the development objective, and the interpretation and dispute settlement processes need to be evaluated from a development perspective. In addition, technical assistance provisions should be included as appropriate.

Following and outside the framework of negotiations, a number of concerns need to be addressed. First, it is necessary to focus on the formation of subsequent agreements or practices that may result in interpretations of provisions. Care should be taken that there is no acquiescence in interpretations that thwart the development objective. Second, it is necessary to ensure that other relevant international agreements entered into before or after negotiations that have a bearing on the trade agreement being negotiated expressly exclude or include its application in the trade relations negotiated. Third, care needs to be taken in the selection of panellists to ensure the inclusion of development-aware individuals on the Panel. Fourth, developing members need to focus on the selection of lawyers in the WTO legal department and the AB. Finally, given that publicists play an important role in shedding light on interpretations of international law, it is important to encourage and promote legal scholarship and publications that are development oriented.

[58] UNCTAD *International Investment Agreements* 128. [59] See chapter 4.

5.3 Textual and teleological approaches and the development dimension

5.3.1 *Factoring in the textual approach* in rein

It has been observed that the textual approach is to be found in the practice of the WTO.[60] This observation needs to be considered with some caution, because the reference to the textual approach has on occasions been made loosely. Thus, if it simply means that the ordinary meaning of the words used, the intentions of the parties and the objects and purposes of the agreement are to be ascertained via the text of the treaty, then this is not of great concern, as it is not necessarily a description of placing the emphasis on the text as opposed to the intention and objects and purposes of the agreement. Indeed, it has been observed that reference to the practice of a textual approach by the AB is precisely that. Thus, Robert Howse rightly points out:

> in emphasizing the importance of the exact words, the AB is not endorsing narrow literalism and eschewing teleological interpretation; rather it is taking the words as the necessary beginning point for an interpretative exercise that includes teleological dimensions. Most importantly, it is rejecting the tendency of the panels to assume a certain purpose prior to careful textual interpretation, thereby taking a shortcut to the establishment of treaty meaning that bypasses the exact text.[61]

This view of the textual approach is in accordance with the general view, and this is what is meant when it is stated that Article 31 of the VC adopts the textual approach – that is, that the intentions of the parties or the objects and purposes of the agreement cannot be resorted to *ab initio* without reference to the text. This is the sense of the 'hierarchy' of the ordinary meaning that is set out in the order of the materials in Article 31 of the VC.[62]

[60] See for example C.-D. Ehlermann, 'Six Years on the Bench of the "World Trade Court": Some Personal Experiences As Member of the Appellate Body of the World Trade Organization' (2002) 36(4) *JWT* 605–39.

[61] R. Howse 'Adjudicative Legitimacy and Treaty Interpretation in International Trade Law: The Early Years of WTO Jurisprudence' in J.H.H. Weiler (ed) *The EU, The WTO and the NAFTA* (Oxford UP, Oxford 2000) chapter 2.

[62] Contra D.F. Vagts 'Treaty Interpretation and the New American Ways of Law Reading' (1993) 4 *EJIL* 472–505, 484, where he asserts that 'most observers see this as establishing hierarchy with "ordinary meaning" at the top'. Vagts appears to be using 'hierarchy' in a more weighted and relative sense, which I dispute. Vagts does not fully substantiate the conclusion that most observers take this view, nor does he explain how certain international agreements (particularly the constitutions of international organisations,

However, if the reference to the textual approach is in fact a description of a particular emphasis that puts more weight on the literal and therefore strict approach to interpretation, then the next question is whether in fact in the WTO there is an actual trend or practice along these lines that can be empirically substantiated. Certainly, there are generalised claims and scattered observations to this effect. Thus, Claus-Dieter Ehlermann states:

> According to Article 31.1 of the Vienna Convention, 'a Treaty shall be interpreted in good faith in accordance with the ordinary meaning to be given to the terms of the treaty in their context and in the light of its object and purpose'. Among these three criteria, the Appellate Body has certainly attached the greatest weight to the first, i.e., 'the ordinary meaning of the terms of the treaty'. This is easily illustrated by the frequent references in Appellate Body reports to dictionaries, in particular to the Shorter Oxford Dictionary, which, in the words of certain critical observers, has become 'one of the covered agreements'. The second criterion, i.e., 'context' has less weight than the first, but is certainly more often used and relied upon than the third, i.e., 'object and purpose'.... the Appellate Body clearly privileges 'literal' interpretation ...[63]

A number of points need to be made here in relation to the claim that the 'literal' option has become a trend in the practice of the WTO.[64] First, frequent reference to dictionary meanings is not in itself conclusive evidence of a trend in which primacy is given to 'the ordinary meaning of the terms of the treaty'. Second, the claim of a WTO practice is couched in too certain and sweeping terms. In fact, an evaluation of such a WTO practice itself involves inter alia the exercise of judgement as to whether there is a trend towards a literal approach. It involves judgement as to whether at any given time the AB has given undue weight to one material or another, which Article 31 of the VC enjoins a treaty interpreter to factor in. Furthermore, it is questionable whether the claim has been substantiated by sufficient AB practice. The focus in this analysis of the AB jurisprudence, such as it has been, has been essentially on some sensational WTO cases that have been in the limelight rather than on any systematic consideration of the case law from this specific perspective. In the same vein, observations made by

whose practice he documents and which emphasise more the teleological approach) can be reconciled in terms of international law with the view of hierarchy that he propounds.

[63] Ehlermann 'Six Years' 615. [64] Ibid.

internal participants in the AB, however authoritative the participant, need to be objectively considered. AB judges may well want to project this 'safe' image in public. Finally, however, if what is being claimed is in fact the case, then this does indeed call for a review of AB decisions, since neither the VC nor the WTO Agreements authorise such an interpretative approach.

The option in favour of a predominantly literal approach is justified by Ehlermann in terms of the provision of clear guidance to the AB members working in different divisions, the Panels and the members of the WTO, thus providing 'security and predictability' in accordance with Article 32 of the DSU.[65]

This justification raises two questions. First, what is the nature of this clarity and predictability – if indeed this is the case? Second, is predictability really being engineered if the intentions of the members and the expressed objects and purposes of the agreements are in fact being diluted?

Furthermore, this judicial conservatism is justified by Ehlermann as providing protection to the AB from criticism that 'its reports have added to or diminished the rights and obligations provided in the covered agreements', as per Article 3.2 of the DSU. It is questionable whether this is borne out. In addition, although this judicial conservatism, this acknowledged 'defensive adjudication', may not have added to or diminished members' rights and obligations, it still raises the question whether it has in fact preserved their rights and obligations – which should be the sole driving force.

Finally, Ehlermann adds: 'The choice has been approved both by Members of the WTO and by critical observers, in particular by experts of international [trade] law.' Unfortunately, it is not clear where and how members of the WTO are supposed to have approved of the literal approach. Can such an insight into the practice of the AB be imputed to the DSB of the WTO – still less approval of that practice? Nor is it explained who the critical observers are who are being relied upon. Certainly, there are trade experts who are critical of the literal approach,[66] as indeed there are critical developing members.[67]

In conclusion, in the light of the nature of the justifications that have been offered for the literal approach – grounded as they appear to be in considerations of expediency and defensiveness – there is a serious question whether the literal approach really is an established and

[65] Ehlermann 'Six Years' 615.

[66] See for example Shankar 'Vienna Convention'. [67] See note 13 above.

accepted practice or is in fact a *desideratum* that is being advanced and that needs to be checked.

This perception of a textual approach is reinforced by the characterisation variously of the WTO Agreements as being essentially contractual in nature and as representing a bargain of concessions whose balance needs to be maintained. Thus, G. Marceau states:

> This obligation to read the WTO as a whole and in a coherent manner reinforces the idea that members wanted to set up an international system of rules and obligations specific to their trade relations, a system that would be coherent in itself and within which rights, obligations and related State action would be the result of an overall balance of concessions.[68]

In the same vein, Joost Pauwelyn makes the distinction between reciprocal and integral obligations:[69]

> Under reciprocal obligations set out, for example, in a multilateral treaty binding equally on all state parties, a promise is made towards each and every state individually. Integral obligations, in contrast imply a promise not towards individual states, but towards the collectivity of all state parties taken together.[70]

Although he concedes that not all WTO obligations are of one character, he nevertheless contends that 'most WTO obligations are of the reciprocal type'.[71] In his view, the WTO integral obligations are those relating to the operation of WTO bodies and those calling for harmonisation – for example, in TRIPS.[72] The reciprocal nature of the obligations would tend towards a textual approach to interpretation of the WTO provisions.

A number of observations need to be made here. First, it is no longer possible to characterise the WTO Agreements as being monolithic. In fact, the agreements contain elements of a constitution of an organisation and a trading system, as well as exhibiting legislative and contractual characteristics. Moreover, the agreements contain both rules and concessions. Indeed, in the EC–Computer Equipment case, the AB is considered to have determined 'that the WTO is to be considered a rule-based constitutional body, not a negotiation based contractual body'.[73]

[68] 'WTO Dispute Settlement' 772. [69] See Pauwelyn *Conflicts of Norms* 55.
[70] Ibid 65. [71] Ibid 69. [72] Ibid 71.
[73] See P.C. Maki 'Interpreting GATT Using the Vienna Convention on the Law of Treaties: A Method to Increase the Legitimacy of the Dispute Settlement System' (2000) 9 (Winter) *Minnesota J Global Trade* 343–60; EC–Computer Equipment (AB).

Second, because a Single Undertaking is arrived at as a consequence of a balance of bargains, it does not necessarily follow that its post-interpretation should be driven by the imprimatur of that pre-final-agreement process. After all, all agreements are a process of bargaining and represent the bargain, but once they are established, they acquire an independent life of their own, and the individual provisions need not necessarily be interpreted with reference to the nature of the balance (or imbalance) of the bargain finally established among the parties. In any event, the notion of the balance of a bargain in the negotiations is distorted here by the fact that developed members have not expected reciprocity from developing members in the negotiations.[74] It follows, therefore, that that non-reciprocity principle in the negotiation of concessions between developed and developing members should also be mirrored in the interpretation process of the WTO Agreements – so that the intention behind the non-reciprocity practice in negotiations of accommodating and facilitating development also permeates the process of interpretation.

Third, the obligation to interpret the Single Undertaking in a coherent and harmonious manner elicits the role of the objects and purposes of the Single Undertaking more than its contractual character.[75] Once development has been recognised in a trade agreement, its dye is cast deeper than other colours. Development is so fundamental a concept in international economic relations and law, that once it is taken into account, it must have a profound impact among the palette of colours. Its colour can, therefore, be coherently and harmoniously taken into account only by recognising its significance as an important informing agent in the process of interpretation.

Finally, for a number of reasons, I take issue with Pauwelyn's distinction between reciprocal and integral obligations within the normative framework of the WTO. First, the distinction conflates the process of negotiation in the multilateral trading system with the actual agreement once it has been arrived at. It also undermines the impact of the most-favoured-nation (MFN) standard following agreement in informing the nature of the norms reciprocally formulated at the level of negotiations. Second, individual market access negotiations are not conducted by way of individually directed promises in a bilateral framework but rather in the knowledge (indeed acknowledgement) that

[74] See for example Article XXXVI [8] of GATT 1994.

[75] Marceau 'WTO Dispute Settlement' 772; Korea–Dairy Safeguard (AB).

such promises are subject to the MFN standard. Third, the distinction between economic interests and rights that underpins Pauwelyn's distinction between reciprocal and integral obligations is eschewed in the WTO dispute settlement system:[76] in particular, for example, economic effect on a member is not a requirement for a cause of action.[77] I maintain this point despite Pauwelyn's interpretation of the EC–Bananas case and his criticism of it with reference to the AB's pronouncement that 'no legal interest' is required for standing in the dispute settlement system. This is inter alia because he considers the AB decision in the EC–Bananas case an indication that members are contracting out of the 'general international law rules on standing'. Thus he states:

> WTO members (or for that matter, the Appellate Body) could well decide that, for whatever policy reason, it is desirable to make breach of WTO law challengeable by all WTO members, irrespective of the breach. Such would not, in and of itself, change the nature of WTO obligations as reciprocal obligations.[78]

However, Pauwelyn does not demonstrate that the AB justified its pronouncement with a policy reason (even if we assume the will of the membership can be attributed to the AB) and was, in effect, for that reason contracting out of general international law rules on standing. An analysis of the EC–Bananas case reveals that the nature of the WTO obligations informed its decision. Indeed, Pauwelyn almost concedes this himself when he states that economic interest will generally be easy to prove 'given that trade potential or missed trade opportunities will be easily proven, in particular given the economic interdependence of WTO members'.[79] They will be easily proven because of the very nature of the reciprocal trade bargains subject to the MFN standard. These impart to third parties an expectation that they will not be robbed of potential or missed trade opportunities. This expectation is also integral to the reciprocal bargain and promise that is subject to the MFN standard. Finally, the stand taken here is supported by both academic writing and AB determination. Thus, in his case note of the AB decision in EC–Customs Classification, involving the interpretation of bound tariffs, Peter C. Maki observes: 'Since, under the Most Favored Nation

[76] See for example US–Malt Beverages (BISD 39S/206, 270–1) para 5.6. in relation to Article III [1] of GATT 1994.

[77] EC–Bananas (AB). [78] Pauwelyn *Conflict of Norms*. [79] Ibid 83.

(MFN) clause, all countries receive the benefit of the bound tariff, it is important to define the term by reference to all of them.'[80]

5.3.2 Factoring in the rehabilitation of the teleological approach for the development dimension

At the outset, it needs to be stated that the call here for the rehabilitation of the teleological approach in the context of the development dimension is a harnessed or moderate one;[81] that is, it is

- limited to its inclusion as required by the rules of the customary international law of treaty interpretation[82] that due weight should be given to the objects and purposes of the WTO Agreements as they relate to the development dimension;
- limited by the notion of development found in the WTO Agreements and set out here, that is, essentially, alleviating the burdens of trade liberalisation, facilitating fair play between members and facilitating those aspects of the development objectives that are established in the WTO Agreements;
- limited by the text of the WTO Agreements.

The WTO Agreements have constitutional, legislative and contractual characteristics. The development dimension is an important constitutional and legislative tenet of the WTO and international economic law, and therefore particularly calls for a teleological orientation in the interpretative process. In this respect there are important insights

[80] Maki 'Interpreting GATT' 353

[81] See for example Vandevelde 'Treaty Interpretation' 281 footnote 34, where he points out that the teleological approach can be subdivided into a moderate school and an extreme school. The extreme school, he states, 'draws the purpose not merely from the text but from a broader inquiry into the circumstances of the agreement's drafting, its subsequent operation or its role in international life'. See also Vagts 'Treaty Interpretation and the New American Ways' 484: '[a] mild form of teleology is embodied in the notion of interpretation "in good faith" and in the reference to the "object and purpose" of the treaty'. However, I take issue with Vagts if he means that teleology 'gets little room' compared with the other materials in Article 31 of the VC – as opposed to 'little room' in the sense that only the milder/less extreme form of teleology is included in Article 31. In fact, teleology is to be found not only in the reference to good faith and objects and purposes but also in the context of the Preamble. See Article 31 (2); M. Shaw *International Law* (4th edn Cambridge UP, Cambridge 1997) 657.

[82] i.e., at a minimum, the teleology that is subsumed under Article 31 of the VC. There should at least be no dereliction of judicial responsibility with respect to the teleology that is integrated into Article 31 of the VC.

to be gained particularly from a focus on comparative approaches to interpretation in the international economic sphere. Furthermore, there is a case for the WTO interpretative process to be attuned to the practice of other international organisations if the WTO is effectively to discharge its function of achieving greater coherence in global economic policy-making.[83]

In the law and practice of international monetary law, the Articles of Agreement of the IMF are interpreted in accordance with customary international law principles of interpretation, but with a strong teleological orientation.[84] Two main reasons lie behind the use of and preference for this orientation. First, Article I of the IMF Articles of Agreement[85] directs observance of a teleological approach.[86] Second, the Articles of Agreement have a constitutional function and character in terms of international monetary relations and therefore are more suited to such an interpretative approach.[87] These justifications are reinforced by the internalised nature of the IMF interpretative process, in that the organs of the IMF are charged with the function of interpretation to the exclusion of any external body. An internalised process lends itself better to the teleological method, given that the insiders who engage in the interpretation have a better knowledge and understanding of the objects and purposes of the organisation.[88] Thus, the legislative element in the teleological approach is mandated by the IMF Articles of Agreement.[89] This legislative character is, however, limited by the fact that the purposes of the IMF are directives. They are not 'independent norms' that can be applied independently of other provisions.[90] Furthermore, the Articles distinguish between interpretation and amendment.[91]

The IMF approach to interpretation is mirrored in the law and practice of the World Bank Group.[92] The teleological approach is similarly justified on the basis of an express mandate, as set out, for example, in Article I of the International Bank for Reconstruction and

[83] Article III of the Marrakesh Agreement.

[84] See for example J. Gold *Interpretation: The IMF and the International Law* (Kluwer, London 1996) 19, 178.

[85] Article 1 of the IMF Articles of Agreement states: 'The Fund shall be guided in all its decisions by the purposes set forth above.'

[86] Gold *Interpretation* 19.

[87] Ibid 172. [88] Ibid 15. [89] Ibid 222. [90] Ibid 173. [91] Ibid.

[92] I.F.I. Shihata *The World Bank in a Changing World* (Martinus Nijhoff, The Hague 2000) III: chapter 1.

Development (IBRD).[93] It is limited, as in the case of the IMF, by the actual purposes that are set out in the text of the Articles of Agreement of the IBRD[94] and by the fact that interpretations cannot translate into amendments.[95] Thus, I. Shihata stated:

> The Bank's successive General Council have carefully studied the *travaux preparatoires* of the Articles of Agreement in an attempt to identify the intended meaning. They have, however, accorded greater attention to the ultimate objective of the Articles and the overall mandate of the Bank. There was no attempt to adhere to a subjective [intentionist] interpretation. Interpretations have rather served the purposes of the Bank as stated in its Charter as an international institution concerned with the reconstruction and development of its members.... They have enabled the Bank to address many areas related to the economic development of its borrowing countries that were not necessarily deemed to be so related at the time the Articles of Agreement were drafted.[96]

In the field of international investment law, not much specific attention has been given to the interpretation techniques actually employed in relation to IIAs,[97] in particular bilateral investment agreements. There are two main explanations for this dearth of focus on the interpretative practice in terms of bilateral investment treaties (BITs). First, most of the disputes involving BITs have been through the ICSID arbitral process, which lacks the doctrine of precedent. However, it is the case that ICSID arbitrators have engaged in interpretations of BITs by factoring comparative BIT practice into the interpretative process.[98] Second, it has been claimed that not much is 'known on the use that countries and investors have made of BITs', because 'they have been invoked in a few international arbitrations, and presumably in diplomatic correspondence and investor demands'.[99] This insight, even though it comes from a recent UNCTAD study, should not be uncritically accepted in its entirety, because a number of ICSID arbitrations involving in some manner or other BITs are now

[93] I.F.I. Shihata *The World Bank in a Changing World* (Martinus Nijhoff, The Hague 2000) III: chapter 1. See also Article I of the International Bank for Reconstruction and Development, which states: 'The Bank shall be guided in all its decisions by the purposes set forth above.'

[94] Shihata *World Bank* 6. [95] Ibid 7. [96] Ibid 17.

[97] See UNCTAD *Trends in International Investment Agreements: An Overview* (UNCTAD/ITE/IIT/13, 1999); UNCTAD *International Investment Agreements.*

[98] See for example *Asian Agricultural Products Ltd [AAPL]* v. *Republic of Sri Lanka* (May 1991) 30 *ILM* 577 para 40.

[99] UNCTAD *Trends in International Investment Agreements* 47.

evident.[100] The UNCTAD study does, however, acknowledge the need for more attention to be paid to the role of interpretation in this sphere for the development of international investment law.[101]

In this vein, the UNCTAD study acknowledges the role and relevance of the development concerns that are often set out in preambles to IIAs[102] in informing the interpretative process, although it notes that they do not on their own 'directly create rights and obligations for the parties'.[103] Indeed, it is noted that to promote the development objective, express reference to the development objective in the preamble is required, as is flexibility in interpretation.[104] Thus, it is stated: 'The manner in which an IIA is interpreted, and the way it is to be made effective, determine whether its objectives, structure and substantive provisions produce the desired developmental effects.'[105]

In the practice of ICSID arbitrations, the Arbitration Tribunals have in the interpretation process relied on the norms of interpretation found in customary international law. In interpreting BITs, the Tribunals have focused on the intention of the contracting parties[106] and, on a number of occasions, on the objects and purposes of the BITs, as set out in the preamble.[107] It is difficult to arrive at a conclusion on the general trend in the approach adopted by arbitrators in investment arbitrations. However, one anonymous reviewer of this chapter suggested that in investment arbitration the arbitrators 'get the desired result via literal interpretation – the dictionary approach'.

Investment Tribunals have, however, relied on a number of occasions on the objects and purposes of the ICSID in interpreting its provisions[108] – in particular, in relation to one of its key provisions defining its jurisdiction, namely, Article 25. Indeed, one commentator observed recently that the ICSID Tribunals have 'adopted broad and flexible

[100] See for example the cases listed and appearing on the ICSID website (www.worldbank.org/icsid); 41 *ILM* 881; 40 *ILM* 457; 36 *ILM* 1531; 34 *ILM* 935; 30 *ILM* 577; *ICJ Reports* (see below).

[101] UNCTAD *Trends in International Investment Agreements* 85.

[102] Ibid 88. [103] Ibid. [104] Ibid 21. [105] Ibid 99.

[106] See for example *Tradex Hellas S.A. [Greece]* v. *Republic of Albania* ICSID ARB/94/2 [1996] 180; available at http://www.worldbank.org/icsid/cases/tradex_decision.pdf.

[107] See for example *Wena Hotels Ltd* v. *Arab Rep of Egypt* ICSID ARB/98/4 (2002) 41 *ILM* 881; *American Manufacturing and Trading, Inc.* v. *Republic of Zaire* ICSID ARB/93/1 (1997) 36 *ILM* 1531 paras 5.12, 5.36; *Asian Agricultural Product Ltd [AAPL]* para 51.

[108] See for example *In the case of Mihaly International Corporation* v. *Democratic Socialist Republic of Sri Lanka* ICSID ARB/00/2 [2002] 149; available at http://www.worldbank.org/icsid/cases/mihaly-award.pdf; *Wena Hotels Ltd*; *Fedax N* v. *The Republic of Venezuela* ICSID ARB/96/3 (1998) 37 ILM 1378 para 24.

approaches in their interpretation or application of Article 25 [2] [b] of the Convention'.[109]

On those occasions when the ICJ has been involved in interpreting investment agreements[110] – in particular, friendship, commerce and navigation (FCN) treaties – the Court has taken into account the objects and purposes of the agreements in question.[111] Thus, in the ELSI case, the Court stated: 'The Chamber however has some sympathy with the contention of the United States, as being more in accord with the general purpose of the FCN Treaty.'[112]

In the *Case Concerning Oil Platforms*, in interpreting the Treaty of Amity, Economic Relations and Consular Rights between the United States and Iran (1955), the Court stated:

> the Court considers that the objective of peace and friendship proclaimed in Article I of the Treaty of 1955 is such as to throw light on the interpretation of the other treaty provisions, and in particular of Articles IV and X. Article I is thus not without legal significance for such an interpretation, but cannot, taken in isolation, be a basis for the jurisdiction of the Court.[113]

In the *Case Concerning the Gabcikovo-Nagymaros* Project, in interpreting the treaty between Czechoslovakia and Hungary of 1977, the Court noted:

> the 1977 Treaty was not only a joint project for the production of energy, but it was designed to serve other objectives as well.... None of these objectives has been given absolute priority over the other, in spite of the emphasis which is given in the Treaty to the construction of a System of Locks for the production of energy. None of them has lost its importance. In order to achieve these objectives the parties accepted obligations of conduct, obligations of performance, and obligations of result.[114]

Reliance by the ICJ on the objects and purposes of these agreements may be explained by the fact that this is a court that has 'permanent and highly authoritative judges'.[115]

[109] See A.A. Asouzu 'A Review and Critique of Arbitral Awards on Article 25 [2][b] of the ICSID Convention' (2002) 3(3) *J World Invest* 397–454.

[110] See for example *ELSI* case (*United States of America* v. *Italy*) 1989 *ICJ Reports*; *Case Concerning Oil Platforms* (*Islamic Republic of Iran* v. *United States of America*) (Preliminary Objections) 1996 *ICJ Reports*; *Case Concerning the Gabcikovo-Nagymaros Project* (Hungary/Slovakia) 1997 *ICJ Reports*.

[111] The ICJ has on other occasions relied on the teleological approach. See for example the *Certain Expenses Case* 1962 *ICJ Reports* 168.

[112] *ELSI* case para 132. See also para 64. [113] Para 31. [114] Para 135.

[115] Observation made by an anonymous referee for this chapter.

In the sphere of international fiscal law, the manner of and approach to interpreting double taxation agreements have received considerable attention among international tax lawyers.[116] International law principles of interpretation apply to double taxation conventions,[117] which, similar to many international agreements, 'leave considerable room for interpretation'.[118] At the national level, the approach to interpreting double taxation agreements has not been completely uniform. Thus, in Germany, the UK, Norway and Switzerland, a textual approach has generally been adopted.[119] In the United States and the Netherlands, on the other hand, the focus has been on the intent of the contracting parties.[120] However, the role of the teleological approach is unclear. Double taxation agreements have a contractual character, but they also have law-making aspects.[121] This raises the question whether this mixture of functions can in principle 'be taken into consideration when interpreting double taxation conventions'.[122] Thus, it has been stated:

> It is uncertain whether it is admissible or useful to consider the object and purpose in the case of double taxation conventions. It is the purpose of double taxation conventions to fairly distribute tax revenues among Contracting States, to avoid double taxation, eliminate tax barriers to trade, encourage foreign investment, avoid discriminations and tax avoidance etc. However, these purposes cannot help in the interpretation of distributive rules since, conversely, it is precisely those distributive rules that identify the purpose of the treaty. At best it might fill loopholes and avoid a case of double taxation that would not have been eliminated by the convention. Yet such an interpretation of loopholes is neither stipulated by the VCLT nor by the character of double taxation conventions as special tax norms.[123]

However, two situations have been identified where the teleological approach is considered relevant: first, where there is an 'improper use of double taxation conventions'[124] and, second, where there are 'convention provisions that are not directly concerned with the avoidance of double taxation, but with other purposes'.[125] Generally, however, it is maintained that the textual approach, particularly in the interest of legal certainty, should prevail in relation to double taxation agreements.[126]

[116] See for example IFA *Interpretation of Double Taxation Conventions* LXXVIIIa (Kluwer, Deventer, The Netherlands 1993).

[117] Ibid K. Vogel and R.G. Prokish "General Report" 66.

[118] Ibid 67. [119] Ibid 60. [120] Ibid. [121] Ibid 68. [122] Ibid. [123] Ibid 72. [124] Ibid.

[125] Ibid 73. [126] Ibid 74, 83.

In the context of regional economic integration agreements, in the European Union the Court of Justice of the European Communities has adopted both the contextual and teleological approaches, with 'increasing resort to the latter'.[127] The teleological approach is also endorsed in NAFTA. Article 102 [2] of NAFTA specifically obliges parties to the agreement to interpret and apply its provisions in the light of the objectives set out.[128] The emphasis on the teleological approach in the European Union has paralleled the increasingly programmatic nature of the EC treaty.[129] The historical (or intention-based) approach to interpretation is little used by the ECJ, on the other hand, mainly because the European treaties have been negotiated in a state of secrecy, and the intentions of the contacting parties have been difficult to discern.[130] Other factors explaining the use of the teleological approach in interpreting regional integration agreements include the fact that regional groupings constitute something of a 'homogenous epistemological community with common values', often with permanent and authoritative judges.[131]

Given that this does not represent the practice in terms of international economic relations as such, it may be noted in passing here that the emphasis on the teleological approach is also to be found in most continental European legal systems in the interpretation of national legislation.[132] (Indeed, the teleological approach is 'expressly enjoined upon the Swiss Courts by the Swiss Civil Code of 1912'.[133]) There are two main reasons for this.[134] First, civil codes tend to be old and therefore to require adaptations. Second, unlike common law systems,

[127] N. Brown and T. Kennedy *The Court of Justice of the European Communities* (Sweet & Maxwell, London 2000) chapter 14, 324. However, H.G. Schermers and N.M. Blokker, in *International Institutional Law* (Martinus Nijhoff, The Hague 1995) 1350, refer to an earlier study by D. Simon, 'L'Interpretation judiciare des traits d'organisation internationales' *Morphologie des conventions et Fonction Juridictionelle* (Edité par A. pedone, Paris), stating: 'Simon concludes that neither the ICJ nor the European Court emphasizes one or another of the recognized schools of interpretation. On the contrary, his study reveals that both courts display considerable eclecticism in order to achieve the desired result, they do not hesitate to mingle different canons of interpretation.'

[128] See Article 102 [1] and [2] of NAFTA. See also for example *S.D. Myers, Inc.* v. *Government of Canada* (2001) 40 ILM 1408.

[129] Brown and Kennedy *The Court of Justice of the European Communities* 326.

[130] Ibid 330.

[131] Observation made by an anonymous referee for this chapter.

[132] Brown and Kennedy *The Court of Justice of the European Communities* 341. [133] Ibid.

[134] Observation made by an anonymous referee for this chapter.

the civil code legislation tends to be open-ended and therefore to require the aid of the objects and purposes.

In conclusion, in most of the principal spheres of international economic law, a central theme has been the equation of an appropriate interpretative technique with the particular dynamics of the subject, the institution, the judges or the agreement in question. The role of the teleological approach in key spheres of international economic relations is specifically recognised and accepted.[135] It is considered particularly relevant when the agreements have a constitutional or programmatic character. Indeed, its role is recognised even when the constitutional, programmatic or normative provisions in question are established in an agreement of a mainly contractual character. Generally, however, where state sovereignty has been of particular concern, a textual or intentionist approach has been preferred in international organisations.[136]

Three lessons are to be drawn from this comparative insight. First, the teleological approach can be used, and is widely used, in other multilateral and regional economic arrangements. This practice is recognised as well as justified as being appropriate by most international lawyers.[137] Indeed, it may be said to constitute an aspect of the norms of the customary international law of treaty interpretation as they have now developed. This development is relevant because Article 3.2 of the DSU refers to the customary rules of interpretation of public international law and not to Article 31 of the VC. The fact that Article 31 of the VC is said to reflect customary international law does not exclude developments in customary international law from being taken into account in this respect. All that is meant here is that to the extent that Article 31 of the VC is coterminous with customary international law, it reflects customary international law and applies. But if customary international law is more expansive than the rules in Article 31 of the VC, then there is scope for those other aspects of customary international law to be recognised. Furthermore, as has been stated earlier,[138] the interpretation of Article 31 of the VC is itself subject to the interpretative rules contained therein – including 'subsequent practice in the application of the treaty' (Article 31 (3) (b)).

135 See also for example Schermers and Blokker *International Institutional Law* para 1389.

136 Ibid.

137 See for example Shaw *International Law* 658; *Oppenheim's International Law* I: 1273 footnote 13; and Vagts 'Treaty Interpretation and the New American Ways'.

138 See chapter 1.

Second, the WTO Agreements have a variegated character (i.e. in part constitutional, in part legislative, in part contractual), and this variegated character can be reflected in the interpretation process through the eclectic use of interpretative approaches, as appropriate in the circumstances.

Third, the teleological approach can actually be entrenched as a direction for the approach to be adopted for interpretation. Indeed, in relation to LDCs this approach is arguably already entrenched[139] but may need further clarification.

In reflecting upon the role of the teleological approach in the interpretation of the WTO Agreements, we must address some of the deep scepticism that accompanies this approach. First, however, two general points need to be made, given that much of the scepticism in relation to the teleological approach stems from what appears to be a knee-jerk reaction to the idea of teleology in the context of the WTO. First, it must be stressed that there is an important distinction between advancing the teleological approach as a general *modus operandi* and calling for due weight to be attached to it, particularly as a fundamental tenet of international economic law (namely, development) is involved. To reiterate, the teleological approach being advanced here is very much within the parameters of international customary norms of treaty interpretation in relation to the limited extent to which the WTO is concerned with trade-related development issues (the development dimension as defined in this chapter). Indeed, this level of teleology in relation to the development dimension is arguably already to be discerned in the framework of the WTO, although it is threatened by the appearance of the textual approach. Second, sceptical arguments in relation to the teleological approach need to be scrutinised to see whether they are actually arguments about the preservation of national sovereignty rather than observations in relation to the interpretative approach itself.

The sceptical arguments can be summarised as follows:[140]

- The WTO is not yet a mature enough institution for the teleological approach.
- The teleological approach will undermine the balance of concessions in the WTO Agreements.

[139] See for example paragraph 2 [iii] of the December 1993 Ministerial Decision on Measures in Favour of Least-Developed Countries; Article 24 of the DSU.

[140] These points are drawn from the observations of the anonymous reviewers of this chapter.

- The diversity of membership of the WTO implies that there is no community with a common value system – a necessary condition for the application of the teleological approach.
- The WTO objects and purposes are unclear, can be contradictory and may involve difficult questions of prioritisation.
- The teleological approach raises the question of how the development dimension is to be implemented.
- The WTO panellists and AB judges do not have competence in development and economic matters.
- In practice, the teleological approach could be the handmaiden of a 'Western' concept of development emphasising good governance, human rights and environmental issues.[141]

To the extent that each of these sceptical arguments might be levelled against the teleological approach, the following responses can be made. First, scepticism about the teleological approach on the grounds that the WTO is not yet mature enough to sustain the licence of such an approach is rooted in an understanding of the teleological approach that is somewhat divorced from the text. Furthermore, the teleological approach is no more dependent upon the maturity of the system within which it operates than a textual approach is. What is more, GATT/ WTO tradition and practice do indeed compare well with the other mature systems within which the teleological approach operates. Indeed, the WTO judicial tradition is now one of the most successful systems in international economic relations. This scepticism about the teleological approach is also questionable from the viewpoint of law and economic analysis – in particular, on the basis of insights drawn from the application of economic analysis to questions of interpretation in contract law.[142] On this analysis, the WTO Agreements are in effect akin to 'incomplete contracts', which raises the question of how the judicial organs ought to engage in their interpretation.[143] In contract law, the courts can adopt either a restrictive textual approach or the contextual approach, which here can be assimilated to the less restrictive

[141] See also Vagts 'Treaty Interpretation and the New American Ways' 494, where he points out that former communist countries were concerned that 'if teleology were invoked, it would be capital in character. Therefore they consistently called for narrow and literal construction.'

[142] For an overview of issues and literature see G.M. Cohen 'Implied Terms and Interpretation in Contract Law' http://encyclo.findlaw.com/tablebib.html, 78–98. However, even in this sphere of law and economics there remains much scope for research.

[143] Ibid.

teleological approach. The choice between the two interpretative methodologies, according to law and economic analysis in contract law, would depend upon three main considerations: the transaction cost of drafting the WTO Agreements fully, the risk of opportunistic behaviour on the part of members of the WTO and the relative likelihood of panel or AB error.[144] In terms of the WTO Agreements, the transaction costs of ensuring a complete contract in the context of negotiating, monitoring and enforcing would be high.[145] Arriving at a consensus, let alone a consensus on all matters in multilateral trade negotiations, is indeed very difficult. The incompleteness of the WTO Agreements can, then, be said to be an 'efficient' alternative, particularly given that the WTO has judicial organs that can, generally speaking, provide flexible and efficient adjustments to various contingencies.[146] Opportunistic behaviour in terms of the WTO Agreements is probably not a problem of significant scale, one might suppose, given that there is a degree of reciprocity in the concessions given and given that one member's opportunistic behaviour can on another occasion be another member's opportunity. Furthermore, international agreements often come to fruition precisely because of a perceived margin for opportunistic behaviour. In any event, both interpretative methodologies can be 'useful for deterring different types of opportunism'.[147] Finally, in relation to the possibility of error on the part of the WTO judicial organs, the following observation by G. M. Cohen in relation to contracts is relevant here:

> the possibility of court error does not always argue in favour of textualism. Both textualist and contextualist methodologies lead to court error. The real question is which methodology has the lowest error rate and at what cost. It is hard to answer this question in the abstract. This may help to explain why courts do not – and never will – use pure interpretative methodologies, but tend to switch back and forth depending on the circumstances.[148]

One might add here that the overall costs to the welfare of the international community of an error that tends in favour of development are likely to be at worst insignificant, and at least beneficial. For some

[144] For an overview of issues and literature see G.M. Cohen 'Implied Terms and Interpretation in Contract Law' http://encyclo.findlaw.com/tablebib.html, 78 in the context of contracts.

[145] Ibid 81 in the context of contracts.

[146] Ibid 82, 89 in the context of contracts.

[147] Ibid 93 in the context of contracts.

[148] Ibid 97.

members of the WTO, however, drafting a particular interpretative methodology into the WTO system could come at a cost, given that it is a second-order concern of little value outside actual litigation.[149]

Second, with respect to the undermining of the balance of concessions that the teleological approach is understood to herald, again it is not proven that the teleological approach any more than the textual approach would result in such a challenge. The textual approach can result in the text being subject 'to more than one reading', which may result in the imposition of a meaning.[150] In any event, the development dimension is an integral part of the balance of concessions. Furthermore, to reiterate, to characterise the WTO normative framework as simply an assimilation of balances of concessions is to ignore the fact that the WTO normative framework is made up of constitutional, legislative and contractual characteristics.

Third, although the WTO community is diverse, that diversity is assimilated into a common or shared sense of a basic international trading system – otherwise, the membership of the WTO would be not so much diverse as non-multilateral. Furthermore, it is not proven that a community and a set of common values is a necessary condition for the application of the teleological approach. The European Union, the IMF and the World Bank have diverse memberships, and the customers of the ICJ are diverse. Indeed, perhaps somewhat cynically, one might state that the teleological approach is precisely important in a diverse situation to maintain the momentum of the consensus reached.

Fourth, there is in fact not much lack of clarity with respect to the development dimension in the WTO Agreements. The WTO Agreements are, at the level of the preambles and the text, replete with references to developing members and the development dimension. This leaves open the question of the relationships between the various objects and purposes and the development dimension. There is a danger here of being unduly alarmist; the problem must be considered in perspective. It is the case that this challenge is also to be found in other international economic organisations, including the IMF/World Bank Group and the European Union, where the teleological approach is used. It is the case also that this challenge is not absent from the textual approach, which has to operate in the shadow of the objects and

149 Ibid 96, in the context of contract law.

150 See for example Vandevelde 'Treaty Interpretation' 288. See also Brownlie *Principles of Public International Law* 637.

purposes of the agreement in question.[151] Furthermore, the weighing of different policy underpinnings is in reality an aspect of the judicial function – even when judges hide under the cover of the textual approach. Finally, although perhaps controversially, the development dimension as defined here is fairly prominent among the objectives of the WTO Agreements and should at the margin of judicial appreciation be allowed to trump other objectives.

Finally, the question of the manner of implementation of the development dimension by the 'judges' in the WTO and their competence in development and economic matters is again a challenge whose ramifications need to be kept in perspective. This is particularly so given the limited role of the teleological approach being advocated here, together with the limited scope of the development dimension. To the extent that this is an issue, however, it does not take much to recognise, for example – as indeed the WTO 'judges' have already demonstrated their competence to do – that allowing private counsel will particularly assist developing members or that the burden of some procedural requirements resulting in non-compliance should not deprive a developing member of the benefits of S&D provisions. Furthermore, the WTO has systems in place in other spheres where it defers to national modes of implementation. Thus, for example, the particular form of a suspension of concessions authorised by the DSB is largely left to the discretion of the member state. There is no reason 'judges', too, should not take their cue here from the developing members concerned – after all, this would be the dictate of the recognised right to development under international law. This also deals with the concern that the development objective may become a handmaiden for a particular 'Western' development paradigm – although one might add here in passing that some form of development perspective is perhaps better than none.

5.4 Proposals for reform in the Doha Round

The Doha Ministerial Declaration articulates the determination of the WTO membership to promote, through trade growth, development and sustainable development and to place the needs and interests of

[151] See for example Vandevelde 'Treaty Interpretation' 285: 'We apply even the clearest of rules only because we sense a more general purpose or standard behind such rules without thinking.'

developing members at the heart of the Work Programme adopted in the declaration.

The Work Programme under the Doha Ministerial Declaration appears to address the problems of interpreting the WTO Agreements, particularly from the perspective of developing members, principally in the following ways:

- in a general manner, under the title 'implementation-related issues and concerns' (para 12 of the Declaration);
- through a focus on S&D provisions (para 44);
- through a focus on the relationship between WTO provisions and multilateral environmental agreements (MEAs) (para 32);
- in the framework of individual topics identified in the Doha agenda – in particular, review of the DSU (para 30).

More specifically, the approach adopted is one of clarification of selected provisions of the WTO Agreements by the membership of the WTO; S&D engineering to clarify, strengthen and make operational these provisions; consideration of how S&D provisions 'may be incorporated into the architecture of the WTO rules'; clarification of the relationship between WTO provisions and MEAs; and, last but not least, the opportunity specifically to reform the interpretative process through the review of the DSU.

However, the Doha agenda does not expressly identify the process of interpretation of the WTO Agreements for developing countries as an issue. Rather, the agenda mainly engages or sets in motion an actual 'politicised' interpretative process only on selected provisions and issues. The list of clarifications provided and provisions identified for review by no means seems to be exhaustive. The general review of S&D provisions provides only a partial accommodation of the development perspective: development-related issues arise from non-S&D provisions as well. However, it may be that the call for S&D provisions to be 'incorporated into the architecture of the WTO rules' in the Ministerial Declaration facilitates the enunciation of a general approach to interpretation for development.[152]

Certainly, developing members have made proposals and observations, particularly in relation to the process of interpretation, in the review of the DSU. The noteworthy proposals related to the elements of

[152] See chapter 4.

the development dimension identified here and concerned mainly with the process of interpretation are as follows:

- the need for an agreed negotiating history to assist Panels and the AB in accordance with the VC;[153]
- provision for dissenting judgements in the DSU;[154]
- explicit indication of how account is taken of S&D provisions in favour of developing countries and LDCs in the DSU (Article 12.11 of the DSU);[155]
- transparency in the inputs provided by the WTO Secretariat to Panels;[156]
- clarification of the circumstances in which *amicus curiae* briefs can be submitted;[157]
- at least one panellist to be from a developing member in disputes between developed and developing members;[158]
- operationalising S&D provisions through amendment and/or authoritative interpretation under Article 9 [2] of the Marrakesh Agreement and the setting up of an S&D monitoring body;[159]
- regular and periodic review by the General Council of the jurisprudence developed by the DSB.[160]

Although these proposals are constructive, they have been variously put forward, generally in a piece-meal and unconnected fashion, mainly in reaction to some interpretative practices that have become apparent. They do not appear to form part of a focused, organised and proactive attempt to develop a coherent approach to the process of interpretation with a development dimension. Indeed, the Doha agenda, along with the contribution of developing members thus far, has been mainly concerned with actual interpretation of particular provisions, including S&D provisions, rather than with the fundamental and underlying process of interpretation that will facilitate the attainment of the development objective on a permanent basis.

[153] Jamaica (TN/DS/W/21, 10 October 2002).

[154] LDC Group (TN/DS/W/17, 9 October 2002). [155] Ibid.

[156] India on behalf of Cuba, Honduras, India, Malaysia, Pakistan, Sri Lanka, Tanzania and Zimbabwe (TN/DS/W/18, 7 October 2002).

[157] Ibid.

[158] Proposal on Special and Differential Treatment by the African Group in the WTO (TN/DS/W/15, 25 September 2002).

[159] TN/CTD/W/3/Rev1. [160] African Group (TN/DS/W/15, 25 September 2002).

Furthermore, the proposals are not set within a conceptual framework but appear at random. It is important to identify in an appraisal of the process of interpretation with a development dimension the pegs on which the development dimension can be hung, so that the full strain of the peg can be ascertained. With this methodology, the range of possibilities is increased, and a coherent strategy for reform is more likely to emerge. For example, the focus on the range of materials that shapes a particular interpretative outcome is to be welcomed. Thus, reference has been made to the historical texts, the material from the WTO Secretariat to the Panels and clarification on the acceptance of *amicus curiae* briefs. However, this focus is not complete. For example, no reference is made to the appropriateness of a narrow or a teleological approach to interpretation. Nor is there any reference to the type of relationship that other international agreements, except MEAs, may have to the process of interpreting the WTO Agreements. Similarly, there is no allusion to nurturing legal writings on development-oriented trade, despite the fact that Article 38 of the Statute of the ICJ specifically mentions publicists as a law-determining source in international law.

By the same token, there has been a focus on issues relating to good governance. For example, there is reference to the inclusion of at least one panellist from a developing member in disputes between developed and developing members. Similarly, allowing for dissenting opinions (in addition to their value per se in the development of the jurisprudence of the WTO) increases the chances of a diverse Panel being composed – as opposed to a panel that will comprise a like-minded body of individuals. However, here also other issues need to be considered. For example, should there not always be a panellist from a developing member – after all, to reiterate, systemic issues that touch upon development can also feature in disputes between developed members.

In conclusion, it is suggested that developing members adopt a strategy in favour of an interpretative process that has a development dimension along the lines suggested here. This strategy should specifically include the following:

- adoption in a limited manner of the teleological approach to interpretation as it affects the development dimension as described here, along with a strengthening of the development objective in the Preamble to the Marrakesh Agreement;
- introduction of a rule that exceptions and derogations to facilitate development should not be strictly interpreted.

6

'Interpreting' in external concerns

6.1 Introduction

Interpreting in external concerns has been among the most considered topics of scholarly and political discourse. It remains one of the most challenging tasks for anyone interested in fair trade and a WTO that has a holistic approach to international and domestic affairs. The legal discourse in the field has, however, been mainly inspired by the desire to incorporate environmental and human rights concerns into trade norms. It has also been primarily concerned with interpreting external concerns legally enshrined in international agreements into the WTO normative framework.[1] Thus, of necessity, the analysis has been chiefly in terms of reconciling conflicts of norms in international law. In this respect, without a doubt the most exhaustive and scholarly work has been that of Joost Pauwelyn.[2] In the circumstances, this chapter will be brief and, in particular, will not touch upon the closely aligned topic of conflict resolution in public international law.

6.2 Apparatus for interpreting in external concerns

A number of definitions need to be given at the outset, before focusing on the approaches that might facilitate interpreting in external concerns. First, the apparatus for interpreting external concerns into the WTO Agreements can be considered from the narrow perspective of interpretation, namely, as set out in Articles 31–2 of the VC. However, it can also be considered from the broader perspective of interpretation, along the lines of law as a process of decision-making. In this manner, the apparatus includes not merely rules but also the relevant interpreters actually involved in the process of interpretation, together with the

[1] See now, however, Lindroos and Mehling 'Dispelling the Chimera'. See also Pauwelyn *Conflict of Norms*.

[2] Pauwelyn *Conflict of Norms*.

broader framework of the process. The broader perspective provides better insights into the process of interpreting in external concerns. Second, external concerns can be trade or non-trade concerns not set out in the WTO Agreements. However, the particular concerns tend usually to be of a non-trade character. These concerns may or may not already be found in other normative frameworks, whether international agreements or domestic legislation.

The legal perspective on internalising external concerns within the WTO embraces not just the challenge of reconciling conflicting norms but also the effective use of the interpretative apparatus (both narrowly and broadly defined) to include external concerns into the body of international trade norms. This interpreting in is not simply to be equated with the process of trumping WTO norms; it is also concerned generally with external influences integrating and tampering with, influencing and informing WTO norms.

6.2.1 Narrow interpretative perspective

From the narrow interpretative perspective, the various techniques of interpreting in external concerns have been thoroughly analysed by Pauwelyn from the perspective of resolving conflicts of different international norms. These need to be reviewed here (although briefly, in light of his work), as they are equally relevant in terms of effective interpretation. First and foremost, the treaty interpretation apparatus in the WTO is to be viewed against the now-established fact that the WTO regime is part of public international law. The WTO Agreements are set against the 'background of already existing norms, in particular norms of general international law'.[3] The point to note here is that this opens up a broader source of law and therefore brings interplay between WTO and other norms. Also of note is the supremacy of international law over domestic law. This supremacy has an impact on domestic practices of interpreting international agreements, albeit within the constraints of national constitutions. It can also have an impact on the interpretation of national obligations in the light of international treaty commitments.

Second, and in particular, Articles 31–2 of the VC expressly open up a wider normative framework than the WTO Agreements:[4]

[3] Ibid 201, 240. See also Lindroos and Mehling 'Dispelling the Chimera'.

[4] Pauwelyn *Conflict of Norms* 351.

- 'any subsequent agreement between the parties regarding the interpretation of the treaty or the application of its provisions' (Article 31 (3) (a)), subject to Article IX of the Marrakesh Agreement;
- 'any subsequent practice in the application of the treaty which establishes the agreement of the parties regarding its interpretation' (Article 31 (3) (b));
- 'any relevant rules of international law applicable in the relations between the parties' (Article 31 (3) (c));
- 'supplementary means of interpretation' of Article 32, particularly the circumstances of the conclusion of the treaty, and its historical background.

In addition, these guidelines for treaty interpretation not only open up normative sources but are themselves a potential subject of interpretation, further expanding the pool of sources of law. Thus, Pauwelyn points to the difference between interpretation in the light of the law in force at the time the treaty came into force and interpretation according to when the treaty is applied.[5] Interpreting according to when the treaty is applied allows for a contemporaneous interpretation.[6] By the same token, arguing that the reference to 'parties' in Article 31 (3) (c) of the VC is a reference to the 'parties' to a particular dispute and arguing that an agreement that reflects the 'common intentions of the parties'[7] also carries with it the *express* endorsement of the agreement by all the 'parties' to the WTO[8] are endeavours to facilitate the inclusion of wider sources of influence.

Third, the context of the WTO Agreements itself provides a pool of sources internal to the WTO Agreements. This context is a requirement based on Article 31.[9] Thus, it is noteworthy that the WTO Preamble and provisions provide for a diversity of considerations, albeit mainly in a trade framework. The parameters of this context and its relevance can be, and often are, the subject of legal argumentation in themselves.

Fourth, an array of principles of treaty construction have a role in facilitating the incorporation of external concerns – for example, the principle *in dubio mitius*, according to which 'if the meaning of a term is ambiguous, that meaning is to be preferred which is less onerous to the party assuming an obligation, or which interferes less with the

[5] Pauwelyn *Conflict of Norms* 351 [6] Ibid 204. [7] Ibid 260–1.
[8] Ibid 259, referring to D. Palmeter and P. Mavroidis *Dispute Settlement in the WTO: Practice and Procedure* (Kluwer, The Hague 1999); Marceau 'Conflicts of Norms' 1087.
[9] Pauwelyn *Conflict of Norms* 247.

territorial and personal supremacy of a party, or involves less general restrictions upon a party'.[10] In this manner, national policies, often a primary source of external concerns, can carry weight. Another example is the principle of effective treaty interpretation, *ut res magis valeat quam pereat*, according to which all the provisions in the treaty need to be taken into account.[11] '[An] interpreter is not free to adopt a reading that would result in reducing whole clauses or paragraphs of a treaty to redundancy or inutility.'[12] Thus, provisions that point to external concerns cannot be ignored. In addition, the principles of *lex specialis*, according to which the *lex specialis* must prevail over the general rule (*lex generalis*),[13] and of *lex posterior derogat legi priori*, according to which the later in time prevails,[14] can both be instrumental in validating external concerns, even if within the confines of the agreements.

Finally, somewhat peculiar to Pauwelyn, the view is advanced that

> inter se 'modifications' to the WTO treaty must be tolerated as long as (i) they are not explicitly prohibited in the WTO (as are certain regional arrangements, not meeting the conditions in GATT Art XXIV); and (ii) they do not affect the rights of other WTO members.[15]

This argument is rejected here as it is based on the controversial distinction between reciprocal and integral norms in the WTO Agreements and goes against the fundamental tenet of the multilateral trading system based on the MFN standard. Nevertheless, it is noted as an argument that facilitates inclusion and variation, both of which enable external influences to be incorporated into the WTO trading system.

6.2.2 *Broader interpretative perspective*

From a broader perspective of interpretation, the background of the relevant interpreters and their advisors becomes significant. Under

[10] Ibid 186, quoting EC–Hormones (AB) para 165 footnote 154.
[11] Pauwelyn *Conflict of Norms* 247.
[12] Ibid 249, quoting US–Gasoline (AB) 23, confirmed by the AB Reports in Japan–Taxes on Alcoholic Beverages and other cases.
[13] Pauwelyn *Conflict of Norms* 385, 414. [14] Ibid 126, 173.
[15] Ibid 316. Pauwelyn bases his view on the distinction he makes in his book between reciprocal and integral norms in the WTO. This is not a position I accept. It is also not accepted by Marceau ('Conflicts of Norms' 1105).

Article 8 of the DSU, the qualifications of panellists are set out as follows:

> 1. Panels shall be composed of well-qualified governmental and/or non-governmental individuals, including persons who have served on or presented a case to a panel, served as a representative of a Member or of a contracting party to GATT 1947 or as a representative to the Council or Committee of any covered agreement or its predecessor agreement, or in the Secretariat, taught or published on international trade law or policy, or served as a senior trade policy official of a Member.
> 2. Panel members should be selected with a view to ensuring the independence of the members, a sufficiently diverse background and a wide spectrum of experience.

In relation to the AB, under Article 17 of the DSU:

> 3. The Appellate Body shall comprise persons of recognized authority, with demonstrated expertise in law, international trade and the subject matter of the covered agreements generally. They shall be unaffiliated with any government. The Appellate Body membership shall be broadly representative of membership in the WTO.

It will be noted that with respect to both panellists and AB judges, the criteria are not *stricto sensu* based on legal qualifications. Panellists can include a pool of diplomats not necessarily qualified in law. Similarly, for AB judges, it appears that the requirement can be qualifications in international trade, not necessarily legal qualifications. Furthermore, a merit-based system is tempered by the requirement that the AB should broadly reflect the membership of the WTO. In the same vein, although not stated explicitly, the qualifications and background of the lawyers in the Legal Department of the WTO and the AB are significant. These lawyers have an input into the legal advice and drafting of the judgments and into the manner of interpretation of the WTO Agreements. How this background actually affects interpretative decisions, if at all, is difficult to assess.

However, this much can be observed. The very process of interpretation in a judicial framework is inherently an engagement, a discourse, a response involving the processing and evaluation of the interplay between a complex set of norms and an equally complex set of facts. This is an organic process and not a mechanical application of or response to a series of norms and facts. The guidelines for interpretation in the VC are only disciplines for a trained response; they cannot embrace completely the multitude of processes involved in the shaping of an interpretation. Furthermore, interpretation is an engagement with justice and an according of justice. Conceptions of justice, therefore, have a bearing on the interpretative process. Interpreting in external concerns needs to strike a chord with this very human reality, the backdrop against which the interpretative process takes place.

6.2.3 *The nature of trade, goods and services*

Interpreting in external concerns is also informed by the very nature of trade and the goods and services being traded. The inherent characteristics of trade, of goods and of services act as cues or receptors for non-trade concerns. This is in addition to the exceptions, preambles and development-related provisions in the WTO Agreements.

It is received wisdom that trade is not a value in itself. For example, Pauwelyn observes:

> unlike, for example, the prohibition of genocide or the protection of human rights or the environment, trade and the liberalisation of trade is not a value. . . . Trade is not a value, it is only an instrument. It is an instrument to increase the economic welfare of all states.[16]

This is profoundly true in that trade is a facilitator and there may be valid reasons for not making a fetish out of it. However, there is an inherent aspect to trade that does have a value. International trade is an engagement between two peoples. It is an accord that partakes of good relations between two peoples. It does not merely facilitate good relations (which it does) but is also inherently an act of good relations. This is why before trading, people ask whether they should trade with an enemy or a mass murderer. In the same vein, trading in itself has economic value beyond mere facilitation of increased wealth. This is why trade can take place without any immediate profit maximisation and can continue despite indifference to it. Was this not the sentiment that the AB itself was echoing when it accepted the potential trading interest of a non-banana-producer in recognising its standing to bring a dispute in the WTO?[17] Is the WTO not the custodian of the very act of trading? One of the functions of the WTO is to further the objectives of the Marrakesh Agreement and the Multilateral Trading

[16] Pauwelyn *Conflict of Norms* 316. [17] EC–Bananas (AB).

Agreements.[18] This objective cannot be achieved without recognition of the fundamental value of the very act of trading. In short, a necessary prelude to trading is the very act of trading. The WTO does not focus only on how trade takes place; it is also very much the custodian of the conditions under which trade takes place. One aspect of this condition is the safeguarding of the act of trading, which derives its value from what it facilitates and also intrinsically – including from what it might lead to. Interpreting in external concerns is informed by this value of trade as much as anything else.

Similarly, goods and services can have an inherent quality that can raise a host of concerns. Some of these concerns are covered by the WTO Agreements and find expression, for instance, in the WTO exceptions. For example, international and national policy with respect to the proliferation of nuclear weapons is specifically covered in the WTO security exception provisions. Equally, there is something inherent in a nuclear weapon that itself calls out for concern with respect to trading in it. Other such goods and services are not covered explicitly, but concerns rest in and emanate from the domestic domain of a member that is not subject to WTO disciplines. These are nevertheless national responses to the inherent quality, value and character of such goods and services. It is therefore possible within the WTO disciplines to take into account in the manner of trading such goods and services, including intellectual property matters, domestic non-trade policies that take their cue from the very nature of these goods and services. The interpreters of the WTO disciplines would be under pressure to mirror and be informed by the inherent quality of such goods, services and intellectual property rights claims in their interpretation and application of the WTO disciplines. Indeed, the 'diplomatic' input into international trade adjudication may be said to bring to bear on international trade law precisely this dimension, which a strictly legal approach might overlook.

6.2.4 National policies as a basis for interpreting in external concerns

National policies may take their cue from or respond to the very nature of goods, services and claims to intellectual property rights. Equally, there may be other reasons for national policies. The parameters of these national policies are delineated in a number of ways. First, they

[18] Article III (I) of the Marrakesh Agreement.

rest in the scope for differential treatment that the national standard in the WTO Agreements tolerates between domestic and imported goods and services. The national standard embodies the domestic policies. This national differential standard hinges mainly on the determination of what constitutes a 'like' product or service, given that the national standard needs to be accorded to all 'like' products or services. A 'non- like' product or service is the basis for the non-application of the national policy or the application of a different policy. Thus, it has been recognised

> that the treatment of imported and domestic products as like products under Article III may have significant implications for the scope of obligations under the General Agreement and for the regulatory autonomy of contracting parties with respect to their internal tax laws and regulations: once products are designated as like products, a regulatory product differentiation, e.g., for standardization or environmental purposes, becomes inconsistent with Article III even if the regulation is not 'applied . . . so as afford protection to domestic production'. In the view of the Panel, therefore, it is imperative that the like product determination in the context of Article III be made in such a way that it not unnecessarily infringe upon the regulatory authority and domestic policy options of contracting parties. The Panel recalled its earlier statement that a like product determination under Article III does not prejudge like product determinations made under other Articles of the General Agreement or in other legislative contexts.[19]

This freedom to pursue domestic policy was further endorsed by the AB, again in the context of Article III of GATT 1994, when it observed:

> Members of the WTO are free to pursue their own domestic policy goals through internal taxation and regulation so long as they do not do so in a way that violates Article III or any of the other commitments they have made in the WTO Agreement.[20]

[19] US–Malt Beverages (GATT Panel) (1992) para 5.72.

[20] Japan–Taxes on Alcoholic Beverages (AB) 16. See also US–Auto Taxes (GATT) (1994): 'The US concern that a broad definition of "like product" could foreclose governments' autonomy to distinguish between products for purposes of achieving legitimate environmental, tax and standards objectives, was misplaced. The Japan–Taxes on Alcoholic Beverages Panel directly addressed this concern by emphasising that a finding of "like product" did not foreclose differences in taxation, as long as such differentiation (1) arose from objective product differences, and (2) reflected the application of a trade-neutral system of taxation applied equally to all like or directly competitive imported and domestic products.'

Second, the exhaustive or non-exhaustive nature of existing exceptions in the WTO has a bearing on the extent to which national policies can flourish independent of such exceptions. In this respect, the European Communities' argument on the nature of Article XX of GATT 1994, and the AB's response in the EC–Asbestos case, deserve to be set out extensively here. The European Communities pointed out:

> The Panel's approach misconstrues the relationship between Articles III:4 and XX of GATT 1994, requires the 'likeness' of two products to be determined solely on the basis of commercial factors and, in the view of the European Communities, entails a serious curtailment of national regulatory autonomy. If non-commercial considerations may only be considered at the Article XX stage of the analysis, then the list of policy purposes for which regulators may distinguish between products is unduly limited to the categories listed in Article XX.[21]

To this the AB responded:

> The scope and meaning of Article III: 4 should not be broadened or restricted beyond what is required by the normal customary international law rules of treaty interpretation, simply because Article XX (b) exists and may be available to justify measures inconsistent with Article III: 4. The fact that an interpretation of Article III: 4, under those rules, implies a less frequent recourse to Article XX (b) does not deprive the exception in Article XX (b) of effet utile.[22]

Third, there is a default setting within which national policies flourish. This is the domain wherein as long as no violations of WTO disciplines occur there is scope for national freedom. Thus, in US–Gasoline, the AB explained:

> WTO Members have a large measure of autonomy to determine their own policies on the environment (including its relationship with trade), their environmental objectives and the environmental legislation they enact and implement. So far as concerns the WTO, that autonomy is circumscribed only by the need to respect the requirements of the *General Agreement* and the other covered agreements.[23]

Similar pronouncements can be found in terms of other policies. For example, in relation to the use of subsidies to facilitate production of particular goods, it has been observed that a 'national policy of promoting the domestic production of certain goods could likewise be

[21] EC–Asbestos (AB) para 34. [22] Ibid para 115. [23] (AB) (1996) 30.

pursued in conformity with the General Agreement (e.g., by means of production subsidies) without discriminating or protective taxation of imported goods'.[24] In relation to GATS, it has been affirmed that there is a 'large degree of regulatory autonomy which WTO Members, individually and collectively, retain under the GATS . . . '.[25]

Finally, in relation to autonomy in the implementation of the WTO obligations, it has been observed:

> The obligation on Members to bring their laws into conformity with WTO obligations is a fundamental feature of the system and, despite the fact that it affects the internal legal system of a State, has to be applied rigorously. At the same time, enforcement of this obligation must be done in the least intrusive way possible. The Member concerned must be allowed maximum autonomy in ensuring such conformity and, if there is more than one lawful way to achieve this, should have the freedom to choose that way which suites it best.[26]

Thus, there is clear evidence of interpretative activity that has focused on the WTO disciplines in terms of their impact on national policies. The national domain is, indeed, recognised as a legitimate basis informing the interpretative process. It is a vehicle for interpreting external concerns into the international trading system. This interpreting in involves identifying the scope for national policies within the WTO disciplines and focusing on the interpretation of such opportunities.

6.3 Conclusion

The capacity of a legal system to import in external concerns, and thereby steer clear of trade fundamentalism, while also safeguarding the commitments of members, will always be under pressure. Interpretation narrowly and broadly defined has a built-in capacity for the reception of external concerns. At the same time, the very nature of trade, the subject matter of the WTO Agreements and the nature of the membership of the WTO all have a role in informing the interpretative process, and thus the text of the WTO Agreements.

[24] Japan–Taxes on Alcoholic Beverages (Panel) (1996).
[25] See Mexico–Telecommunications (Panel) (2004).
[26] US–Section 301 of the Trade Act (Panel) para 7.102.

7

Interpreting the agreements on trade remedies

7.1 Introduction

The authority and the scope of the ability of members of the WTO to impose anti-dumping, countervailing and safeguard measures (collectively referred to as trade remedies) is to be found in the different WTO multilateral agreements on trade in goods.[1] These agreements share some similarities in concepts, procedures and language, as well as economic and political underpinnings. At the same time, the theoretical, political and historical dissimilarities in the remedies have contributed to their being arranged in different agreements. As responses to 'unfair' international trade and 'exceptional emergency' situations, the remedies essentially rely on national trade restrictive measures. These national measures are sometimes to be found in one domestic piece of legislation, while drawing upon the same national administrative apparatus. Trade remedies thus constitute a discrete branch of international trade regulation, with allied interpretative issues and concerns.

A focus on interpretative issues surrounding trade remedies is important for three main reasons. First and foremost, from an external perspective the trade remedies are set against the general liberal trade ethos in the WTO. They focus attention, therefore, on the interpretative tensions between that ethos and what is enshrined in the agreements by way of authority for the use of trade restrictions in prescribed circumstances. Second, as they are national defensive, as well as potentially offensive, measures, the manner in which these remedies are allowed to operate is of particular interest to national authorities and the membership of the WTO as a whole. Third, the agreements on remedies have generated considerable WTO jurisprudence and are likely to continue to do so. They are at the forefront of some of the WTO

[1] i.e., the Agreement on Implementation of Article VI of the General Agreement on Tariffs and Trade 1994 (ADA); the Agreement on Subsidies and Countervailing Measures (ASCM); and the Agreement on Safeguards (SA).

Agreements of particular concern to domestic importers, exporters, industries and consumers. The manner in which these agreements are translated in practice is therefore of considerable importance to non-state entities.

Generally in the context of WTO dispute settlement, the agreements are to be interpreted in accordance with 'customary rules of interpretation of pubic international law'.[2] In the case of the ADA, this is specifically reiterated in the agreement.[3] On the other hand, national trade remedies legislation giving effect to the WTO Agreements operates in a domestic legal setting – along with the initiation, investigation and determination of injury to the domestic industry and the authorisation for the use of trade restrictive retaliation. Thus, the first decision-makers involved in the application and interpretation of the WTO Agreements in question are national operators. They engage in the interpretation of domestic trade remedies rules, in accordance with relevant domestic principles and procedures of interpretation.[4] The relevant domestic rules of interpretation may be established to give effect to WTO obligations, but whatever the domestic procedures and rules of interpretation, as a matter of international law and WTO law the WTO obligations prevail.

In the circumstances, a number of questions arise that are specific to the interpretation of trade remedies agreements and their implementing national legislation. For example, are the objects and purposes of the international trade remedies norms transparent, and if not, how can they be discerned? What is the locus of trade remedies norms in the overall WTO trading system? What is the standard of review in the WTO dispute settlement system with respect to the examination of the national application of trade remedies norms? What are the influences that engage the interpreters of these norms at the national level? What are the sources and aids to interpretation of the trade remedies agreements? What lessons from the WTO jurisprudence can be learnt from the perspective of understanding the interpretative processes involved? These are among the principal queries that trade remedies give rise to and are the subject of focus here.

[2] See Article 3 (2) of the DSU. [3] See Article 17 (6) (ii) of the ADA.

[4] For example in accordance with Article 43 of the Chinese Provisional Rules of Ministry of Trade and Economic Cooperation on Initiation of Antidumping Investigations, it is MOFTEC that is responsible for the interpretation of the rules.

7.2 Discerning the objects and purposes of the trade remedies agreements

The objects and purposes of the WTO trade remedies agreements are not transparently set out. Although the Agreement on Safeguards (SA) has a preamble, the ADA and the ASCM do not. Therefore, their objects and purposes are not readily discernible. In the circumstances, what should guide relevant decision-makers when applying these agreements? Can and do these agreements operate merely technically, in an objects and purposes vacuum? Can any guiding principles be fathomed from the historical antecedents of the agreements or the practice in the dispute settlement system? Is it appropriate for adjudicators to discern the principles that underpin the agreements? Given that the objects and purposes of an agreement serve to inform the interpretation of its text, the questions raised by their apparent absence underline the difficulties posed in the interpretative processes, highlight second-best solutions in their location and raise the spectre of conflation between the functions of the WTO judicial and legislative organs.

It is the case, however, that the trade remedies agreements were not established merely as technical norms, and they cannot operate without some semblance of objects and purposes informing the provisions. It is not possible for international agreements to be established and to operate in an objects and purposes vacuum. The political expediency or lapse that displaced the articulation of the objects and purposes at the time of the negotiations of the agreements during the Uruguay Round could not have displaced the objects and purposes of these agreements as such. It might, however, have had an impact on their subsequent character – their discernment being more of a hostage to the perceptions of relevant interpreters. For this reason, some commentators have called for the United States to work towards the articulation of the object and purposes in the Doha Round.[5] However, since the trade remedies agreements (in particular the ASCM and the ADA) are integral parts of the WTO Single Undertaking, these agreements are informed inter alia by the Preamble of the Marrakech Agreement – including GATT 1994.

The importance of the objects and purposes of an agreement generally to the process of interpretation are evident. However, when the agreements are very technical, it is all the more important to have an

[5] R.O. Cunningham and T.H. Cribb 'Dispute Settlement through the Lens of "Free Flow of Trade": A Review of WTO Dispute Settlement of US Anti-Dumping and Countervailing Duty Measures' (2003) 6(1) *JIEL* 155–70, 169.

overall perspective, which may all too easily be lost in the minutiae of the procedural details. H. Horn and P. C. Mavroidis provide an interesting illustration of the nuances that can emerge from differing perspectives in the context of the SA:

> The appropriate interpretation of the term 'serious injury' depends on the objectives of the Member governments. A government that is only concerned with aggregate social welfare might care about aggregate adjustment costs caused by too rapid adjustment to external shocks, and use these costs to measure injury. A government that is more concerned with the situation of particular politically influential groups might judge injury from reductions in the level of production in specific sectors, reduced profitability or financial viability of specific domestic industries, unemployment . . .[6]

7.2.1 The ADA

Both the Kennedy Round[7] and the Tokyo Round agreements[8] on the implementation of Article VI of GATT had preambles. However, these were not identical – the latter being more elaborate. The common premise in these agreements was the desire to interpret Article VI of

[6] H. Horn and P.C. Mavroidis 'US–Lamb United States–Safeguard Measures on Imports of Fresh, Chilled or Frozen Lamb Meat from New Zealand and Australia: What Should Be Required of a Safeguard Investigation?' (2003) 2(3) *World Trade Rev* 395–430, 411.

[7] The relevant parts of the Kennedy Round preamble read as follows: 'Recognizing that anti-dumping practices should not constitute an unjustifiable impediment to international trade and that anti-dumping duties may be applied against dumping only if such dumping causes or threatens material injury to an established industry or materially retards the establishment of an industry; Considering that it is desirable to provide for equitable and open procedures as the basis for a full examination of dumping cases; and Desiring to interpret the provisions of Article VI of the General Agreement and to elaborate rules for their application in order to provide greater uniformity and certainty in their implementation'. See BISD 15th Supplement (1968) 24.

[8] The Tokyo Round preamble read as follows: 'Recognizing that anti-dumping practices should not constitute an unjustifiable impediment to international trade and that anti-dumping duties may be applied against dumping only if such dumping causes or threatens material injury to an established industry or materially retards the establishment of an industry; Considering that it is desirable to provide for equitable and open procedures as the basis for a full examination of dumping cases; Taking into account the particular trade, development and financial needs of developing countries; Desiring to interpret the provisions of Article VI of the General Agreement on Tariffs and Trade . . . and to elaborate rules for their application in order to provide greater uniformity and certainty in their implementation; and Desiring to provide for the speedy, effective and equitable settlement of disputes arising under this Agreement'. See GATT *The Texts of the Tokyo Round Agreements* (1986) 127.

GATT 1947. In that framework, the common objectives and purposes as set out in the preambles essentially aimed at providing disciplines in the application of anti-dumping measures. These can be summarised as follows:

- anti-dumping duties to be applied only if there is an injury to the domestic industry;
- anti-dumping practices not to constitute an unjustifiable impediment to international trade;
- equitable, open and full examination of dumping cases;
- provision for uniformity and certainty.

The Tokyo Round Agreement added two more considerations:

- the trade, development and financial needs of developing countries;
- the speedy, effective and equitable settlement of disputes.

Both these additions informed the interpretation of the agreement in question. It is notable that the Uruguay Round ADA has no preamble.

The debate over the appropriate policies underlying an agreement on dumping stretches as far back as the negotiations involving the drafting of the original Article VI of GATT 1947 itself. Then, the debate was polarised with respect to the very fundamental questions of whether dumping itself should be condemned and the type and degree of response to dumping that should be permitted.[9] In the final analysis, dumping was condemned, but in prescribed circumstances, and the responses to such dumping were subject to certain disciplines.[10] Article VI of GATT 1947 is not itself immediately preceded by a formal preamble, although the first sentence of paragraph 1 is similar to a preamble, condemning dumping if it negatively affects the domestic industry. Indeed, this first sentence was formulated at the Havana Conference 'as a preamble to Article VI'.[11] The original draft Article VI of GATT 1947 was replaced by the corresponding Article 34 of the Havana Charter precisely because the text adopted contained 'a useful indication of the principle governing the operation of that article . . .'.[12] Thus, the recognition of the usefulness of the principle underlying the article in the operation of the provision dates back to the origins of Article VI of GATT 1947. In the Kennedy Round, as indeed in the

[9] See T.P. Stewart (ed) *The GATT Uruguay Round: A Negotiating History (1986–1992)* (Kluwer, Deventer 1993) 1406.

[10] Ibid. [11] GATT *Analytical Index* (6th edn GATT, Geneva 1994) 204. [12] Ibid 231.

Tokyo Round, with further fine-tuning, the need to focus on 'broad conceptual and philosophical aspects of anti-dumping' was accepted by the United States, the United Kingdom[13] and developing countries[14] – hence, it would seem, the preambles included in those agreements.

In the Uruguay Round, the quest to clarify further the objects and purposes of the anti-dumping code continued. Different opinions surfaced in a re-visitation of the debate over what the objects and purposes should be:[15]

- to combat injurious dumping;
- to combat injurious dumping where price discrimination caused an inefficient use of resources;[16]
- to combat only price discrimination that is not in accordance with customary business practice and commercial considerations;[17]
- to establish a principle of comparative advantage to restrain anti-dumping practices; to make the anti-dumping code an exception to Articles I–III of GATT;[18]
- to take into account wider public interest, namely, consumers and user industries; to perform a cost–benefit analysis of anti-dumping measures;[19]
- to take into account international public interest;[20]
- not to operate anti-dumping measures in a protectionist manner[21] or as an unjustifiable impediment to international trade;[22]
- to establish efficient and effective anti-dumping measures;[23]
- to ensure predictability in anti-dumping investigations.[24]

It is clear that perceptions as to the appropriate policy underpinnings of the anti-dumping code expressed during the Uruguay Round varied, leaving aside the abundance of external economic analysis for the rationale of an international anti-dumping code. The debate was

[13] Stewart *GATT Uruguay Round* 1421. [14] Ibid 1454.

[15] See for example 'Meeting of 18th May 1989' GATT document MTN.GNG/NG8/10 (June 1989); 'Principles and Purposes of Antidumping Provisions: Communication from the Delegation of Hong Kong' GATT document MTN.GNG/NG8/W/46 (3 July 1989); 'Proposed Elements for a Framework for Negotiations: Principles and Objectives for Anti-dumping Rules, Communication from the Delegation of Singapore' GATT document MTN.GNG/NG8/W55 (October 1989), cited in Stewart *GATT Uruguay Round* 1499, 1504.

[16] See Stewart *GATT Uruguay Round* 1500. [17] Hong Kong: ibid 1502 footnote 702.

[18] Hong Kong: ibid 1499. [19] Ibid 1501. [20] Singapore: ibid 1504.

[21] Singapore: ibid. [22] EC: GATT document MTN.GNG/NG8/15, 3 (March 1990).

[23] Ibid. [24] Ibid.

sufficiently heated to be characterised as polarised[25] between strengthening the mandate of members to respond to dumping and strengthening the disciplines within which that response needs to be exercised.[26] Underlying these two stand-points was the question whether anti-dumping measures are exceptions to the general principles of GATT 1994.

Despite the debate focusing on the objects and purposes of an anti-dumping code, and despite the precedents of preambles in the Kennedy Round and Tokyo Round codes, the Uruguay Round negotiations resulted in no clear, express articulation of the objects and purposes of such a code. Neither the Dunkel Draft nor the final agreement contained a preamble or any other clear elaboration of the underlying principles.[27] In the circumstances, what problems from the perspective of interpreting the ADA are raised by the negotiations and final result with respect to the objects and purposes of the ADA?

In the first instance, the full set of papers of the *travaux preparatoires* relating to the debate on the objects and purposes of the ADA in the Uruguay Round is not readily available. For example, the Chairman's paper dated 19 January 1990, in which the Chairman attempted to describe the basic issues of principle in the section titled 'Objectives and Principles of Rules on Anti-dumping Practices', is difficult to trace.[28] In the Chairman's opinion, the 'objectives and principles provided the parameters for the negotiations and would have to be constantly kept in mind during all phases of the negotiations on the specific issues listed in the latter part of the paper'.[29] Although one delegate understood the word 'parameters' not to reflect agreement on the policy underpinning the code,[30] the insights the Chairman's paper provided cannot be readily ascertained given the difficulty in accessing this document.

Second, what conclusions can be drawn from the absence of a preamble in the ADA? Does this omission render the Preamble to the Marrakesh Agreement more prominent and therefore colour the agreements more as being in the category of exceptions to the general WTO normative framework? If so, a restrictive approach to interpreting the agreement may be called for.[31] Does this absence reflect a resolution of the shades of opinion in the debate on the objects and principles

[25] See Stewart *GATT Uruguay Round* 1503 footnote 703. [26] Ibid 1536. [27] Ibid 1685.
[28] GATT document MTN.GNG/NG8/15, 4 (March 1990).
[29] Ibid 5; Stewart *GATT Uruguay Round*. [30] Stewart *GATT Uruguay Round*.
[31] See chapter 4.

during the negotiations? Does it reflect the fact that the school advancing the policy for introducing further disciplines in anti-dumping practices lost in the negotiations? Or is the omission neutral in terms of the policy underpinnings of the ADA considered during the negotiations? The last explanation seems most likely: the negotiators, having failed to arrive at a consensus, simply abandoned the task of clarifying the objects and purposes of the agreement, addressing their attention instead to the more operational provisions of the agreement.

This leaves open the separate question of the role of the preambles in the Tokyo Round and Kennedy Round anti-dumping codes in the interpretation of the Uruguay Round ADA. The codes in question bound only their signatories and had separate dispute settlement systems. Nevertheless, there are persuasive reasons that suggest those preambles may have a bearing on the existing Uruguay Round ADA. First and foremost, as all the ADAs to date are in fact implementing codes of Article VI of GATT 1947/1994, they must reflect to a degree the collective understanding of that provision. This understanding must include what is encapsulated in the respective preambles – particularly given that there is no subsequent clearly expressed contradiction of the continuance of this understanding. Indeed, as each code has been an implementing code, there would seem to be a presumption that the codes incrementally contribute to an understanding of Article VI of GATT 1994.

Second, preambles are introductory statements or explanations of the objects and purposes of a treaty. Their inclusion, although desirable, is not mandatory as a matter of treaty law. Furthermore, they are not exclusive in terms of the objects and purposes, which may be found elsewhere or be implicit in the provisions or agreements as a whole. Consequently, the omission of a preamble is at worst unhelpful, and its inclusion is simply an explanation or indication of the objects and purposes of what follows. On its own, a preamble is not norm generating. Therefore, the lack of a preamble in the current ADA is unfortunate but not conclusive. It does not displace the prior preambles helpfully included in the predecessor codes. Finally, the 'precedential' value of the preambles is also suggested by the injunction in the WTO for consistency with prior decisions and practices within the GATT,[32] including the accepted relevance of past GATT Panel decisions

[32] See Article XVI (1) of the Marrakesh Agreement.

involving the previous codes, set against the background of their preambles, to decision-making in the settlement of disputes.[33]

The historical antecedents of the objects and purposes of the ADA are thus not clearly traceable. Its Article 1 (titled 'Principles'), apart from essentially reinforcing the obligations contained within the agreement, is not very revealing. It does, however, refer to Article VI of GATT 1994. Under this article, the principle is set out under which dumping is condemned if it causes or threatens material injury to an established industry or materially retards the establishment of a domestic industry. Thus, the dumping that is relevant is dumping that has a negative effect on the domestic industry. The language or notion of 'unfairness' is absent from this causal relationship. By the same token, the rule of law is enunciated in the application of anti-dumping measures. A significant aspect of this rule of law is the notion of due process.

Preambles are also to be found in domestic legal systems. National legislation is often accompanied by a preamble – normally words indicating that the legislation is intended to give effect to the relevant WTO trade remedy agreement. However, the preamble may also contain additions, or what may be construed as glosses to the relevant WTO remedies agreement. For example, in the Preamble to the Pakistan Anti-Dumping Duties Ordinance 2000, it is stated that the 'imposition of anti-dumping duties to offset injurious dumping is in the public interest'. On the other hand, Article 9 (1) of the ADA states with respect to duties that it is 'desirable that the imposition be permissive in the territory of all Members, and that the duty be less than the margin if such lesser duty would be adequate to remove the injury to the domestic industry'. The gloss on the imposition of duties also assumes that it is, in fact, in the public interest and that lesser measures, for example price undertakings, are not in the same category. In other national implementing legislation, the objects and purposes of the legislation are couched in terms of unfair competition or market distortion. For example, in the Turkish legislation, the aim of the Statute is described as 'protecting a domestic industry against injury caused by unfair competition practices in imports namely, dumped or subsidised imports . . . '.[34] In Peru, the aim of the legislation is to 'prevent and remedy distortion of market competition caused by dumping and

[33] Argentina–Measures Affecting Imports of Footwear, Textiles, Apparel and Other Items (AB).

[34] Article 1.

subsidies'.[35] In Uruguay, the purpose of the legislation is to provide for 'an efficacious means of counteracting unfair trading practices involving the importation of dumped products which are causing or threatening injury to the domestic industry . . . '.[36] However, the WTO rules on dumping are not confined to dumping that is 'unfair'.[37] The preambles in the national legislation are, of course, of relevance in informing the interpretative outcomes at the domestic level; however, they are also of consequence in terms of the particular member's WTO obligations, where the preamble informs the legislative interpretation towards a departure from WTO obligations.

There has been little express elaboration by the AB, in its deliberations on the ADA, of the general objects and purposes that underpin much of the detail of the agreement. In a recent panel decision, however, the Panel seems to have missed the opportunity, taking a somewhat pessimistic view of the task.[38] This much may be gleaned – although it pertains mainly to the institutional and procedural aspects of anti-dumping investigation and determination. In principle, members are free to structure their anti-dumping systems as they choose, subject to the provisions of the ADA.[39] The ADA is underpinned by a 'framework

[35] Article 1 of the Supreme Decree 006–2003-PCM 'Regulations on Dumping and Subsidies', which replaces Supreme Decree 043–97-EF and amendments thereto.

[36] WTO G/ADP/N/1/URY/2 (5 December 1996).

[37] For example 'predatory dumping'.

[38] See US–'Zeroing' Dumping Margins (Panel) para 292: 'We note that Article 31 of the *Vienna Convention* provides that the object and purpose of a treaty must be taken into account in establishing the ordinary meaning of the terms used therein. Since Article 31 refers to "the object and purpose" of *the treaty* and not of its individual provisions, the argument of the European Communities regarding Article 9.3 might be better characterized as a further contextual argument rather than an argument relating to object and purpose. We further note that since the *AD Agreement* contains no discrete statement of objectives, one can only derive or deduce its objectives from the operational provisions of the Agreement. While it is perhaps possible at a very high level of generality to deduce from the operational provisions of the *AD Agreement* as a whole that for instance, one of the "objectives" of the *AD Agreement* is to provide a multilaterally agreed framework of rules governing actions against injurious dumping, claims of more specific objectives are difficult to discern with any facility or compelling force due to the lack of anything that could properly be described as constituting a clear statement of the objectives of the *AD Agreement*. In this regard, we note that the European Communities refers to "the object and purpose of the *AD Agreement* regarding the consistent application of basic economic concepts" in the measurement of international price discrimination between two markets. The precise meaning the European Communities ascribes to these concepts and the manner in which the European Communities derived them from the text of the *AD Agreement* are unclear.'

[39] US–Corrosion-Resistant Steel Sunset Review (AB) 158.

of procedural and due process obligations'.[40] Its provisions are informed by the principle of 'good faith'.[41] This principle imposes on the national investigating authorities a standard of reasonableness,[42] fundamental fairness and impartiality.[43] Indeed, implicit in the jurisprudence of the WTO is the construct of the 'reasonable competent authority', which must act in good faith, with regard to due process, fairness, reasonableness and balance between its own rights and the legitimate interests of the parties.[44] This standard of the reasonable competent authority is reinforced by the deferential standard of review set out in the ADA, which focuses on proper establishment and unbiased, objective evaluation of facts rather than the merits of the actual determinations.[45] Substantively, the AB has observed that 'the Anti-Dumping Agreement deals with counteracting injurious dumping and that an anti-dumping duty can be imposed and maintained only if dumping (as properly established) causes injury to the domestic industry'.[46]

On the other hand, a number of external observers have taken the view that whereas the words may not be found in the precedents outlining the objects and purposes of the ADA, in general the actions and deeds of the AB point towards an interpretation of the ADA through the lens of the free flow of trade.[47] This view is not universally shared, however,[48] which serves to highlight the dangers of construing objects and purposes from actions and deeds. Certainly, the customary rules of treaty interpretation do not invite scrutiny of deeds and actions in this sense to fathom the objects and purposes of an agreement.

7.2.2 The ASCM

The problems in discerning the objects and purposes of the ASCM mirror in important respects those in interpreting the ADA. The ASCM's predecessor under the Tokyo Round was titled 'Agreement on Interpretation and Application of Articles VI, XVI and XXIII of the

[40] Thailand–Antidumping Duties on Angles (AB) para 109.
[41] US–Anti-Dumping Measures on Certain Hot-Rolled Steel Products (AB) para 97.
[42] Ibid. [43] Ibid para 192. [44] Ibid para 81.
[45] See below and Article 17 (6) of the ADA.
[46] US–Anti-Dumping Measures on Oil Country Tubular Goods (OCTG) from Mexico para 117.
[47] See for example Cunningham and Cribb 'Dispute Settlement'.
[48] J.P. Durling 'Deference, but Only When Due: WTO Review of Anti-Dumping Measures' (2003) 6(1) *JIEL* 125–53.

General Agreement (hereinafter referred to as the Tokyo Round Subsidies Code). The agreement contained a preamble setting out a number of objectives and purposes:

- Subsidies should be recognized to constitute an important national policy instrument that also has the potential to harm trade and production.
- The emphasis of the agreement should be on the effects of subsidies in the context of the internal economic circumstances of the member as well as the state of international economic relations.
- The application of subsidies should not adversely affect the interests of members, nor should the imposition of countervailing measures unjustifiably impede international trade.
- Relief should be made available to adversely affected producers within an agreed international framework.
- The interests of developing countries should be taken into account.
- The provisions of Articles VI, XVI and XXIII should be interpreted so as to provide greater uniformity and certainty in their application.

The Uruguay Round ASCM does not have a preamble; however, the importance of clarifying the objectives of the proposed agreement and the underlying principles of Articles VI and XVI of GATT 1947 was generally accepted, and repeatedly stated, at the time.[49] Indeed, discussion on fundamental principles took place, and several shades of opinion on the underlying principles can be discerned. The views were set against the background of two schools of thought: on the one hand, the school led by the United States, which emphasised the need for stronger disciplines for subsidies on the basis that economic theory called for the elimination of market distortions caused by subsidies; on the other, the school that emphasised the function of subsidies as a tool for policy-makers in the national development process.[50] The views on the objects and purposes may be summarised as follows:[51]

- that there was a need to strengthen subsidies disciplines;
- that there was a need to strengthen disciplines in the use of countervailing measures so that their use does not become protectionist;

[49] See for example Stewart *GATT Uruguay Round* 846–8; GATT document MTN.GNG/NG10/7 (8 June 1988); GATT document MTN.GNG/NG10/W/9/Rev.3 (May 1988).

[50] See for example Stewart *GATT Uruguay Round* 844.

[51] See for example GATT document MTN.GNG/NG8/10/7 (23 June 89).

- that there was a need for further disciplines in both subsidies and countervailing measures;
- that there was a need to focus only on the adverse international effects of subsidies, regardless of the kind of subsidy (this is what Article XVI of GATT disciplines were intended to do);
- that there was a need to categorise subsidies into permitted and prohibited ones;
- that there was a need to manage subsidies multilaterally through Article XVI of GATT rather than unilaterally through Article VI of GATT;
- that the provision of countervailing measures under Article VI of GATT constituted an exception in GATT: the purpose of countervailing measures was not to offset comparative advantage; therefore, the requirement for their application was clearly set out – there had to be a subsidy that caused injury to the domestic industry;
- that there were linkages between Articles VI and XVI of GATT – between disciplines in the sphere of subsidies and the parameters for the application of countervailing measures; consequently, there was a need to ensure balance between the disciplines in both spheres;
- that there was a need for S&D for developing members;
- that there was a need for predictability for producers;
- that there was a need among procedures for dispute settlement and remedies.

Against this background, and in the absence of a preamble, the discernment and the inculcation of the objects and purposes in the process of interpretation of the ASCM posit a number of problems. First and foremost, the absence of a preamble is unfortunate. The single source of some limited assistance is the Punta del Este Ministerial Declaration, which in the relevant part read:

> Negotiations on subsidies and countervailing measures shall be based on a review of Articles VI and XVI and the MTN [Multilateral Trade Negotiations] agreement on subsidies and countervailing measures with the objective of improving GATT disciplines relating to all subsidies and countervailing measures that affect international trade. A negotiating group will be established to deal with these issues.

This is noteworthy in that it makes clear that the negotiations were based on Articles VI and XVI of GATT, as well as the Tokyo Round Subsidies Code, and that the focus of the negotiations is to be subsidies and countervailing measures that affect international trade.

Second, the arguments that tend towards the application of the Tokyo Round Subsidies Code Preamble, insofar as the ADA is concerned, are also relevant here. Those arguments are reinforced by the Punta del Este Declaration, which specifically refers to the MTN agreement on subsidies and countervailing measures.

Third, how do the differences in perceptions of the fundamental objectives affect the manner of interpreting the ASCM? In particular, given that the ASCM has essentially two tracks – focusing both on subsidies and on countervailing measures – how do the differences during the negotiations over the manner in which each should be accorded emphasis translate into the process of interpretation? Given the view taken by some that Article VI was an exception to GATT, should the interpretation of Part V influence the manner of its interpretation? If so, how is that approach affected by the fact that much of Part V of the ASCM is interpreted and applied in the first instance by national authorities?

Similar to the case of the ADA, national legislation implementing the ASCM can also have its own preambular gloss, with possible consequential orientation in terms of its application and interpretation. Thus, the Pakistan Countervailing Duties Ordinance 2000 states: 'And whereas the imposition of countervailing duties to offset injurious subsidization is in the public interest'. Similarly, the Philippines Republic Act No. 8751 states:

> An Act strengthening the mechanisms for the imposition of countervailing duties on imported subsidization products, commodities or articles of commerce in order to protect domestic industries from unfair trade competition . . .

Neither 'public interest' nor 'unfair trade competition' is an objective set out as such in the ASCM.

In the deliberations of the AB, references to and elucidation of the objects and purposes of the ASCM are more frequent than in the case of the ADA. For example, in Canada–Certain Measures Affecting the Automotive Industry, the AB chided the Panel for failing to 'examine other contextual elements for Article 3.1 [b], and to consider the object and purpose of the SCM Agreement'.[52] In the same case, the AB stated that 'a finding that Article 3.1[b] extends only to contingency "in law" upon the use of domestic over imported goods would be contrary to the object and purpose of the SCM Agreement because it would make

[52] Canada–Certain Measures Affecting the Automotive Industry (AB) para 138.

circumvention of obligations by Members too easy'.[53] In US–Carbon Steel the AB was more forthcoming:

> Looking beyond the immediate context of Article 21.3, we turn to the object and purpose of the *SCM Agreement*. We note, first, that the Agreement contains no preamble to guide us in the task of ascertaining its object and purpose. In *Brazil–Desiccated Coconut*, we observed that the '*SCM Agreement* contains a set of rights and obligations that go well beyond merely applying and interpreting Articles VI, XVI and XXIII of the GATT 1947.'[54] The *SCM Agreement* defines the concept of 'subsidy', as well as the conditions under which Members may not employ subsidies. It establishes remedies when Members employ prohibited subsidies, and sets out additional remedies available to Members whose trading interests are harmed by another Member's subsidization practices. Part V of the *SCM Agreement* deals with one such remedy, permitting Members to levy countervailing duties on imported products to offset the benefits of specific subsidies bestowed on the manufacture, production or export of those goods. However, Part V also conditions the right to apply such duties on the demonstrated existence of three substantive conditions (subsidization, injury, and a causal link between the two) and on compliance with its procedural and substantive rules, notably the requirement that the countervailing duty cannot exceed the amount of the subsidy. Taken as a whole, the main object and purpose of the *SCM Agreement* is to increase and improve GATT disciplines relating to the use of both subsidies and countervailing measures. (Footnote renumbered)[55]

In the same vein, in US–Softwood Lumber, the AB stated:

> Moreover, to accept Canada's interpretation of the term 'goods' would, in our view, undermine the object and purpose of the *SCM Agreement*, which is to strengthen and improve GATT disciplines relating to the use of both subsidies and countervailing measures, while, recognizing at the same time, the right of Members to impose such measures under certain conditions. It is in furtherance of this object and purpose that Article 1.1 (a) (1) (iii) recognizes that subsidies may be conferred, not only through monetary transfers, but also by the provision of non-monetary inputs. (Footnotes omitted)[56]

[53] Canada–Certain Measures Affecting the Automotive Industry (AB) para 138, para 66.
[54] 'Brazil–Desiccated Coconut (AB) 181.'
[55] US–Carbon Steel (AB) para 73.
[56] US–Final Countervailing Duty Determination with Respect to Certain Softwood Lumber from Canada (AB) para 64.

Thus, the jurisprudence of the WTO would suggest a measure of balancing between the disciplines in the two spheres of the ASCM and the rights of members.[57]

7.2.3 *The SA*

The SA is the first specific agreement on safeguard measures – the Tokyo Round having failed to bring any improvements to Article XIX of GATT.[58] The agreement does have a short preamble, which starts off by affirming the need to 'improve and strengthen the international trading system based on GATT 1994'. Safeguards need to be considered in this context. In that light, the SA is intended to clarify and reinforce the disciplines of GATT 1994, in particular its Article XIX. Furthermore, the need to ensure increased competition in international markets and the importance of structural adjustment in the event of increased imports are noted.

Of relevance also in discerning the objects and purposes of the SA is the Punta del Este Declaration. This called for efficiency, predictability, clarity, security and equity for both importing and exporting countries.[59] The declaration also called inter alia for objectivity, degressivity and a temporary time frame for safeguard measures.

The following observations can be made about the objectives as set out in the SA. First, the SA Preamble seems to be directed mainly at limiting the scope of the use of safeguard measures. Second, no clear, explicit explanation of the underlying rationale for the use of safeguard measures is given. Somewhat in contrast, certain instances of relevant implementing legislation are more transparent in terms of the reasons for the use of safeguard measures. Third, the Preamble does not reflect all the desiderata that the Ministerial Declaration launching the negotiations called for; for example, there is no mention of degressivity. By the same token, the Preamble is silent on the question of non-discrimination, a consideration over which there was some

[57] See also US–DRAMS CVD Investigation (AB) para 115: 'the object and purpose of the SCM Agreement . . . reflects a delicate balance between the Members that sought to impose more disciplines on the use of subsidies and those that sought to impose more disciplines on the application of countervailing measures. Indeed, the Appellate Body has said that the object and purpose of the SCM Agreement is "to strengthen and improve GATT disciplines relating to the use of both subsidies and countervailing measures, while recognising at the same time, the right of Members to impose such measures under certain conditions" ' (footnotes omitted).

[58] Stewart *GATT Uruguay Round* 1717–19. [59] Ibid 1753.

disagreement among members at the time of the negotiations.[60] However, the 'application of safeguards on a "most-favoured-nation" (MFN) basis, that is, without discriminating between supplying Members, is a major guiding principle of the SA, and indeed a fundamental achievement compared to Article XIX of the GATT'.[61]

At the national level, the objectives of safeguard measures legislation are variously stated. For example, in the Indonesian legislation, they are set out inter alia as follows:

> Considering:
>
> (a) that the implementation of commitment to liberalize trade under the Agreement Establishing the World Trade Organization through the reduction of tariffs and the abolition of non-tariff barriers may lead to a surge in the import of goods causing serious losses to the domestic industry;
> (b) that the serious losses and/or foreseeable serious losses as meant in letter (a) can be prevented through the National legislation on safeguard of the domestic industry, so that the industry suffering losses can be make lawful structural adjustments based on the Agreement on Safeguards as referred to in Law No. 7/1994 on the Ratification of the Agreement Establishing the World Trade Organization;
> (c) that based on the considerations in letter (a) and letter (b), it is deemed necessary to stipulate Presidential Decree on the Safeguard of the Domestic Industry Against a Surge in the Import of Goods.[62]

In the Philippines safeguards legislation, the objectives of the Act are stated as follows:

> Sec. 2. Declaration of Policy: The State shall promote the competitiveness of domestic industries and producers based on sound industrial and agricultural development policies, and the efficient use of human, natural and technical resources. In pursuit of this goal and in the public interest, the State shall provide safeguard measures to protect domestic industries and producers from increased imports which cause or threaten to cause serious injury to those domestic industries and producers.[63]

[60] Stewart *GATT Uruguay Round*, 1768–9.

[61] E. Montaguti *UNCTAD Course on Dispute Settlement Safeguard Measures* 3.8 (UNCTAD, Geneva 2003).

[62] The Safeguard of the Domestic Industry against a Surge in the Impact of Goods (Presidential Decree no. 84/2002 dated 16 December 2002).

[63] Act Protecting Local Industries by Providing Safeguard Measures to Be Undertaken in Response to Increased Imports and Providing Penalties for Violation Thereof (Republic Act no. 8800).

The Vietnam safeguards legislation states:

> In order to enhance the State management over the economy, create conditions for the Vietnamese economy to effectively integrate into the international economy, restrict unfavourable impacts causing serious harm to the domestic production due to abnormal increases in the import of goods into Vietnam.[64]

There are clear differences here in orientation between the different national preambles and the SA Preamble, as well as some differences in emphasis. Thus, the SA Preamble emphasises liberal trade in its reference to the general GATT 1994 framework, competition in international markets and the strengthening of the disciplines in Article XIX of GATT 1994. On the other hand, the national SA implementing legislation in the Philippines sets out to promote the competitiveness of domestic industry, and in the case of Vietnam the objective is to create conditions for the Vietnamese economy to participate effectively in the international market. In the case of Indonesia, structural adjustment is a purpose, whereas in the SA Preamble its importance is simply noted.

The Preamble of the SA has been drawn upon in the jurisprudence of the WTO.[65] Indeed, the objects and purposes of the SA have been further clarified through judicial pronouncement. Thus, a principal reason for the establishment of the SA has been described as the need for a safety valve 'for situations in which, following trade liberalization, imports increase so as to cause serious injury or threat thereof to a domestic industry', thereby giving members confidence to engage in further trade liberalisation.[66] Safeguard measures are thus intended to be emergency measures – in effect, extraordinary remedies to be used only on a temporary basis.[67] Furthermore, the formulation in the Preamble is understood to inform a restrictive approach to the interpretation of the SA, such that safeguard measures are available only in limited circumstances – more limited circumstances than for anti-dumping and countervailing measures.[68]

[64] Ordinance no. 42/2002/PL-UBTVQH10 on Safeguards in the Import of Foreign Goods into Vietnam.

[65] See for example WTO *Analytical Index* Agreement on Safeguards paras 1–2. See also Korea–Dairy Safeguard (AB) paras 88; Argentina–Footwear (AB) paras 94–5; US–Lamb Safeguards (AB) paras 7.76–7, 7.124.

[66] Argentina–Footwear (AB). [67] Ibid.

[68] Ibid; WTO *Analytical Index* Agreement on Safeguards Preamble paras 1–3; US–Lamb Safeguards (AB) para 124.

Thus, in Korea–Dairy Safeguard, the AB stated:

> The object and purpose of Article XIX is to allow a Member to re-adjust temporarily the balance in the level of concessions between that Member and other exporting Members when it is faced with 'unexpected' and, thus, 'unforeseen' circumstances which lead to a product 'being imported' in 'such increased quantities and under such conditions as to cause or threaten serious injury to domestic producers . . . of like or directly competitive products'. This allows an importing Member to give the domestic industry in question enough time to adjust to the new competitive conditions caused by the increased imports. We should not lose sight of the fact that taking safeguard action results in restrictions on imports arising from 'fair' trade. The application of a safeguard measure does not depend upon 'unfair' trade actions, as is the case with anti-dumping or countervailing measures.[69]

In US–Line Pipe, the AB set about extensively elucidating the objects and purposes of the SA.[70] It affirmed that safeguard measures are 'extraordinary remedies to be taken only in emergency' circumstances where there is an 'absence of any allegation of an unfair trade practice'.[71] The AB reiterated what it had said earlier in Argentina–Footwear (EC) – that the extraordinary nature of safeguard measures rested on the basis of the context and the objects and purposes of Article XIX of the GATT 1994 and of the SA. The AB explained that the emergency and extraordinary nature of the remedy was based on the text of Article XIX of GATT 1994 and Article 11.1 (a) of the SA, which contained references to 'emergency action', and the intentions of the drafters, as evidenced by the text of Article XIX of GATT 1994. The title of Article XIX was 'Emergency Action on Imports of Particular Products'. Furthermore, the safeguard was to be implemented only when the developments in imports were not foreseen or expected. In addition, the remedy was only temporary. In particular, the AB reiterated what it had said in Argentina–Footwear with respect to the objects and purposes of Article XIX [1] [a] and the SA:

> This reading of these phrases is also confirmed by the object and purpose of Article XIX of the GATT 1994. The object and purpose of Article XIX is, quite simply, to allow a Member to re-adjust temporarily the balance in the level of concessions between that Member and other exporting

[69] Korea–Dairy Safeguard (AB) para 87. [70] US–Line Pipe (AB) paras 80–4.
[71] Ibid para 80.

> Members when it is faced with 'unexpected' and, thus, 'unforeseen' circumstances which lead to the product 'being imported' in 'such increased quantities and under such conditions as to cause or threaten serious injury to domestic producers of like or directly competitive products'. In perceiving and applying this object and purpose to the interpretation of this provision of the *WTO Agreement*, it is essential to keep in mind that a safeguard action is a 'fair' trade remedy. The application of a safeguard measure does not depend upon 'unfair' trade actions, as is the case with anti-dumping or countervailing measures. Thus, the import restrictions that are imposed on products of exporting Members when a safeguard action is taken must be seen, as we have said, as extraordinary. And, when construing the prerequisites for taking such actions, their extraordinary nature must be taken into account.
>
> ... In furthering this statement of the object and purpose of the *Agreement on Safeguards*, it must always be remembered that safeguard measures result in the temporary suspension of concessions or withdrawal of obligations, such as those in Article II and Article XI of the GATT 1994, which are fundamental to the *WTO Agreement*. (Original emphasis, underlining added; footnotes omitted)[72]

The AB further stated:

> There is, therefore, a natural tension between, on the one hand, defining the appropriate and legitimate scope of the right to apply safeguard measures and, on the other hand, ensuring that safeguard measures are not applied against 'fair trade' beyond what is necessary to provide extraordinary and temporary relief. A WTO Member seeking to apply a safeguard measure will argue, correctly, that the *right* to apply such measures must be respected in order to maintain the *domestic* momentum and motivation for ongoing trade liberalization. In turn, a WTO Member whose trade is affected by a safeguard measure will argue, correctly, that the *application* of such measures must be limited in order to maintain the *multilateral* integrity of ongoing trade concessions. The balance struck by the WTO Members in reconciling this natural tension relating to safeguard measures is found in the provisions of the *Agreement on Safeguards*.[73]

It should be noted that the elaboration of the objects and purposes of the SA has indeed been almost without restraint. Furthermore, this elaboration is notable for its emphasis on its illiberal trade characteristics and its limited scope. As if this were not enough, the elaboration

[72] Ibid. [73] Ibid paras 83–4.

touches upon the significance of this gloss on the objects and purposes to the construction and interpretation of the SA. This is to be contrasted with the restraint in elaboration of the objects and purposes of the ADA.

Most academics take the view that safeguards are 'inefficient protectionism, generally discouraging the redeployment of resources from declining industries to competitive ones'.[74] However, safeguards can facilitate entry into trade liberalisation because they give political cover with respect to some of the burdens that ensue from liberalisation[75] and can serve to 'temporarily reduce the pace of adjustment in order to reduce adjustment costs' – although at the risk of abuse.[76]

7.3 Aids in the interpretative processes: lessons from the WTO trade remedies jurisprudence

The primary sources of law in trade remedies cases are the covered agreements, as interpreted in the WTO jurisprudence. The interpretation of the trade remedies agreements is firmly established within the framework of the customary rules of international law for the interpretation of treaties as set out in Articles 31–3 of the VC. In addition, of note in dispute settlement proceedings are the arguments of the parties in the proceedings,[77] academic writings[78] and the Panel's right to seek information under Article 13 of the DSU, in particular in the form of *amicus curiae* briefs.[79] Such briefs have been submitted in trade remedies cases.[80]

It is, however, always a quest for studies that focus on interpretative practices to examine which sources are in reality used in the interpretative processes – indeed, to consider the extent to which the various

[74] A.O. Sykes 'The Persistent Puzzles of Safeguards: Lessons from the Steel Dispute' (2004) 7(3) *JIEL* 523–64, 524.

[75] A.O. Sykes 'The Safeguards Mess: A Critique of WTO Jurisprudence' (2003) 2(3) *World Trade Rev* 261–95, 288.

[76] Horn and Mavroidis 'US–Lamb' 399. Contra Sykes 'Persistent Puzzles of Safeguards'; Sykes 'Safeguards Mess'.

[77] See M. Oesch *Standards of Review in WTO Dispute Settlement Resolution* (Oxford UP, Oxford 2003) 185.

[78] Ibid. See also Article 38 (1) (d) of the Statute of the International Court of Justice.

[79] Ibid.

[80] See for example US–Countervailing Duties on Certain Hot-Rolled Lead and Bismuth Carbon Steel Products (AB); *amicus curiae* briefs from the American Iron and Steel Institute and the Specialty Steel Industry of North America.

permitted aids within the context of the VC are actually resorted to. The aids to interpretation can be divided into the intrinsic and extrinsic techniques used in the interpretative process, that is, intrinsic to the trade remedies agreements and extrinsic to them.[81] This analytical framework is used loosely here to facilitate construction of the relevant WTO practice as an aid to elucidation alone.

7.3.1 Intrinsic techniques

Recourse to intrinsic techniques is far more evident. In this respect, foremost among these techniques are those used to interpret the text of the trade remedies agreements. First, in construing a treaty provision one is reminded that the process 'is rooted in the ordinary meaning of the terms used'.[82] That said, dictionary definitions are considered to be only starting-points and to have their limitations.[83] Furthermore, to determine the meaning of words, various dictionaries have been used, both American and British.[84] This prompts the question of which version of the English language is richer – American or British – and indeed of which should be given more weight. The question it seems has not arisen yet.

Second, words can also be rooted in municipal systems, in the sense of the manner in which the municipal law of a member characterises property or transactions. For example, what is encompassed by the notion of 'personal property'? The guidance provided here is that municipal law can be relevant in providing evidence of meaning but is not conclusive. This is because

> municipal laws – in particular those relating to property – vary amongst WTO Members. Clearly, it would be inappropriate to characterize, for purposes of applying any provisions of the WTO covered agreements,

[81] See Sinclair *Vienna Convention* 118; C. de Vissecher *Problemes d'interpretation judiciaire en droit international public* (Edité par A. pedone, Paris 1963).

[82] US–Final Countervailing Duty Determination with Respect to Certain Softwood Lumber from Canada (AB) para 58.

[83] Ibid.

[84] For example *Webster's Third New International Dictionary* (Encyclopaedia Britannica Inc, Chicago 1966); *Black's Law Dictionary* (6th edn West Publishing Company, St. Paul, MN, 1990); *The New Shorter Oxford English Dictionary* (Oxford UP, Oxford 1993); *Shorter Oxford English Dictionary* edited by W.R. Trumble and A. Stevenson (5th edn Oxford UP, Oxford 2002).

> the same thing or transaction differently, depending on its legal categorization within the jurisdictions of different Members.[85]

Third, as the trade remedies agreements are written not just in English but also in French and Spanish, the meaning of the words used in the Spanish and French texts is also relevant. Thus, in the US–Corrosion-Resistant Steel Sunset Review case, the AB confirmed its reading of Article 3 of the ADA with reference to the French and Spanish versions of Article 3 [1].[86] In particular, in the light of Article 33 (3) of the VC,

> the terms of a treaty authenticated in more than one language – like the *WTO Agreement* – are presumed to have the same meaning in each authentic text.[87] It follows that the treaty interpreter should seek the meaning that gives effect, simultaneously, to all the terms of the treaty, as they are used in each authentic language.[88] (Footnotes renumbered)[89]

Fourth, in addition to the overall objects and purposes of the agreement, the interpreter may well look at the particular object of the provision in question.[90]

Fifth, context can include the seeking of support in other provisions. For example, in Thailand–Antidumping Duties on Angles, the AB, in interpreting Article 3, sought contextual support for its reading in

[85] US–Final Countervailing Duty Determination with Respect to Certain Softwood Lumber from Canada (AB) para 56..

[86] US–Corrosion-Resistant Steel Sunset Review (AB) para 277.

[87] 'Article 33(3) of the Vienna Convention . . . provides: "(t)he terms of the treaty are presumed to have the same meaning in each authentic text." '

[88] 'See Appellate Body Report, EC–Bed Linen (Article 2.15–India), footnote 153 to para. 123. We also note that, in discussing the draft article that was later adopted as Article 33 (3) of the Vienna Convention, the International Law Commission observed that the "presumption (that the terms of a treaty are intended to have the same meaning in each authentic text) requires that every effort should be made to find a common meaning for the texts before preferring one to another". (Yearbook of the International Law Commission (1966), Vol. II, p. 225) With regard to the application of customary rules of interpretation in respect of treaties authenticated in more than one language, see also International Court of Justice, Merits, Case Concerning Elettronica Sicula S.p.A. (ELSI) (United States v. Italy) 1989, ICJ Reports, para. 132, where, in interpreting a provision of the Treaty of Friendship, Commerce and Navigation between the United States of America and the Italian Republic of 1948, the International Court of Justice noted that it was possible to interpret the English and Italian versions "as meaning much the same thing", despite a potential divergence in scope.'

[89] US–Final Countervailing Duty Determination with Respect to Certain Softwood Lumber from Canada (AB) para 58.

[90] See for example Brazil–Export Financing Programmes for Aircraft (AB) para 149, where the AB discusses the purposes of Articles 25 and 27 of the ASCM.

Articles 6 and 12 of the ADA. Indeed, even a footnote can represent context.[91] Furthermore, context can involve identifying and characterising a provision as an overarching provision, and thus as informing subsequent paragraphs.[92]

Sixth, to ascertain the intentions of the drafters, inferences about their intentions can be drawn from the provisions of the agreements alone, without necessarily resorting to the negotiating text.[93]

Seventh, the interpreter's capacity to discern, characterise and indeed construct a provision as an exception is evident in the AB deliberations. For example, in US–Corrosion-Resistant Steel Sunset Review, the AB characterised the continuation of an anti-dumping duty as an exception after five years.[94] Similarly in US–Carbon Steel, the AB held that the termination 'of a countervailing duty is the rule and its continuation is the exception'.[95] In passing, it may be added here that there is not much evidence of the characterisation of any of the trade remedies agreements as exceptions to the general liberal trade ethos.[96]

Eighth, generally words cannot be read into an agreement that are not there. This has been stated in the context of other WTO Agreements, as well as of the trade remedies agreements.[97] However, there are circumstances when this may well be possible. For example:

> when a provision refers, without qualification, to an action that a Member may take, this serves as an indication that no limitation is intended to be imposed on the manner or circumstances in which such action may be taken. However, because the task of interpreting a treaty provision does not end with a bare examination of its text, the absence of an express limitation on Members' ability to take a certain action is not dispositive of whether any such limitation exists. (Footnote omitted)[98]

In the same vein, with respect to the interpretation of omissions,[99] generally absence from the text suggests an absence of the obligation – for

[91] Ibid with respect to footnote 55 to Article 27.4 of the ASCM.

[92] For example Article 3 of the ADA in Thailand–Antidumping Duties on Angles (AB).

[93] See for example US–Corrosion-Resistant Steel Sunset Review (Panel) para 111.

[94] Ibid para 178. [95] US–Carbon Steel (AB) paras 86–90.

[96] On exceptions see chapter 4.

[97] US–Line Pipe (AB) para 250. See also India–Patent (AB).

[98] US–Carbon Steel (AB) para 104.

[99] See for example N.P. Meagher 'The Sound of Silence: Giving Meaning to Omissions in Provisions of World Trade Organization Agreements; A Note on the World Trade Organization Appellate Body Decision in United States–Countervailing Duties on Certain Corrosion-Resistant Carbon Steel Flat Products from Germany' (2003) 37(2) *JWT* 411–27.

example, the absence of an obligation on investigating authorities to calculate or rely on dumping margins in sunset reviews.[100] In particular, when there is an absence, omission or silence in one provision with respect to a certain matter and explicit reference in another or other provisions to that matter, the inference to be drawn is that the silence was intended by the negotiators.[101] However, this reading of the omission, and of the intentions of the drafters, does not necessarily mean that this would be the case under any circumstances.[102] Thus, in Canada–Certain Measures Affecting the Automotive Industry, the AB stated:

> In our view, the Panel's analysis was incomplete. As we have said, and as the Panel recalled, 'omission must have some meaning'. Yet omissions in different contexts may have different meanings, and omission, in and of itself, is not necessarily dispositive. Moreover, while the Panel rightly looked to Article 3.1(a) as relevant context in interpreting Article 3.1(b), the Panel failed to examine other contextual elements for Article 3.1(b) and to consider the object and purpose of the *SCM Agreement*. (Footnote omitted)[103]

In this case, the AB held that the 'fact that Article 3.1[a] refers to "in law or in fact", while those words are absent from Article 3.1[b], does not necessarily mean that Article 3.1[b] extends only to *de jure* contingency'.[104]

Similarly, in US–Carbon Steel, the AB stated:

> We have previously observed that the fact that a particular treaty provision is 'silent' on a specific issue 'must have some meaning'. In this case, the lack of any indication, in the text of Article 21.3, that a *de minimis* standard must be applied in sunset reviews serves, at least at first blush, as an indication that no such requirement exists. However, as the Panel itself observed, the task of ascertaining the meaning of a treaty provision with respect to a specific requirement does not end once it has been determined that the text is silent on that requirement.[105] Such silence does not exclude the possibility that the

[100] Para 123.

[101] See for example US–Final Dumping (AB) para 100; US–Corrosion-Resistant Steel Sunset Review (AB) para 152; EC–Malleable Cast Iron (AB) para 98.

[102] US–Final Dumping (AB) para 135.

[103] Canada–Certain Measures Affecting the Automotive Industry (AB) para 138.

[104] Para 141. [105] '(Panel) paras 8.27–30.'

> requirement was intended to be included by implication. (Some footnotes omitted)[106]

Finally, the ADA[107] and the ASCM[108] feature provisions that cross-reference each other. These have been noted. In US–Corrosion-Resistant Steel Sunset Review,[109] the AB saw significance in the fact that Article 3 was not cross-referenced in Article 11.3 of the ADA,[110] and therefore concluded that investigating authorities were not mandated to follow the conditions under Article 3 when considering a 'likelihood-of-injury' test.

Similarly, in US–Carbon Steel, the AB stated:

> We observe, in this regard, that the technique of cross-referencing is frequently used in the *SCM Agreement.* Article 21.4 refers to the obligations set forth in Article 12, and Article 21.5 subjects undertakings given in accordance with Article 18 to the review mechanisms contemplated in Article 21. Similarly, Article 22.7 of the *SCM Agreement* explicitly applies the provisions of Article 22, entitled '*Public Notice and Explanation of Determinations*', to reviews carried out under Article 21. Furthermore, Article 11.9 is specifically referred to in Article 15.3 of the *SCM Agreement,* and the provisions of Article 11, more generally, are referred to in a number of other provisions of the *SCM Agreement.*[111] These cross-references suggest to us that, when the negotiators of the *SCM Agreement* intended that the disciplines set forth in one provision be applied in another context, they did so expressly. In the light of the many express cross-references made in the *SCM Agreement,* we attach significance to the absence of any textual link between Article 21.3 reviews and the *de minimis* standard set forth in Article 11.9. (Footnote renumbered)[112]

[106] US–Carbon Steel (AB) para 65.
[107] US–Corrosion-Resistant Steel Sunset Review (AB) para 125.
[108] US–Carbon Steel (AB) para 69. [109] (AB) para 125. [110] Ibid.
[111] 'See for example Articles 12.13, 13.1, 17.1 and 22.1 of the SCM Agreement. Moreover, as the Panel noted (para 8.26 footnote 261): "(a) number of provisions in the SCM Agreement also apply independently of cross-references in that they contain explicit statements of their scope of application: definition of 'subsidy' in Article 1 ('For the purpose of this Agreement'); definition of 'interested parties' in Article 12.9 ('for the purposes of this Agreement'); calculation of the amount of a subsidy under Article 14 ('For the purpose of Part V'); definition of 'initiated' in footnote 37 ('as used hereinafter'); definition of 'injury' under Article 15 and in footnote 45 ('Under this Agreement'); definition of 'like product' in footnote 46 ('Throughout this Agreement'); definition of domestic industry in Article 16 ('For the purposes of this Agreement'); and definition of 'levy' in footnote 51 ('As used in this Agreement')." '
[112] (AB) para 69.

The AB continued:

> Given that the requirements of Articles 11 and 12 are placed consecutively in the Agreement, and the fact that both Articles expressly set out obligations in relation to *investigations*, we read the express reference in Article 21.4 to Article 12, but not to Article 11, as an indication that the drafters intended that the obligations in Article 12, but not those in Article 11, would apply to reviews carried out under Article 21.3.[113]

Similarly, in US–Corrosion-Resistant Steel Sunset Review,[114] the AB stated:

> The Panel observed that the technique of cross-referencing is frequently used in the *Anti-Dumping Agreement*. For example, Article 11.4 indicates that the 'provisions of Article 6 regarding evidence and procedure shall apply' to reviews under Article 11. Similarly, Article 11.5 applies the provisions of Article 11 to price undertakings accepted under Article 8. The Panel observed that, by contrast, Article 11 contains no cross-reference to Article 2,[115] which prescribes how to calculate a dumping margin. In this context, we agree with the Panel that the absence of a cross-reference in Article 11 to Article 2 may be of some significance. (Footnote renumbered)[116]

In the same vein, in US–Carbon Steel, the AB stated:

> Before leaving our analysis of the *text* of Article 21.3 of the *SCM Agreement*, we, lastly, note that the provision contains no explicit cross-reference to evidentiary rules relating to initiation, such as those contained in Article 11.6. We believe the absence of any such cross-reference to be of some consequence given that, as we have seen, the drafters of the *SCM Agreement* have made active use of cross-references, *inter alia*, to apply obligations relating to *investigations* to review proceedings. In our view, the omission of any express cross-reference thus serves as a further indication that the negotiators of the *SCM Agreement* did not intend the evidentiary standards applicable to the self-initiation of *investigations* under Article 11 to apply to the self-initiation of *reviews* under Article 21.3. (Footnote omitted)[117]

With respect to the *travaux preparatoires* of the trade remedies agreements, GATT Panel Reports and general principles from the trade remedies agreements that might inform the interpretative process, the following may be observed.

[113] Para 74. [114] AB. [115] '(Panel) para 7.166.' [116] (AB) para 123. [117] Paras 86–90.

First, the negotiating text of the trade remedies agreements has not been very frequently referred to, although it has been resorted to. Equally, the AB has been prepared to exclude it when it is not necessary in accordance with the VC. Thus, there is evidence of recourse to both the Havana Conference and the Uruguay Round. It has been observed that the Havana Conference of the International Trade Organization (ITO) Charter has played an important role in the interpretation of Article XIX.[118] It should be noted that Article XXIX of GATT 1994 makes reference to the Havana Conference. In particular, the changes made by way of an interpretative note[119] to Article 40 of the ITO – the corresponding escape clause in the ITO – have influenced the non-discriminatory application of Article XIX of GATT.[120] Although the binding character of the interpretative note has been challenged on the grounds that it was added to the charter after the signing of GATT,[121] the weight with which it informs the interpretative process must now be determined with reference to the weight of the subsequent practice in its application. Be that as it may, the negotiating history of Article XIX of GATT is well documented.[122] This type of documentation of the negotiating history of the text of the provisions of the trade remedies agreements is not, however, to be found throughout the provisions and agreements.

Furthermore, the approach of the AB to resort to the *travaux preparatoires* seems somewhat ambivalent, although it is generally in the context of Article 32 of the VC.[123] Thus, in US–Carbon Steel,[124] the AB observed with respect to the use by the Panel of a 1987 note prepared by the Secretariat for the Uruguay Round Negotiating Group on Subsidies and Countervailing Measures, (1) that its use of and reliance on this note was not explained by the Panel, that is, 'whether the Panel considered the Note to form part of the preparatory work of the treaty and intended to use it as a supplementary means of treaty interpretation within the meaning of Article 32 of the Vienna Convention'; (2) that the note was in any event equivocal; (3) that there was 'no evidence

[118] See Stewart *GATT Uruguay Round* 1720–1.

[119] Ibid. See also GATT Doc L/4679 (1978). [120] Stewart *GATT Uruguay Round* 1720.

[121] Ibid footnote 18. See M. Bronckers *Selective Safeguard Measures in Multilateral Trade Relations: Issues of Protectionism in GATT, European Community and United States Law* (Kluwer, Deventer and Boston 1985), cited in Stewart *The GATT Uruguay Round* 1720 footnote 17.

[122] For the negotiating history of Article XIX of the GATT 1994 and the SA see US–Line Pipe (AB) footnote 171.

[123] See also chapter 1. [124] (AB) para 77.

adduced before the Panel suggesting that the negotiators of the SCM Agreement considered [it]'; and (4) that the interpretation did 'not lead to irrational or absurd results'. Therefore, the AB concluded that it did not 'consider it strictly necessary to have recourse to supplementary means of interpretation identified in Article 32 of the Vienna Convention'.[125] However, having said that, the AB went on to state: 'In any event, we consider that recourse to the negotiating history of the SCM Agreement tends to confirm our view as to the meaning of Article 21.3.'

Second, with respect to GATT Panel Reports, the following is to be noted. In the framework of the SA, previous GATT Panel Reports also have a bearing on interpretation, even though the SA does not have a predecessor agreement.[126] Indeed, GATT Panel Reports relating to comparable provisions in the Tokyo Round Agreement on Interpretation and Application of Articles VI, XVI and XXII of the GATT have been relied upon.[127]

Finally to be noted are principles that are derivatives from the agreements – in particular, from the objects and purposes of the agreements – that colour in a general manner the interpretative process. Thus, in the Argentina–Footwear case, the AB underlined the fact that safeguard actions needed to be considered in the context of the notion of 'fair' and 'unfair' trade when it stated:

> it is essential to keep in mind that a safeguard action is a 'fair' trade remedy. The application of a safeguard measure does not depend upon 'unfair' trade actions, as is the case with anti-dumping or countervailing measures.[128]

This 'principle of fair trade' has affected the interpretation of the SA at least.

[125] GATT document MTN.GNG/NG10/W/4 (1987).

[126] See for example US–Lamb Safeguards (AB) paras 79–92.

[127] See US–Lamb Safeguards (AB) para 92, referring to Canada–Imposition of Countervailing Duties on Imports of Manufacturing Beef from the EEC. In the same case the AB referred (footnote 46) to various GATT Panel decisions in the context of interpreting 'domestic industry' in the SA. The GATT Panel reports noted to have been examined earlier by the Panel in US–Lamb Safeguards were US–Definition of Industry Concerning Wine and Grape Products, adopted 28 April 1992, BISD 39S/436; Canada–Imposition of Countervailing Duties on Imports of Manufacturing Beef from the EEC, 13 October 1987, unadopted, SCM/85; New Zealand–Imports of Electrical Transformers from Finland, adopted 18 July 1985, BISD 32S/55.

[128] (AB) paras 93–5. The reference to the notion of 'fair trade' is also endorsed in Korea–Dairy Safeguard (AB) paras 83–4.

7.3.2 Extrinsic techniques

The extrinsic techniques comprise general principles of interpretation, deliberations in respective WTO trade remedies committees, previous trade round agreements and international law.

First, the main principles that stand out are logic, good faith and effectiveness, and these are engaged with in the modus operandi of interpretation. With respect to the invocation of logic, for example, in Korea–Dairy Safeguard, the AB stated:

> the first clause describes certain *circumstances* which must be demonstrated as a matter of fact in order for a safeguard measure to be applied consistently with the provisions of Article XIX of the GATT 1994. In this sense, we believe that there is a logical connection between the circumstances described in the first clause – 'as a result of unforeseen developments and of the effect of the obligations incurred by a Member under this Agreement, including tariff concessions . . . ' – and the conditions set forth in the second clause of Article XIX:1(a) for the imposition of a safeguard measure.[129]

Similarly, in Canada–Measures Affecting the Export of Civilian Aircraft, the AB attributed logic to the members of the WTO when it observed:

> There is no logical reason why the members of the WTO would, in conceiving and concluding the SCM Agreement, have granted panels the authority to draw inferences in cases involving actionable subsidies that may be illegal if they have certain trade effects, but not in cases that involve prohibited export subsidies for which the adverse effects are presumed. To the contrary the appropriate inference is that the authority to draw adverse inferences from a Member's refusal to provide information belongs a fortiori also to panels examining claims of prohibited subsidies.[130]

In the same vein, there has been some ado about good faith in the interpretation of trade remedies agreements. Generally, the fact that good faith plays a role in the interpretation and implementation processes is clear,[131] and this has been affirmed in a number of trade

[129] (AB) para 85. See also US–Line Pipe (AB) para 169. The word 'logic' appears several times in approximately twenty-one AB deliberations involving trade remedies cases, including those cases where it appears in the pleadings of the parties. This figure comes from a count on the Worldtradelaw.net website, 27 January 2005.

[130] (AB) para 202. [131] See for example Articles 31 and 26 of the VC.

remedy cases.[132] The role of good faith is set not only in the context of the organs of the DSU[133] but also when the national authorities are involved in implementing the agreements, interpreting the agreements and resting their authority on 'permissible interpretations'.[134] Recent WTO decisions have provided insights into the function of good faith in the interpretative processes; equally, they have left some questions unanswered. Thus, in US–Offset Act, the United States claimed that there is

> no basis or justification in the WTO Agreement for a WTO dispute settlement panel to conclude that a Member has not acted in good faith or to enforce a principle of good faith as a substantive obligation agreed to by WTO Members.[135]

The AB responded by affirming the role of good faith in the interpretation and implementation processes of WTO agreements, in terms of its own jurisprudence and international law. However, it also concluded that clearly 'there is a basis for a dispute settlement panel to determine, in an appropriate case, whether a Member has not acted in good faith'. This raises the question of what constitutes an appropriate case. Was the AB asserting that a Panel may in any appropriate case determine whether a member has not acted in good faith. The AB must be taken to be referring here to appropriate cases in the context of interpretation or implementation or otherwise to agreed-upon good faith obligations by the membership. However, might there be a suggestion here of other appropriate cases, given that the statement stands on its own? In any event, insofar as appropriate cases are concerned with interpretation or implementation of existing WTO obligations, the AB clarified that a violation of a provision does not necessarily imply bad faith.[136] By a different Panel it has been stated that there cannot be bad faith when a measure has not been violated.[137] It appears, therefore, that good faith has been ascribed a role, but one that is of a limited character.

There remains the question whether good faith plays a role in the authorities' choice of permissible interpretations under the ADA.[138] Are permissible interpretations *a fortiori* in good faith? There will be

[132] See for example US–Offset Act (AB) para 296; US–Anti-Dumping Measures on Certain Hot-Rolled Steel Products (AB) para 101; and EC–Bed Linen Article 21.5 (Panel) .

[133] Article 31 of the VC. [134] See Article 17.6 (ii) of the ADA. [135] (AB) para 297.

[136] US–Offset Act (AB) para 298. [137] EC–Bed Linen Article 21.5 (Panel) para 6.91.

[138] See Article 17.6 (ii) of the ADA and below on standard of review.

interpretations in the penumbra where the permissible interpretations are determined by the good faith requirement.

Mention must also be made of the principle of effectiveness, namely, the duty to interpret all applicable provisions of a treaty to give meaning to all of them in a harmonious fashion.[139] This has been discussed elsewhere already in the context of the relationship of the trade remedies agreements to the remainder of the WTO Agreements.

Second, the ongoing deliberations within the respective WTO trade remedies committees are important. Thus, in the context of the SA, although the deliberations of the Committee on Safeguards with respect to notification requirements under Article 12 of the SA are not legally binding, they are nevertheless important.[140] By the same token, of import are the deliberations of the committee when it reviews the request of a member to suspend concessions or other equivalent obligations to determine whether they are 'substantially equivalent' to those suspended through the safeguard measure,[141] and also its deliberations when it observes whether procedural requirements have been complied with upon a request by a member.[142] It will be noted that notifications of laws and regulations under Article 12.6 of the SA are accompanied by questions and answers.[143]

The relationship between the deliberations of such committees and the dispute settlement process has been described as complex.[144] In principle, it has been observed that the deliberations of the committees, subject to the express provisions of the relevant agreements, cannot generally affect the jurisdiction of the Panels and the AB to adjudicate on the relevant issues *de novo*.[145] Furthermore, in theory the Panels, on the one hand, may 'exercise a certain deference towards findings and recommendations of special bodies'[146] and, on the other hand, have the option to consider the issues *de novo*.[147] The general consensus, however, seems to be against deference.[148] This would appear to relate to the question of justiciability or competence. Leaving such questions of jurisdiction aside, the AB has suggested that Panels 'should [take] into account the deliberations and

[139] Argentina–Safeguard Measures on Imports of Footwear (AB).

[140] See WTO *Analytical Index* on Article 12 of the Agreement on Safeguards para 200; Korea–Dairy Safeguard (Panel) paras 7.131–3.

[141] Article 13.1 (c) of the SA. [142] Article 13.1 (b) of the SA.

[143] See for example replies by Honduras to questions posed by the United States (WTO/SG/Q1/HND/3).

[144] Oesch *Standards of Review* 37. See also chapter 2 above.

[145] Oesch *Standards of Review* 38. See also Article 11 of the DSU.

[146] Oesch *Standards of Review* 38. [147] Ibid 39. [148] Ibid 40.

conclusions' of such bodies.[149] Having considered these deliberations, Panels may, however, reject them. When he concludes with respect to the practice in the WTO that 'Panels and the AB have been exercising the same policy of full *de novo* review towards special bodies' interpretative deliberations as they have been applying towards members' authorities', Mathias Oesch does not make clear whether he is asserting that there is no obligation to consider the deliberations.[150] If so, this would appear to go against the specific and clear statement by the AB: 'Moreover, we are convinced that, in considering the justification of balance-of-payments restrictions, panels should take into account the deliberations and conclusions of the BOP Committee . . . '.[151]

Third, the AB has relied on the relevant trade remedies Tokyo Round Agreements to show the difference and progress in thinking in the relevant trade remedies Uruguay Round Agreements.[152]

Finally, there is evidence of recourse to international law, in particular customary international law, in the context of trade remedies. Thus, in US–Line Pipe, the AB considered that the principle of proportionate counter-measures was relevant.[153] As trade remedies are essentially counter-measures, this principle would appear to be of relevance across the trade remedies agreements. In FSC, the AB referred to 'certain widely recognised principles of taxation', including principles of international taxation and the 'widely recognised principles which many States generally apply in the field of taxation'.[154] Reliance has also been placed on the jurisprudence of the ICJ and publicists, for example, in relation to the principle of effectiveness.[155]

7.3.3 Conclusion

There are interesting lessons for the interpreter of trade remedies agreements. These lessons are as much of general relevance as they are

[149] Standards of Review 176. See also India–Quantitative Restrictions on Imports of Agricultural, Textile and Industrial Products (AB) para 103.

[150] Oesch *Standards of Review* 177, relying on Turkey–Textile and Clothing Products (AB) and US–Shirts and Blouses (Panel).

[151] India–Quantitative Restrictions on Imports of Agricultural, Textile and Industrial Products (AB) para 103.

[152] See for example EC–Malleable Cast Iron (AB) para 99, a comparison between the Uruguay Round ADA and the Tokyo Round AD.

[153] Paras 257, 259.

[154] FSC Recourse to Article 21 (AB) para 142.

[155] See Korea–Dairy Safeguard (AB) paras 80, 81.

specific to the trade remedies agreements, and they arise both from the particularities of the trade remedies agreements and from their general character as international agreements. The number of cases involving the trade remedies agreements is such that they command attention for the lessons they have generated in the context of the interpretative process in general in the WTO.

7.4 Inter-relationships of the ADA, the ASCM and the SA

According to one observer, given the similarity and common methodology in the respective trade remedies, there has been a measure of 'osmosis between the various trade defence rules' from the dispute settlement interpretation under the WTO.[156] However, there are also fundamental dissimilarities among the trade remedies, stemming in particular from their nature: specifically, anti-dumping and countervailing measures are 'fair' responses to 'unfair' trade practices, unlike safeguard measures. Thus, the requirement of 'serious injury' to the domestic industry under the SA is higher than the 'material injury' standard in the ADA.[157] Furthermore, a strict textual approach to interpretation is discernible in the WTO dispute settlement practice of the SA that is not necessarily seen with the ASCM and the ADA. There arises at the outset, therefore, the question whether this osmosis among the trade remedies agreements of their respective interpretations is appropriate without further consideration. Should interpreters reflect before borrowing an interpretation from another trade remedies agreement or should they automatically borrow?

In addition to the similarities from the perspective of interpretation, there are other sound reasons for drawing from the different trade agreements. First, the WTO Agreements are all part of a Single Undertaking. Therefore, the trade remedies agreements can constitute the context for each of the agreements. Second, as a matter of treaty interpretation, where there are similarities in substance or process in different agreements, those different agreements become relevant. Indeed, where these similarities are accompanied by identity of language, there is a presumption that their meaning will be identical. Third, one Uruguay Round Ministerial Declaration is specifically

[156] See Montaguti *UNCTAD Course* 5.

[157] See US–What Glutton (AB) para 149; Montaguti *UNCTAD Course* 20.

relevant insofar as the ADA and Part V of the ASCM are concerned.[158] The declaration states:

> Ministers, *Recognise* with respect to dispute settlement pursuant to the Agreement on Implementation of Article VI of GATT 1994 or Part V of the Agreement on Subsidies and Countervailing Measures, the need for the consistent resolution of disputes arising from anti-dumping and countervailing duty measures.

Against this background, the very practice of the Panels and the AB is of great relevance. Thus, the jurisprudence of the WTO indicates that the AB has resorted to the three different trade remedies agreements when it has found similarities or identity of language. Thus, the AB has relied on its interpretation of the ADA in interpreting the SA. For example, in considering the non-attribution rule in Article 4.2 (b) of the SA, the AB referred to its interpretation of the similar language in Article 3.5 of the ADA in US–Line Pipe: 'Our statements in *US–Hot-Rolled Steel* on Article 3.5 of the *Anti-Dumping Agreement* likewise provide guidance in interpreting the similar language in Article 4.2(b) of the *Agreement on Safeguards*.'[159] With respect to the definition of domestic industry in the SA, previous cases involving the ASCM and the ADA (or their predecessors) have been considered.[160]

In US–Corrosion-Resistant Steel Sunset Review, in interpreting the ADA the AB referred to its interpretation of the ASCM:

> In considering the nature of a likelihood determination in a sunset review under Article 11.3, we recall our statement in *US–Carbon Steel*, in the context of the *SCM Agreement*, that:
>
> > ... original investigations and sunset reviews are distinct processes with different purposes. The nature of the determination to be made in a sunset review differs in certain essential respects from the nature of the determination to be made in an original investigation. (Footnote omitted)[161]

This observation applies also to original investigations and sunset reviews under the ADA.

[158] Declaration on Dispute Settlement Pursuant to the Agreement on Implementation of Article VI of the General Agreement on Tariffs and Trade 1994 or Part V of the Agreement on Subsidies and Countervailing Measures.

[159] Para 212.

[160] See for example GATT cases cited in US–Lamb Safeguards footnote 46, as listed in note 126 above.

[161] US–Corrosion-Resistant Steel Sunset Review (AB) para 106.

In US–Anti-Dumping Measures on Certain Hot-Rolled Steel Products, in interpreting the ADA the AB referred to its interpretation of the SA:

> We are fortified in our interpretation of Article 3.5 of the Anti-Dumping Agreement by the interpretation we gave to Article 4.2(b) of the Agreement on Safeguards. In two recent Reports, United States–Wheat Gluten Safeguard and United States–Lamb Safeguard, we examined the causation requirements of the Agreement on Safeguards and, in particular, the non-attribution language of Article 4.2(b) of that Agreement.... Although the text of the Agreement on Safeguards on causation is by no means identical to that of the Anti-Dumping Agreement, there are considerable similarities between the two Agreements as regards the non-attribution language. Under both Article 3.5 of the Anti-Dumping Agreement and Article 4.2(b) of the Agreement on Safeguards, any injury caused to the domestic industry, at the same time, by factors other than imports, must not be attributed to imports. Moreover, under both Agreements, the domestic authorities seek to ensure that a determination made concerning the injurious effects of imports relates, in fact, to those imports and not to other factors. In these circumstances, we agree with the Panel that adopted panel and AB reports relating to the non-attribution language in the Agreement on Safeguards can provide guidance in interpreting the non-attribution language in Article 3.5 of the Anti-Dumping Agreement. (Footnote omitted)[162]

In US–Offset Act, the AB considered identical provisions of the ADA and the ASCM:

> We observe that Article 18.1 of the Anti-Dumping Agreement is identical in language, terminology and structure to Article 32.1 of the SCM Agreement, except for the reference to dumping instead of subsidy. The Panel analyzed the terms 'specific' and 'against' in Article 18.1 in the same manner as it did with respect to their use in Article 32.1. We agree with the Panel's approach. We also note that the United States does not challenge such approach and that, at the oral hearing, none of the appellees or third participants expressed the view that the terms, as used in Article 18.1 should have a different meaning as used in Article 32.1.... Given that Article 18.1 of the Anti-Dumping Agreement and 32.1 of the SCM Agreement are identical except for the reference in the former to dumping, and in the latter to a subsidy, we are of the view that this finding is pertinent for both provisions.[163]

[162] (AB) para 229. See also EC–Bed Linen (AB) para 159.

[163] (AB) paras 237–8. See also US–Cotton Subsidies (AB) para 438, wherein the AB in interpreting the SCM referred to the injury provisions in the SA and ADA.

Two points need to be made here. First, in following this identity of interpretation, the AB was not taking its cue from the Ministerial Declaration on Dispute Settlement,[164] as Article 32.1 of the ASCM is a provision of Part XI of that agreement rather than of Part V. Second, the AB did not decide merely on the basis of the identity of wording, but actually considered the respective objects and purposes of the two agreements in question. Thus, the AB stated:

> 252 Turning to considerations of object and purpose, we do not consider that the object and purpose of the Anti-Dumping Agreement and of the SCM Agreement, as reflected in Article 18.1 of the Anti-Dumping Agreement and in Article 32.1 of the SCM Agreement, support the incorporation into these provisions, through the term 'against', of a requirement that the measure must come into direct contact with the imported good, or the entity responsible for it. Both provisions fulfil a function of limiting the range of actions that a Member may take unilaterally to counter dumping or subsidization. Excluding from Article 18.1 of the Anti-Dumping Agreement and Article 32.1 of the SCM Agreement actions that do not come into direct contact with the imported good or the entity responsible for the dumped or subsidized good, would undermine that function. (Footnote omitted)[165]

There is further evidence that the AB's approach in taking its cue from interpretations in other trade remedies agreements or from similarities in the agreements is not automatic but considered. In particular, the AB has preserved its freedom in the manner of its interpretation of the ADA and the ASCM. This is discernible from its interpretation of the Ministerial Declaration on Dispute Settlement[166] in US–Countervailing Duties on Certain Hot-Rolled Lead and Bismuth Carbon Steel Products.[167] In that case, the AB interpreted the declaration narrowly:

> By its own terms, the Declaration does not impose an obligation to apply the standard of review contained in Article 17.6 of the Anti-Dumping Agreement to disputes involving countervailing duty measures under Part V of the SCM Agreement. The Declaration is couched in hortatory language; it uses the words 'Ministers recognize'. Furthermore, the Declaration merely acknowledges 'the need for the consistent resolution

[164] Declaration on Dispute Settlement Pursuant to the Agreement on Implementation of Article VI of the General Agreement on Tariffs and Trade 1994 or Part V of the Agreement on Subsidies and Countervailing Measures.

[165] US–Offset Act (AB) para 252. [166] Ibid.

[167] US–Countervailing Duties on Certain Hot-Rolled Lead and Bismuth Carbon Steel Products (AB) para 47.

> of disputes arising from anti-dumping and countervailing duty measures.' It does not specify any specific action to be taken. In particular, it does not prescribe a standard of review to be applied.[168]

In conclusion, the AB's considered approach to the osmosis of interpretations among the trade remedies agreements is indeed sound. There is, however, some danger of intellectual lapses, not least because of the intellectual convenience. There is a need to be aware of the real differences among these agreements, the consequential differences in approaches to their interpretation and the fact that even where there is identity of words, the context and objects and purposes of the agreement might suggest a different construction.

7.5 Relationship of trade remedies agreements within the WTO Single Undertaking

The web of agreements within which the trade remedies agreements sit includes principally GATT 1994, the DSU and the Marrakesh Agreement. However, given that the WTO Agreements comprise a Single Undertaking, in theory at least the relationships between the trade remedies agreements and other agreements extend further. The trade remedies agreements are part of the family of multilateral agreements on trade in goods described in Annex 1A of the Marrakesh Agreement. Consequently, their relationship to the other agreements within this group is of particular note – especially the relationship to GATT 1994. This is because the trade remedies agreements have cross-references to provisions in GATT 1994 and/or are developments of provisions in GATT 1994.

Nevertheless, the nature of the relationships between the trade remedies agreements and the rest of the Single Undertaking, including GATT 1994, is not that simple. The AB has held that the relationship between GATT 1994 and other multilateral trade agreements on goods is a complex one that needs to be considered on a case-by-case basis.[169] In particular, the complexity arises, as has been pointed, out for the following reasons.[170] First, the circumstances of the Uruguay negotiations

[168] Ibid para 49.

[169] See Brazil–Desiccated Coconut (AB) para 14; US–FSC (AB) para 116. In the latter case the AB stated (para 116): 'In Brazil–Desiccated Coconut, we observed that the "relationship between the GATT 1994 and the other goods agreements in Annex 1A is complex and must be examined on a case-by-case basis".'

[170] Montaguti and Lugard 'The GATT 1994 and Other Annex 1A Agreements: Four Different Relationships?' (2000) 3(3) *JIEL* 473–84.

were such that the Single WTO package was established at the last minute. Second, many of the multilateral trade agreements derive from the side agreements resulting from previous trade rounds. Finally, the general rule with respect to the priority of successive treaties relating to the same subject matter in the case of conflict[171] does not apply because the WTO agreements comprise a Single Undertaking.[172]

All three trade remedies agreements have expressly defined relationships. Thus, the ADA is specifically titled 'Agreement on Implementation of Article VI of the General Agreement on Tariffs and Trade', and its Article 1 reinforces this relationship. Similarly, Part V of the ASCM with respect to countervailing measures refers to Article VI of GATT 1994, and the SA refers both in its Preamble and its Article 1 to Article XIX of GATT 1994. In addition to GATT 1994, there is also cross-referencing to the DSU, particularly in the context of the standard of review set out in Article 17 of the ADA.

Given the framework of the Single Undertaking, the precise nature of the relationships, whether expressly defined or not, is a matter of construction. The possible nature of these relationships has been characterised as one of 'conflict, express derogation, overlap and complementarity'.[173] These categories of relationship are not exhaustive, however. One particular relationship is of context and another is of complexion. Thus, in the US–Shrimp case, the AB took the view that GATT 1994 was informed by the Preamble of the Marrakesh Agreement. Here the relationship is not one of conflict, derogation, overlap or complementarity – nor indeed of context as such – but rather one of influence or complexion. In the same vein, one might add to the categories of relationships a relationship that supplements, clarifies[174] and elaborates.

In the construction of this relationship are a number of guide-posts to assist in interpretation. First, with respect to GATT 1994 and the multilateral trade agreements, the General Interpretative Note to Annex 1A of the Marrakesh Agreement provides direction in the event of conflict:

> In the event of conflict between a provision of the General Agreement on Tariffs and Trade 1994 and a provision of another agreement in Annex 1A to the Agreement Establishing the World Trade Organization . . . , the provision of the other agreement shall prevail to the extent of conflict.

[171] See Article 30 (3) of the VC. [172] Article II (2) of the Marrakesh Agreement.
[173] Montaguti and Lugard 'The GATT 1994 and Other Annex 1A Agreements'.
[174] See for example US–Anti-Dumping Act of 1916 (AB) para 114.

Thus, there has to be conflict between the provision of GATT 1994 and the provision of the trade remedies agreements for the provision of the other agreement to prevail, but only to the extent of the conflict.[175] The integrity of GATT 1994 is thus preserved to the extent of a conflict.

A somewhat similar interpretative rule is to be found in Article 1.2 of the DSU:

> The rules and procedures of this Understanding shall apply subject to such special or additional rules and procedures on dispute settlement contained in the covered agreements as are identified in Appendix 2 to this Understanding. To the extent that there is a difference between the rules and procedures of this Understanding and the special or additional rules and procedures set forth in Appendix 2, the special or additional rules and procedures in Appendix 2 shall prevail.

This has been interpreted by the AB as follows:

> In our view, it is only where the provisions of the DSU and the special or additional rules and procedures of a covered agreement cannot be read as complementing each other that the special or additional provisions are to prevail. A special or additional provision should only be found to prevail over a provision of the DSU in a situation where adherence to the one provision will lead to a violation of the other provision, that is, in the case of a conflict between them.[176]

Here 'difference' has been interpreted as 'conflict'. The DSU criterion has been interpreted strictly to preserve the integrity of the DSU as far as possible. The reason for this was given in the context of the place of the special provision in the overall scheme of the DSU:

> We see the special or additional rules and procedures of a particular covered agreement as fitting together with the generally applicable rules and procedures of the DSU to form a comprehensive, integrated dispute settlement system for the WTO Agreement. The special or additional provisions listed in Appendix 2 of the DSU are designed to deal with the particularities of dispute settlement relating to obligations arising under a specific covered agreement, while Article 1 of the DSU seeks to establish an integrated and comprehensive dispute settlement system for all of the covered agreements of the WTO Agreement as a whole. It is, therefore, only in the specific circumstance where a provision of the DSU and a

[175] See for example Brazil–Desiccated Coconut (AB).

[176] Guatemala–Anti-Dumping Investigation Regarding Portland Cement from Mexico (AB) para 65. See also para 77.

special or additional provision of another covered agreement are mutually inconsistent that the special or additional provision may be read to prevail over the provision of the DSU.

The second interpretative guide in the characterisation of the relationships is the general interpretative principle of effectiveness. In the absence of a conflict, this rule applies. It has been applied by the AB variously, and was explained as follows in Argentina–Safeguard Measures on Imports of Footwear:

> Yet a treaty interpreter must read all applicable provisions of a treaty in a way that gives meaning to *all* of them, harmoniously. And, an appropriate reading of this 'inseparable package of rights and disciplines' must, accordingly, be one that gives meaning to *all* the relevant provisions of these two equally binding agreements. (Footnotes omitted)[177]

The AB went on to state:

> We believe that, with this conclusion, the Panel failed to give meaning and legal effect to all the relevant terms of the WTO Agreement, contrary to the principle of effectiveness (ut res magis valeat quam pereat) in the interpretation of treaties. The Panel states that the 'express omission of the criterion of unforeseen developments' in Article XIX:1(a) from the Agreement on Safeguards 'must, in our view, have meaning.' On the contrary, in our view, if they had intended to expressly omit this clause, the Uruguay Round negotiators would and could have said so in the Agreement on Safeguards. They did not. (Footnotes omitted)[178]

Similarly, in Korea–Dairy Safeguard, the AB elaborated extensively the principle of effectiveness:

> In light of the interpretive principle of effectiveness, it is the *duty* of any treaty interpreter to 'read all applicable provisions of a treaty in a way that gives meaning to *all* of them, harmoniously.' An important corollary of this principle is that a treaty should be interpreted as a whole, and, in particular, its sections and parts should be read as a whole. Article II:2 of the *WTO Agreement* expressly manifests the intention of the Uruguay Round negotiators that the provisions of the *WTO Agreement* and the Multilateral Trade Agreements included in its Annexes 1, 2 and 3 must be read as a whole. (Footnotes omitted)[179]

[177] AB. [178] (AB) para 88.

[179] Korea–Dairy Safeguard (AB) paras 80, 81. The AB (footnote 44) in that case cited various authorities for the principle of effectiveness as follows: 'The duty to interpret a treaty as a whole has been clarified by the Permanent Court of International Justice in

In conjunction with the tie-breaker rules expressly set out and the principle of effectiveness, the relationship among the different agreements has been determined through the normal general principles of treaty interpretation. Thus, the AB has based its decisions on a textual analysis of the provisions – for example, on an analysis of Articles 1 and 2 of the SA, which refer to Article XIX of GATT[180] – and on the basis of the intentions of the negotiators.[181]

A number of specific points with respect to the relationships between the trade agreements and GATT 1994 need to be highlighted. First, GATT Article XIX has been interpreted to apply cumulatively along with the SA.[182] The AB has said that the 'two texts must be read "harmoniously", and as "an inseparable package of rights and disciplines" '.[183] This interpretation has been severely criticised by one eminent commentator. Thus, Alan Sykes observes:

> One can certainly quarrel with the legal soundness of these decisions. Given the uniform practice of ignoring Article XIX [1], first clause, during the latter years of GATT, and its omission from the Safeguards Agreement, one can certainly doubt that the drafters of the Uruguay Round Agreements had any intention of reviving the obligation – had

Competence of the I.L.O. to Regulate Agricultural Labour (1922), PCIJ, Series B, Nos. 2 and 3, p. 23. This approach has been followed by the International Court of Justice in Ambatielos Case (1953) ICJ Reports, p. 10; Reservations to the Convention on the Prevention and Punishment of the Crime of Genocide (1951) ICJ Reports, p. 15; and Case Concerning Rights of United States Nationals in Morocco (1952) ICJ Reports, pp. 196–199. See also I. Brownlie, Principles of Public International Law, 5th ed. (Clarendon Press, 1998), p. 634; G. Fitzmaurice, "The Law and Procedure of the International Court of Justice 1951–1954: Treaty Interpretation and Other Treaty Points", 33 British Yearbook of International Law (1957), p. 211 at p. 220; A. McNair, The Law of Treaties (Clarendon Press, 1961), pp. 381–382; I. Sinclair, The Vienna Convention on the Law of Treaties (Manchester University Press, 1984), pp. 127–129; M.O. Hudson, La Cour Permanente de Justice Internationale (Editions A Pedone, 1936), pp. 654–659; and L.A. Podesta Costa and J.M. Ruda, Derecho Internacional Público, Vol. 2 (Tipográfica, 1985), p. 105.'

[180] Argentina–Safeguard Measures on Imports of Footwear (AB) para 82.

[181] Ibid para 95: 'Our reading, too, is consistent with the desire expressed by the Uruguay Round negotiators in the Preamble to the Agreement on Safeguards "to clarify and reinforce the disciplines of GATT 1994, and specifically those of its Article XIX . . . , to re-establish multilateral control over safeguards and eliminate measures that escape such control . . . '.

[182] See WTO *Analytical Index* Agreement on Safeguards Article 1 paras 4–5. See also Korea–Dairy Safeguard (AB) paras 76–7; Argentina–Footwear (EC) (AB) para 83.

[183] See US–Safeguard Measures on Imports of Fresh, Chilled or Frozen Lamb Meat from New Zealand and Australia (AB) para 69. See also Argentina–Footwear (AB) para 81; Korea–Dairy Safeguard (AB) para 75.

> they wished to alter established GATT practice in this respect, they would have so indicated with clarity.[184]

Elsewhere he states: 'I believe, GATT practice evolved over time towards ignoring the requirements of the first clause in Article XIX[1]. . . . National laws to authorize safeguard measures soon made no mention of them.'[185]

This critique is rather strange given the reference by the AB to the intentions of the drafters and the explanations given for the interpretative approach adopted. Furthermore, it should be noted that Sykes does not provide the evidence of national practice that he refers to, except for the United States – not to mention the fact that as a matter of international law such national practice, were it to be substantiated as being universal, would be relevant only if 'it establishe[d] the agreement of the parties regarding its interpretation'.[186]

Second, the question whether GATT exceptions such as Article XXIV of GATT 1994 'can justify violation under more specialised agreements on trade in goods, such as the Agreement on Safeguards', which has arisen in the context of safeguards, may also have relevance generally in relation to remedies.[187] Joost Pauwelyn takes the view that the exceptions indeed have relevance, although the answer remains somewhat uncertain:

> Since the Agreement on Safeguards is explicitly linked to, and stated as an elaboration of, GATT Article XIX, and the AB has confirmed that the field of safeguards is regulated in the Agreements on Safeguards and Article XIX, there can be no doubt that GATT Article XXIV remains relevant also.[188]

Third, with respect to the ADA, the tensions have essentially been between the DSU and Article 17 of the ADA. Here it can be argued that the AB has taken the opportunity to define the relationship in such a manner as to constrain the use of anti-dumping measures and reinforce the DSU over the weaker enforcement mechanisms in the ADA.

Finally, in relation to the ASCM, the AB has ruled:

> At the outset, we observe that provisions in both the GATT 1994 and the *SCM Agreement* are relevant to this dispute. We note the Appellate

[184] Sykes 'Safeguards Mess' 277. [185] Ibid 4. [186] Article 32 of the VC.

[187] Joost Pauwelyn 'The Puzzle of WTO Safeguards and Regional Trade Agreements' (2004) 7(1) *JIEL* 109–42.

[188] Ibid. 122–3.

> Body's earlier ruling that a provision of an agreement included in Annex 1A of the *WTO Agreement* (including the *SCM Agreement*), and a provision of the GATT 1994, that have identical coverage, both apply, but that the provision of the agreement that 'deals specifically, and in detail' with a question should be examined first.[189] The Appellate Body has also ruled that 'countervailing duties may only be imposed in accordance with the provisions of Part V of the *SCM Agreement* and Article VI of the GATT 1994, taken together',[190] and that '[i]f there is a conflict between the provisions of the *SCM Agreement* and Article VI of the GATT 1994 . . . the provisions of the *SCM Agreement* would prevail as a result of the general interpretative note to Annex 1A.'[191] No conflict between Articles 10 and 32.1 of the *SCM Agreement* on the one hand, and Article VI:3 of the GATT 1994 on the other hand, is alleged in this appeal, nor do we see any such conflict. Therefore, the requirements of these provisions of the *SCM Agreement* and the GATT 1994 apply on a cumulative basis. (Footnotes renumbered)[192]

However, whereas in the case of countervailing measures there is express guidance on the relationship between Article VI of GATT and the ASCM in the ASCM, in the case of Article XVI of GATT there is no 'express textual guidance found in the [ASCM]'.[193] In such circumstances, the relationship is to be considered on the basis of 'the texts of the relevant provisions as a whole'.[194]

In sum, the business of relationships is indeed complex. Furthermore, the process of characterising this relationship may well be underpinned by policy and/or give rise to policy considerations. Thus, it is possible to shift the locus of a norm backwards into GATT, forwards into the trade remedies agreements, to orientate it backwards or forwards, or indeed to disperse it everywhere!

7.6 Standard of review

There has been much focus on the question of the appropriate standard of review to be applied in the WTO dispute settlement process with respect to national decisions in the sphere of trade

[189] 'EC–Bananas III, (AB) para. 204.'

[190] 'Brazil–Desiccated Coconut, (AB) 167, at 181' (original italics; underlining added).

[191] 'Ibid.'

[192] US–Final Countervailing Duty Determination with Respect to Certain Softwood Lumber from Canada (AB) para 134.

[193] US–FSC (AB) para 117.

[194] Ibid.

remedies.[195] The relevant standard of review for the purposes of this chapter essentially refers to the degree of rigour in the review process with which a WTO Panel charged with a dispute involving a national trade remedies measure should examine the relevant national authority's decision.[196] The examination of the national trade remedies measure may involve questions of fact or of law or mixed questions of fact and law. Whatever the nature of these questions, the Panel can essentially review across a spectrum of standards from a *de novo* basis through to a totally deferential basis. In the case of a *de novo* approach, the Panel would examine all the issues, whether of a factual or a legal nature, afresh, whereas in the case of a totally deferential approach the Panel would show deference to the factual or legal determinations of the national authorities, provided certain procedural conditions had been met. In between these two extremes is the intermediate deferential approach, which gives a certain margin of discretion to the national authorities.[197]

Historically, in the general practice of GATT 1947 panels, a deferential but nevertheless rigorous approach to factual issues in anti-dumping and countervailing matters was pursued.[198] In the Uruguay Round, proposals for standards of review were considered, in particular the US proposal specifically in relation to anti-dumping issues, which then came to fruition in the form of Article 17 of the ADA.[199]

7.6.1 General standard of review

The general standard of review to be applied by Panels is that set out in Article 11 of the DSU, that is, that there should be an objective assessment of the matter, including an objective assessment of the facts.

[195] Oesch *Standards of Review*; C.-D. Ehlermann and N. Lockhart 'Standard of Review in WTO Law' (2004) 7(3) *JIEL* 491–521; M. Oesch 'Standards of Review in WTO Dispute Resolution' (2003) 6(3) *JIEL* 635–59; H. Spamann 'Standard of Review for World Trade Organization Panels in Trade Remedy Cases: A Critical Analysis' (2004) 38(3) *JWT* 509–55.

[196] See for example Ehlermann and Lockhart 'Standard of Review in WTO Law' 491; Spamann 'Standard of Review for World Trade Organization Panels' 510; Oesch *Standards of Review* 637.

[197] See for example Spamann 'Standard of Review for World Trade Organization Panels'.

[198] See for example Oesch *Standards of Review* 64–5. See also US–Salmon from Norway (Anti-Dumping Duties) (Panel) para 494; US–Salmon from Norway (Countervailing Duties) (Panel) para 258, cited in Oesch *Standards of Review*.

[199] Oesch *Standards of Review* 73.

This has been interpreted by the AB with respect to questions of fact as involving 'neither *de novo* review nor total deference.... But rather objective assessment of the facts...'.[200]

In relation to law, the customary rules of interpretation for interpreting treaties apply, namely, the *de novo* approach.

7.6.2 Standard of review in the ADA

The general rule set out in Article 11 of the DSU also applies generally to trade remedies cases. However, in the case of the ADA, this standard of review is affected by the provisions of Article 17.6 of the ADA. With respect to questions of fact, Article 17.6 articulates the deferential approach – although it is not entirely clear where in the spectrum between *de novo* review and total deference the benchmark is to be found.[201] In this respect, Article 17.6 (i) in relevant parts reads as follows:

> in its assessment of the facts of the matter, the panel shall determine whether the authorities' establishment of the facts was proper and whether their evaluation of those facts was unbiased and objective. If the establishment of the facts was proper and their evaluation was unbiased and objective, even though the panel might have reached a different conclusion, the evaluation shall not be overturned.

Thus, the focus of Article 17.6 (i) is on the propriety of the review in two respects: first, the establishment of the facts; second, whether the factual determination by the national authorities is based on positive evidence and objective evaluation.[202]

Thus, the standard of review here is deferential inasmuch as the Panel is required to focus only on the process not the substantive outcome. If the process is proper, unbiased and objective, then the Panel may not substitute its own judgement for that of the national authorities, even though the panel may have come to a different substantive conclusion.[203] However, it is not clear what degree of deference in relation to this appraisal of impartiality and objectivity is required.[204]

200 EC–Hormones (AB) para 117.
201 Oesch *Standards of Review* 78.
202 Ibid 89.
203 See EU–Bed Linen (AB) para 108: 'If the establishment of the facts was proper and the evaluation was unbiased and objective, then a Panel shall not overturn that evaluation...'.
204 Oesch *Standards of Review* 89.

In practice, the interpretation placed on Article 17.6 (i) by the AB has generally been considered to be a restricted one, allowing the Panel a fair degree of discretion. This is reinforced by the interpretation that Article 17 of the ADA has to be read against the background of Article 11 of the DSU,[205] even though, according to one commentator, Article 11's role is only 'subsidiarily relevant' to Article 17.6 (i) of the ADA.[206]

With respect to questions of law, Article 17.6 (ii) has been understood as a statement of the *de novo* approach, but with a caveat. Article 17.6 (ii) states:

> the panel shall interpret the relevant provisions of the Agreement in accordance with customary rules of interpretation of public international law. Where the panel finds that a relevant provision of the Agreement admits of more than one permissible interpretation, the panel shall find the authorities' measure to be in conformity with the Agreement if it rests upon one of those permissible interpretations.

The Panel is to adopt the *de novo* approach but defer to national preferences in interpretation if these are within the permissible spectrum of possible interpretations, in conformity with the customary international law rules for interpreting treaties. The permissible interpretation must first satisfy and derive from the application of Articles 31–2 of the VC. However, it has been pointed out that this deference does not sit comfortably with Articles 31–2 of the VC, which, it has been argued, are intended to elicit only one interpretation.[207] This view is shared by Oesch:

> The possibility of arriving at more than one permissible interpretation pursuant to the second sentence is arguably inconsistent with the rules of interpretation stipulated in Articles 31 and 32 of the VCLT. . . . the two provisions provide a complete set of interpretative rules whose application in principle leads to one single, consistent interpretation of a treaty provision . . . based on this view, the second sentence of Article 17.6 [ii] can never come into play, simply because the correct application of the VCLT never leaves an interpreter to choose among a range of permissible interpretations.[208]

[205] See US–Anti-Dumping Measures on Certain Hot-Rolled Steel Products; Thailand–Antidumping Duties on Angles (AB).

[206] Oesch *Standards of Review* 101.

[207] See Ehlermann and Lockhart 'Standard of Review in WTO Law' 500.

[208] Oesch *Standards of Review* 94.

However, Oesch goes on to state that the 'second sentence of Article 17 [6] [ii] of the AD Agreement takes priority over the principle that the customary rules of interpretation result in a single interpretation'.[209]

These observations are based on the contention that the customary rules of treaty interpretation as set out in Articles 31–2 of the VC can lead only to a single interpretation. This is somewhat controversial, not to mention dogmatic, even allowing for the acknowledgement of the existence of a different school on this point.[210] There are several reasons for reacting against such an analysis. First, Articles 31–2 of the VC do not provide a complete set of interpretative rules. Thus, Sinclair, who has been cited (albeit in other contexts) in AB Reports, states:

> few would seek to argue that the rules embodied in Articles 31 to 33 of the Convention are exhaustive of the techniques which may be properly adopted by the interpreter in giving effect to the broad guidelines laid down in those rules. . . . What we have in the Convention is an 'economical code of principles'. (Footnote omitted)[211]

Second, the principles in Articles 31–2 of the VC are 'broad guidelines'.[212] They involve judgement; they do not offer precision leading automatically to correct judgements. Thus, Sinclair states:

> The convention rules are expressed in very general terms and much in the way of discretion and appreciation is left to the tribunal called upon to interpret a particular treaty provision. Our review of recent international case law on treaty interpretation reveals only too clearly that widely differing results can still be achieved even if a conscious effort is being made to apply to convention rules.[213]

Third, the VC by its own terms contemplates the possibility of different interpretations arising from the application of Articles 31–2 of the VC. Thus, Article 33 (4) in the context of plurilingual treaties states:

> Except where a particular text prevails in accordance with paragraph 1, when a comparison of the authentic texts discloses a difference of meaning which the application of Articles 31 and 32 does not remove, the meaning which best reconciles the texts, having regard to the object and purpose of the treaty, shall be adopted.

The problem of divergent interpretations of plurilingual treaties is somewhat similar in that each agreement is in the first instance interpreted

[209] Ibid 95. [210] Ibid 44. [211] Sinclair *Vienna Convention* 153.
[212] Ibid. [213] Ibid.

by applying Articles 31–2 of the VC, before the guidance for resolving conflict is resorted to.

Finally, even leaving aside the question of whether the VC by its own terms allows for different permissible interpretations, permissible interpretations can be generated through its application in the context of Article 17.6 (ii) of the ADA. This is because Article 17.6 (ii) by its own terms places a gloss on the text and context of the ADA by effectively stipulating that the provisions of the ADA can lend themselves to different permissible interpretations. In other words, the ADA is transformed from an iron rod to a cane that has some flexibility. Furthermore, a permissible interpretation can be generated as a consequence of subsequent member practice 'in the application of the treaty which establishes the agreement of the parties regarding its interpretation'.[214] By the same token, Article 17.6 (ii) of the ADA establishes in a sense a mechanism for a term to be given a special meaning as intended by the membership.[215]

It is not clear which of the ADA provisions lend themselves to more than one permissible interpretation. The AB has stated that this can become clearer only in the context of a dispute.[216] Oesch takes issue with this. Thus, he states: 'This finding is questionable from a legal policy point of view although it is understandable from a practical perspective. . . . it does not stand to reason that such a judgement can only be predicted "within the context of particular disputes".'[217]

With respect to this, some observations can be made here. First, it is not the function of the AB to define the discretion that members contemplated a member should have. Second, it is for the member to define which alternative interpretations are preferred and to decide whether to avail itself of those interpretations through the formulation of its national measures. Third, these questions of possible interpretations may alternatively be conceived of and characterised not so much

[214] Article 31 (3) (c) of the VC. [215] Article 31 (4) of the VC.

[216] See Oesch *Standards of Review* 180–1, referring to US–Anti-Dumping Measures on Certain Hot-Rolled Steel Products (AB) paras 59–61. Generally on Article 17.6 of the ADA, see US–Anti-Dumping Measures on Certain Hot-Rolled Steel Products (AB) paras 51–62. In particular in para 61 the AB stated: 'We cannot, of course, examine here which provisions of the Anti-Dumping Agreement do admit of more than one "permissible interpretation". Those interpretive questions can only be addressed within the context of particular disputes, involving particular provisions of the Anti-Dumping Agreement invoked in particular claims, and after application of the rules of treaty interpretation in Articles 31 and 32 of the Vienna Convention. . . .'

[217] Oesch *Standards of Review* 181.

as issues of interpretation but rather, in reality, as about the devolution of discretion to the national level. In this case, the tension between the provision and the VC is even less.

Finally, it needs to be noted that there is a danger here of building a spectre of mushrooming divergent national interpretations. Only certain provisions of the ADA may warrant some flexibility in their application to accommodate the specifics of national anti-dumping systems.

Generally, in relation to the interpretation placed on Article 17 of the ADA and its deferential standard, it has been pointed out the AB has shown a tendency, despite the provision, to substitute its own judgement for that of the national authorities[218] – for example, by stipulating that the permissible interpretation can be arrived at only after the application of the international rules of treaty interpretation under the VC, which falls under the scrutiny of the AB.[219] Similarly, it has been observed that Panels have allowed information to be placed on record in the WTO dispute settlement process that was not available to the national authorities, despite Article 17.5 of the ADA, which prescribes that Panels should examine the matter based on the 'facts made available in conformity with appropriate domestic procedures to the authorities of the importing Member'.[220]

7.6.3 *Standard of review and the ASCM and the AS*

Although the Ministerial Decision on Review of Article 17.6 of the ADA and the Ministerial Declaration on Dispute Settlement Pursuant to the ADA or Part V of the SCM talk about the need for consistent resolution of disputes arising from ADA and countervailing measures, the AB has interpreted these instruments as being merely hortatory.[221] The Ministerial Decision envisaged a review of whether the standard in Article 17.6 could be applied generally. No such decision has yet been taken.[222] Therefore, in relation to the SA[223] and the

[218] Cunningham and Cribb 'Dispute Settlement' 162. [219] Ibid 163. [220] Ibid 164.

[221] See Spamann 'Standard of Review for World Trade Organization Panels' 519; US–Countervailing Duties on Certain Hot-Rolled Lead and Bismuth Carbon Steel Products II (AB) paras 44–55.

[222] See also Oesch *Standards of Review* 89.

[223] See Argentina–Footwear (AB) para 120: 'The Agreement on Safeguards, like the Agreement on the Application of Sanitary and Phytosanitary Measures, is silent as to the appropriate standard of review. Therefore, Article 11 of the DSU, and, in particular, its requirement that "a panel should make an objective assessment of the matter before it,

ASCM,[224] Article 17 of the ADA does not apply, and the general rule as set out in Article 11 of the DSU, and as interpreted by the AB in EC–Hormones, applies. However, the general view seems to be that the legal

including an objective assessment of the facts of the case and the applicability of and conformity with the relevant covered agreements", sets forth the appropriate standard of review for examining the consistency of a safeguard measure with the provisions of the Agreement on Safeguards.' See also US–Steel Safeguards WT/DS248/AB/R: 'As we have said before, a panel may not conduct a de novo review of the evidence or substitute its judgement for that of the competent authorities. Therefore, the "reasoned conclusions" and "detailed analysis" as well as "a demonstration of the relevance of the factors examined" that are contained in the report of a competent authority, are the only bases on which a panel may assess whether a competent authority has complied with its obligations under the Agreement on Safeguards and Article XIX:1(a) of the GATT 1994' (footnote omitted).

[224] See US–Countervailing Duties on Certain Hot-Rolled Lead and Bismuth Carbon Steel Products (AB) para 47: 'Article 17.6 of the Anti-Dumping Agreement sets out a special standard of review for disputes arising under that Agreement. The Declaration on Dispute Settlement Pursuant to the Agreement on Implementation of Article VI of the General Agreement on Tariffs and Trade 1994 or Part V of the Agreement on Subsidies and Countervailing Measures (the "Declaration") provides as follows: "Ministers, Recognize, with respect to dispute settlement pursuant to the Agreement on Implementation of Article VI of GATT 1994 or Part V of the Agreement on Subsidies and Countervailing Measures, the need for the consistent resolution of disputes arising from anti-dumping and countervailing duty measures. The United States argues that, by virtue of the Declaration, the standard of review specified in Article 17.6 of the Anti-Dumping Agreement also applies to disputes involving countervailing duty measures under Part V of the SCM Agreement. In the view of the United States, the Panel erred in applying the standard of review set out in Article 11 of the DSU in this case. . . . We consider this argument to be without merit. By its own terms, the Declaration does not impose an obligation to apply the standard of review contained in Article 17.6 of the . . . Anti-Dumping Agreement to disputes involving countervailing duty measures under Part V of the SCM Agreement. The Declaration is couched in hortatory language; it uses the words 'Ministers recognize'. Furthermore, the Declaration merely acknowledges 'the need for the consistent resolution of disputes arising from anti-dumping and countervailing duty measures'. It does not specify any specific action to be taken. In particular, it does not prescribe a standard of review to be applied. . . . Furthermore, the Decision on Review of Article 17.6 of the Agreement on Implementation of Article VI of the General Agreement on Tariffs and Trade 1994 (the 'Decision') provides: 'The standard of review in paragraph 6 of Article 17 of the Agreement on Implementation of Article VI of GATT 1994 shall be reviewed after a period of three years with a view to considering the question of whether it is capable of general application.' This Decision provides for review of the standard of review in Article 17.6 of the Anti-Dumping Agreement to determine if it is 'capable of general application' to other covered agreements, including the SCM Agreement. By implication, this Decision supports our conclusion that the Article 17.6 standard applies only to disputes arising under the Anti-Dumping Agreement, and not to disputes arising under other covered agreements, such as the SCM Agreement. To date, the DSB has not conducted the review contemplated in this Decision' (footnotes and paragraph numbers omitted).

basis for the standard of review in the SA and the ASCM is in the agreements themselves[225] rather than in Article 11 of the DSU,[226] because Article 11 of the DSU does not specify whether the objective assessment should take a *de novo* or a deferential approach.[227] In other words, the particular standard of review in these trade remedies cases is informed by the balance of jurisdictional competences created in these agreements between the member and the WTO.[228] This is because in the EC–Hormones case itself, the AB prescribed that the relevant standard of review was informed by the same balance established in that agreement.[229] This is reinforced, it has been claimed, by the actual practice of the WTO in such cases.[230] From this perspective, it has been suggested that the standard of review in the SA and the ASCM is similar to that set out in Article 17.6 (i) of the ADA,[231] given that these agreements are similar to the ADA in that they also have WTO-mandated investigation and procedural guarantees.[232] Thus, in these cases, the AB has described the function of the Panel in matters of fact as involving a critical evaluation of whether the national authorities considered all the relevant facts and adequately explained how those facts supported the determinations made,[233] regardless of whether the actual determination was correct.[234] However, the AB qualified the

[225] See Spamann 'Standard of Review for World Trade Organization Panels' 527.

[226] Ibid 528, relying on A.J. Desmedt and others.

[227] See for example Ehlermann and Lockhart 'Standard of Review in WTO Law' 510; Spamann 'Standard of Review for World Trade Organization Panels'. Spamann refers to this as the jurisprudential standard of review in the case of the SA and the ASCM.

[228] See for example Ehlermann and Lockhart 'Standard of Review in WTO Law' 491.

[229] See EC–Hormones (AB) para 115.

[230] See Spamann 'Standard of Review for World Trade Organization Panels' 530.

[231] See for example Ehlermann and Lockhart 'Standard of Review in WTO Law' 510.

[232] Ibid 507.

[233] See Argentina–Footwear (AB) para 121; US–Lamb Safeguards (AB) para 106; US–Countervailing Duties on Certain Hot-Rolled Lead and Bismuth Carbon Steel Products II (AB) paras 44–51; US–Carbon Steel (AB) para 142. See also US–DRAMS CVD Investigation (AB) para 151: 'a panel's analysis usually should seek to review the agency's decision on its own terms . . . panels may not conduct a *de novo* review of agency determinations'. See also paras 186, 188.

[234] See US–Carbon Steel (AB) para 303: 'Moreover, we cannot accept the United States' interpretation that a failure to explain a finding does not support the conclusion that the USITC "did not actually perform the analysis correctly, thereby breaching Article 2.1, 4.2, or 4.2(b) (of the Agreement on Safeguards)" [footnote:] As we stated above, because a panel may not conduct a de novo review of the evidence before the competent authority, it is the explanation given by the competent authority for its determination that alone enables panels to determine whether there has been compliance with the requirements of Article XIX of the GATT 1994 and of Articles 2 and 4 of the Agreement

emulation of other agreements when it pointed out: 'we recall that an "objective assessment" under Article 11 of the DSU must be understood in the light of the obligations of the particular covered agreement at issue in order to derive the more specific contours of the appropriate standard of review'.[235] This statement confirms Article 11 of the DSU as the basis for the standard of review, as much as the particular agreement in question. In the case of questions of law in relation to the SA and the ASCM the *de novo* approach applies.

7.6.4 Standard of review and domestic trade remedies legislation

How domestic trade remedies legislation should be interpreted in the WTO dispute settlement system is also a matter that touches upon the question of standard of review. Should Panels treat domestic trade remedies legislation *de novo* and interpret it themselves or approach it with a degree of deference? Two prior issues must be addressed, namely, the character of domestic trade remedies law and when it becomes justiciable in the WTO system. First, generally with respect to justiciability, when the domestic legislation is not mandatory but gives the executive branch discretion that might mean it is applied in a WTO-inconsistent manner, the legislation can be challenged only on the basis of its specific application.[236] However, that is not necessarily to preclude the justiciability of discretionary legislation in terms of its consistency with WTO law in the WTO dispute settlement process[237] – particularly when the legislation might, say, have a chilling effect on international trade.[238] Second, it appears settled in the WTO jurisprudence that domestic law is a matter of evidence and therefore a question of fact.[239]

In relation to the standard of review, a certain degree of deference is given to the domestic authorities with respect to their interpretation of their own legislation.[240] This is reinforced by the jurisprudence of the

on Safeguards. It may well be that, as the United States argues, the competent authorities have performed the appropriate analysis correctly.'

235 US–DRAMS CVD Investigation (AB) para 184.

236 See US–Anti-Dumping Act of 1916 (AB) paras 10, 57–61. See also Oesch *Standards of Review* 190.

237 See for example Oesch *Standards of Review* 190.

238 US–Section 301 of the Trade Act of 1974 (Panel).

239 See for example US–Section 301 of the Trade Act of 1974 (Panel) para 7.18; Oesch *Standards of Review* 194.

240 US–Section 301 of the Trade Act of 1974 (Panel) para 7.19.

WTO in general, which suggests that a *de novo* approach is not applied to the interpretation of domestic law.[241] However, where there is uncertainty or division in the domestic law, the Panel and the AB can 'weigh the jurisprudence of the municipal courts'.[242] During such an exercise, the Panel needs to take into account 'all the relevant aspects of the domestic law'.[243] However, it is not for the Panel to develop an independent interpretation of domestic legislation.[244] Once an interpretation has been discerned, the question of conformity or compliance with WTO law needs to take into account the 'wide ranging diversity in the legal systems' and the fact that 'conformity can be ensured in different ways in different legal systems'.[245]

With respect to interpreting the national measure in question, the following guidance should be noted. In US–Corrosion-Resistant Steel Sunset Review, the AB held that the approach to interpreting the national measure under dispute should take as its starting-point analysis of the measure at face value.[246] Furthermore, 'if the meaning and content of the measure are clear on its face, then the consistency of the measure as such can be assessed on that basis alone. If however, the meaning or content of the measure is not evident on its face, further examination is required.' The AB then quoted itself in US–Carbon Steel:

> The party asserting that another party's municipal law, as such, is inconsistent with relevant treaty obligations bears the burden of introducing evidence as to the scope and meaning of such law to substantiate that assertion. Such evidence will typically be produced in the form of the text of the relevant legislation or legal instruments, which may be supported, as appropriate, by evidence of the consistent application of such laws, the pronouncements of domestic courts on the meaning of such laws, the opinions of legal experts and the writings of recognized scholars. The nature and extent of the evidence required to satisfy the burden of proof will vary from case to case. (Footnote omitted)[247]

Similarly, in the FSC case the AB looked at the US legislative history but did not take at face value the quotations in the US Senate

[241] Oesch *Standards of Review* 205.
[242] Ibid 198; see also Oesch's citation of US–Anti-Dumping Act of 1916 (Panel) para 6.52.
[243] US–Anti-Dumping Act of 1916 (Panel) para 6.47.
[244] Oesch *Standards of Review* 205, referring to US–Anti-Dumping Act of 1916 (Panel) para 6.52.
[245] US–Section 301 of the Trade Act of 1974 (Panel) para 7.24; Oesch *Standards of Review* 206.
[246] (AB) para 168. [247] (AB) para 157.

legislative report on the FSC Repeal and Extraterritorial Income Exclusion Act.[248]

7.6.5 Standard of review and the process of interpretation

The topic of the standard of review intersects with the process of interpretation in a number of ways. First, it can determine the identity or location of the interpreter. Thus, if the standard of review is complete deference, the identity of the interpreter is located within the national system. In the case of partial deference, the standard of review can still inform the methodology employed in the interpretative process. On the other hand, although the *de novo* standard of review has little impact on the substantive methodology of the interpretation as such, it nevertheless affirms the identity and location of the interpretative process. Second, the standard of review may also influence the particular approach by which the agreements are interpreted – for example, teleological/textual or trade restrictive/trade liberalising. The more deferential the approach, the more likely it will be trade restrictive. Third, standards of review relate both to questions of fact and to questions of law. It is well understood that questions of fact and law are often mixed. Indeed, the distinction between the two spheres can sometimes be blurred; for example, the characterisation of a fact can be a question of law. Thus, this tension between questions of law and questions of fact, this malleable character of factual matter,[249] can as a matter of fact involve a synergy among the respective standards of review, as they relate to questions of fact and law, where these differ. Thus, in the case of mixed questions of law and fact, the deferential factual standard may have the consequence of colouring the legal aspects with the deferential standard.

[248] FSC Recourse to Article 21 (AB) para 150.

[249] See for example the differences between the United States and Canada in US–Final Dumping (AB) para 163: 'In our view, the issue raised by Canada – whether an investigating authority has exercised its discretion in an even-handed manner – is a question of law. The fact that such an "obligation (is) not found in Article 2.2.1.1" is not dispositive. Whether a particular approach of an investigating authority is, or is not, even-handed is, ultimately, a matter of the "legal characterization" of facts and, as such, a matter of law. We are thus unable to agree with the United States that the issue raised by Canada with respect to the lack of even-handed treatment on the part of USDOC is beyond the scope of appellate review' (footnote omitted).

7.7 Conclusion

It is not a simple matter to discern the approaches that have been adopted in the context of dispute settlement practice to interpreting the trade remedies agreements. This is for the following reasons in particular. First, there is no single criterion for evaluating the approaches. The focus here is on the manner in which the agreements have been interpreted. However, that still raises the question of what is meant by the 'manner in which the agreements have been interpreted'. For example, the agreements can be interpreted literally/textually or teleologically, the former connoting a restrictive approach and the latter a more objects-and-purposes-orientated approach. Of equal relevance is whether the interpretative approaches have been oriented towards liberal trade or, recognising the legitimacy of the trade remedies agreements, have tended to underscore the policy underpinning the availability of these remedies in favour of the members. Simply focusing on the textual or the teleological orientation of the interpretations does not necessarily give a full flavour of whether the interpretations are liberal trade friendly or member friendly. Second, it can be misleading to treat the trade remedies agreements as a monolithic group for such an exercise, although some academic commentators have taken such an approach and thus may have opened themselves up to challenge. Thus, John Greenwald states:

> in order to find anti-dumping duties, countervailing duties, or safeguard measures 'illegal', the panels and the Appellate Body have (1) read language out of an applicable agreement, (2) read language into an agreement that is nowhere to be found in the text, and (3) interpreted the language of the applicable agreement in a manner that is unreasonably restrictive.[250]

Finally, the number and volume of trade remedies cases is very substantial indeed, and they cover a host of issues. Therefore, assessments of this type can only be partial. Indeed, the circumstances can be such that different conclusions can be arrived at depending on which set of decisions is made.

With respect to challenges to the consistency of national measures under the SA, certainly none of the challenges has thus far been successfully defended by the member imposing the measure. Furthermore,

[250] See J. Greenwald 'WTO Dispute Settlement: An Exercise in Trade Law Legislation?' (2003) 6 *JIEL* 113–24, 115.

on the basis of a reading of the AB decisions, there is discernible a restrictive approach to interpretation. Indeed, the AB has been accused of 'imposing requirements for the use of safeguards that are economically and logically incoherent . . . '.[251] Thus, it has been pointed out that although the SA does not 'specify a time frame for the required increase in imports and does not prescribe the types of increases in imports' – for example, 'sudden, sharp or significant'[252] – these are the requirements that the AB has read into the SA.[253] Such requirements, it is claimed, do not represent a commitment to strict textual interpretation of international agreements[254] but an institutional policy preference based on the belief that safeguards are almost never justified and therefore require very tight restrictions on their use 'even if these restrictions go beyond the language of Article XIX and the Safeguard Agreement that was actually negotiated and agreed by WTO Members'.[255]

In relation to the ADA, the general approach to interpretation does not appear to be very textual. However, writing in 2003, Greenwald observed that all WTO cases 'challenging anti-dumping decisions by national authorities have succeeded'.[256] He pointed out that neither the AB nor the Panels would concede that an interpretation of the national authorities is 'permissible'.[257] However, to this it may be said that the AB has not ruled the possibility out. Similarly, in the context of the Byrd Amendment in relation to Article 18 of the ADA, which talks about measures against dumping, Greenwald observed that the AB interpreted 'against' very widely. However, this is a matter of opinion. Similarly, Cunningham and Cribb observe:

> AD and CVD [countervailing] measures, as limitations on the free flow of trade, are viewed sceptically in WTO decisions, no matter which country is the defendant. Consequently, Panels and the Appellate Body [1] are likely to strike down substantive or calculational decisions unless made in strict compliance with their view of the text of the Agreements; [2] are tough on issues of perceived procedural harshness; and [3] are unreceptive to arguments based on the limitations on the scope of the review.[258]

[251] Sykes 'Persistent Puzzles of Safeguards' 524.
[252] See Greenwald 'WTO Dispute Settlement' 116. [253] Argentina–Footwear.
[254] Greenwald 'WTO Dispute Settlement' 116. [255] Ibid. [256] Ibid 117. [257] Ibid 118.
[258] Cunningham and Cribb 'Dispute Settlement'.

In contrast to Greenwald, Durling,[259] also writing in 2003, observed that the 'critics have exaggerated both the frequency and severity of WTO decisions on anti-dumping measures'.[260]

In relation to the ASCM, the AB Reports have not shown an undue orientation towards a textual approach. Indeed, in relation to the ASCM, the evidence suggests that the AB's approach to interpretation has been one of form over substance, although there may be subtle differences in approach in terms of Part V with respect to countervailing measures, where a greater reliance on the textual approach may be found. In relation to countervailing measures, it has been observed that it is 'not yet clear whether countervailing duties will be subjected to the degree of WTO scrutiny that has emerged in the review of the [ADA]'.[261]

[259] Durling 'Deference'. [260] Ibid 141.
[261] Cunningham and Cribb 'Dispute Settlement' 164.

Conclusion

Trends in the jurisprudence of the WTO are difficult to assess. In the first instance, the criteria against which the trends can be measured vary. Thus, the jurisprudence can be assessed according to how strict or liberal the interpretation is, how free or fair trade orientated it is, and how environmentally or development friendly it is. Second, trends have a temporal dimension. Thus, the particular time frame chosen to assess the trend can have a bearing on the assessment. Finally, assessing trends involves judgements. These can and do vary. More important, however, trends are ultimately only symptomatic of the underlying conditions within which the jurisprudence of the WTO is processed. Therefore, an examination of the underlying conditions is a much more fundamental exercise. In this vein, the focus of this monograph is very much set against the background of the underlying conditions of interpretation that give rise to the jurisprudence of the WTO.

The apparatus of interpretation is at the very core of enforcing the rights of members in the WTO dispute settlement system. As such, it has a bearing on the assertion of the development dimension by developing members within the context of the dispute settlement system. It is also very much an aspect of implementing the WTO Agreements at the national level. The WTO apparatus for interpretation, therefore, not only needs to be neutral and efficient but also, given that it is a judicial apparatus, must itself be characterised by justice and fairness. It is this latter aspect that is often lost sight of. In particular, the justice and fairness aspect of the interpretative process is pertinent to the development dimension. Thus, the development dimension calls for an evaluation of the principles of treaty interpretation as set out in the VC against the background of justice and fairness, burdens on developing members arising from the very process of treaty interpretation, the interpretation of S&D provisions as exceptions, national policy space through deferential standards of interpretation, the inclusion of relevant development norms in the interpretation of WTO

Agreements and the conditions of interpretation of particular disciplines of special interest to developing members, such as trade remedies and S&D provisions. There is thus a whole agenda from a development dimension to the interpretation of the WTO Agreements that calls for their examination from such a perspective. The assertion here is that the development dimension has a legitimate claim for being inculcated in the very apparatus of interpretation of the WTO Agreements.

One vehicle for such a focus that emerges as a leitmotif comprises the objects and purposes of the WTO Agreements. This is so for two specific reasons: first, development is a long-term goal established in the objects and purposes of the WTO Agreements; second, whereas text can be skewed through interpretation, and post-agreement discovery of the intentions of the parties can be a complex exercise, the objects and purposes of the WTO Agreements are relatively more objectively ascertainable.

However, the problems arising from the interpretation of the WTO Agreements are not confined to the concerns of developing members. Thus, the lack of clarity in the principles of treaty interpretation, the problems that stem from interpreting institutional issues in the WTO, the manner of characterising exceptions and their treatment for the purposes of interpretation, the issues that emerge from the interpretation of national legislation, the incorporation of international law into the process of interpreting the WTO Agreements and, finally, the conditions for interpreting the trade remedies agreements are all matters of general concern that need to be highlighted as a prelude to their resolution. The perspectives on these issues are very much connected with the furthering of the objectives of the WTO and its efficient functioning.

Annexes

1 Relevant WTO provisions

Marrakesh Agreement Establishing the WTO

Article IX (2)

The Ministerial Conference and the General Council shall have the exclusive authority to adopt interpretations of this Agreement and of the Multilateral Trade Agreements. In the case of an interpretation of a Multilateral Trade Agreement in Annex 1, they shall exercise their authority on the basis of a recommendation by the Council overseeing the functioning of that Agreement. The decision to adopt an interpretation shall be taken by a three-fourths majority of the Members. This paragraph shall not be used in a manner that would undermine the amendment provisions in Article X.

Article XVI (3)

In the event of a conflict between a provision of this Agreement and a provision of any of the Multilateral Trade Agreements, the provision of this Agreement shall prevail to the extent of the conflict.

Annex 1. Annex 1A Multilateral Agreements on Trade in Goods

General interpretative note to Annex 1A:
In the event of conflict between a provision of the General Agreement on Tariffs and Trade 1994 and a provision of another agreement in Annex 1A to the Agreement Establishing the World Trade Organization (referred to in the agreements in Annex 1A as the 'WTO Agreement'), the provision of the other agreement shall prevail to the extent of the conflict.

Article 3 (2) of the DSU

The dispute settlement system of the WTO is a central element in providing security and predictability to the multilateral trading system.

The Members recognize that it serves to preserve the rights and obligations of Members under the covered agreements, and to clarify the existing provisions of those agreements in accordance with customary rules of interpretation of public international law. Recommendations and rulings of the DSB cannot add to or diminish the rights and obligations provided in the covered agreements.

Article 17.6 of the Agreement on Implementation of Article VI of the General Agreement on Tariffs and Trade 1994

In examining the matter referred to in paragraph 5:

(i) in its assessment of the facts of the matter, the panel shall determine whether the authorities' establishment of the facts was proper and whether their evaluation of those facts was unbiased and objective. If the establishment of the facts was proper and the evaluation was unbiased and objective, even though the panel might have reached a different conclusion, the evaluation shall not be overturned;

(ii) the panel shall interpret the relevant provisions of the Agreement in accordance with customary rules of interpretation of public international law. Where the panel finds that a relevant provision of the Agreement admits of more than one permissible interpretation, the panel shall find the authorities' measure to be in conformity with the Agreement if it rests upon one of those permissible interpretations.

2 Relevant provisions of the Vienna Convention on the Law of Treaties 1969

Section 3. Interpretation of Treaties

Article 31

General rule of interpretation

1. A treaty shall be interpreted in good faith in accordance with the ordinary meaning to be given to the terms of the treaty in their context and in the light of its object and purpose.
2. The context for the purpose of the interpretation of a treaty shall comprise, in addition to the text, including its preamble and annexes:
   (a) any agreement relating to the treaty which was made between all the parties in connection with the conclusion of the treaty;

(b) any instrument which was made by one or more parties in connection with the conclusion of the treaty and accepted by the other parties as an instrument related to the treaty.

3. There shall be taken into account, together with the context:
   (a) any subsequent agreement between the parties regarding the interpretation of the treaty or the application of its provisions;
   (b) any subsequent practice in the application of the treaty which establishes the agreement of the parties regarding its interpretation;
   (c) any relevant rules of international law applicable in the relations between the parties.
4. A special meaning shall be given to a term if it is established that the parties so intended.

Article 32

Supplementary means of interpretation

Recourse may be had to supplementary means of interpretation, including the preparatory work of the treaty and the circumstances of its conclusion, in order to confirm the meaning resulting from the application of article 31, or to determine the meaning when the interpretation according to article 31:

(a) leaves the meaning ambiguous or obscure; or
(b) leads to a result which is manifestly absurd or unreasonable.

Article 33

Interpretation of treaties authenticated in two or more languages

1. When a treaty has been authenticated in two or more languages, the text is equally authoritative in each language, unless the treaty provides or the parties agree that, in case of divergence, a particular text shall prevail.
2. A version of the treaty in a language other than one of those in which the text was authenticated shall be considered an authentic text only if the treaty so provides or the parties so agree.
3. The terms of the treaty are presumed to have the same meaning in each authentic text.
4. Except where a particular text prevails in accordance with paragraph 1, when a comparison of the authentic texts discloses a difference of meaning which the application of articles 31 and 32 does not remove, the meaning which best reconciles the texts, having regard to the object and purpose of the treaty, shall be adopted.

INDEX

Made in the USA
Lexington, KY
25 February 2013